Inner London: Policies for dispersal and balance

Shankland Cox Partnership
Institute of Community Studies

View of the study area from the south.
Millbank Tower, Big Ben, the Barbican
and other central area buildings are on
the skyline.

DEPARTMENT OF THE ENVIRONMENT

Inner London: Policies for dispersal and balance

Final Report of the Lambeth Inner Area Study

Graeme Shankland, Peter Willmott and David Jordan

LONDON   HER MAJESTY'S STATIONERY OFFICE

© *Crown copyright 1977*

First published 1977

Designed by HMSO Graphic Design

ISBN 0 11 751141 2

Foreword

by the Minister of Housing and Construction

This report is the outcome of one of the three studies undertaken by consultants for the Department of the Environment in the inner areas of major cities – Birmingham, Liverpool and London.

For over four years the consultants, in collaboration with the local authority, worked in the part of Lambeth known as Stockwell carrying out research into a wide range of issues. At the same time they have carried out action projects which in addition to shedding light on the issues have brought some practical benefits to the residents of the study area. Reports on many of the action projects have been published and are available from the Inner Cities Directorate of the Department, together with reports of particular research studies done by the consultants.

It is well over a decade since some of us started to advocate a 'total' approach to urban renewal, urging that this should be brought to the centre of politics rather than continue as a peripheral issue. During these last four years, while the studies continued, concern about the multiple problems and challenges of inner urban areas has grown. Peter Shore's statement in the House of Commons on 6 April 1977 made this a central issue of the Government's social, economic and planning policies. The work of the inner area studies has contributed much to our understanding of these problems. The Summary Reports published in January of this year have already stimulated many valuable comments as to the future directions of urban policy and have contributed to the discussions which led to the Commons statement and then to the preparation of the Government's White Paper. But the Summary Reports could only set out the consultants' arguments and conclusions in outline. The present report sets them out in full, with their supporting vidence, and contains a great deal of additional material.

It has been my privilege during the greater part of the consultants' study to serve as Chairman of the Joint Steering Committee which has guided their work. I am grateful to the members and officers of the Lambeth Borough Council for their help and co-operation. These studies will prove to be of lasting value to everyone concerned with renewing the conditions and opportunities for life in the old urban areas which lie at the hearts of our cities. I hope this report, and those from the other two studies, will be read widely and closely. They certainly deserve to be.

Reg Freeson

Chairman of the Steering Committee

June 1977

Contents

Foreword   *page* v

Introductory note   ix

1   The Inner City and the Stockwell Study   1

2   The people and their views   25

3   Poverty and deprivation   55

4   The job market   77

5   Stresses in housing   101

6   The housing trap   115

7   Balanced dispersal   127

8   Planning and housing policies   141

9   The delivery of welfare   165

10 From study to action   183

11 Policies for dispersal and balance   203

Appendices

1   Announcement of Inner Area Studies and Terms of Reference   222

2   The Household Survey   224

3   Additional tables   226

4   References   235

Index   239

Introductory note

This book reports and interprets the study undertaken for the Department of the Environment between December 1972 and the summer of 1976 by an interprofessional team from the Shankland Cox Partnership and the Institute of Community Studies. The study was directed jointly by Graeme Shankland and Peter Willmott, and David Jordan was its full-time project leader. The team averaged 12 members during the main work period; most were part-time and its composition changed according to the work programme.

The team were guided in their work by a Steering Committee under the Chairmanship of a Minister of the Department of the Environment. It included members of the London Borough of Lambeth, the Greater London Council and the Inner London Education Authority.

Most of the material on which the book is based has been drawn from separate subject reports including 14 already published by the Department of the Environment and others in the press, together with the experience of the various action projects.

The labour market studies, including the local employers' survey, were carried out by Glen Bramley, who also worked on the examination of housing stress and made a particularly valuable contribution to the study as a whole. A study of the housing stock and of differences between various types and tenures was carried out by Jean MacDonald, Oliver Cox, Jean Cox, David Heath and Jennifer Moss, who was also responsible for population projections and demographic studies. Oliver Cox, Jean Cox, Bill Brisbane and Glen Bramley worked on the enquiry into housing management. Bill Brisbane was also responsible for the review of social ownership. Tony Bowhill and Al Simmonds carried out an analysis of the local housing market. Phyllis Willmott carried out the research on the 'delivery of local services'. A study of policies and structure was undertaken by David Jordan and Michael Collins. Peter Willmott, David Jordan and Jennifer Moss carried out the analysis of changes in the socio-economic structure of London and Lambeth in particular. The household survey was directed by Peter Willmott; Wyn Tucker acted as survey supervisor, assisted by Michael Willmott. A study of multiple deprivation was carried out by Peter Willmott with the assistance of Phyllis Willmott, Wyn Tucker, Hilary Dowling and Mollie Richards; Ian Cullen was responsible for the statistical analysis for this study and also gave advice and help with computing problems generally. Barrie Needham gave specialist advice on economic aspects of the Study as a whole, as did J. B. Cullingworth on policy issues in the later stages.

The team members mainly responsible for the action projects were as follows: schools project, Jean Cox and Jenny Mills; salaried childminders ('Groveway project'), Phyllis Willmott; local information posts, Phyllis Willmott; multi-service project, Phyllis Willmott and Peter Willmott; multi-space project, David Jordan, Len Harris, Jon Rowland and Jenny Cox; 'frustrated movers' (survey and action project), David Jordan, Lynda Thorn and Alice Hemmings.

The main burden of secretarial work and typing was carried by Doris Cheetham, Mischa Spallone, Marie Wain and Sue Chisholm. Oliver Cox and Audrey Tyrer prepared the illustrations to the book and David Heath and Paul Cox the photographs. Ruth McIver and Sue Steer worked as assistants in the team's office in Stockwell.

The main body of this book summarises our findings from the four years of the study and sets out our recommendations. Some extra information is given in the Appendices and for further details the reader may refer to the subject reports published by the Department of the Environment. In the footnotes to the text we have abbreviated references to works cited. Titles in italics are published books or reports, and those in inverted commas are articles. Full references can be found in Appendix 4.

December 1976

1 The Inner City and the Stockwell Study

This book is about what is happening to Inner London. For some time there has been growing recognition that, in common with the inner areas of other British cities, it is suffering from major social and environmental problems. In particular, it is thought that the place and its people have been 'left behind' by prosperity, and that this gap has been widening. In the study reported in this book we have tried to discover if this is true. Is there a distinctive inner city problem? And are special measures needed to deal with it?

For nearly a century the population of Inner London has been falling as people, mostly on their own initiative, have left for the suburbs and beyond. More recently, the population of Outer London has also fallen. But these reductions have been more than matched by an increase in the Outer Metropolitan Area, the country ring stretching out some 50 miles from Charing Cross. Thus, in one sense, the metropolis has been expanding, its population spreading over a broader area.

During most of this time Greater London has remained an expanding labour market, despite people moving further out. In the 1950s London gained well over a quarter of a million jobs. Now the total number of jobs is declining. Some firms have moved out, some have been 'merged', others have disappeared. As a result, in the ten years between 1961 and 1971, Greater London lost nearly a quarter of a million jobs, some 10 per cent of the total, and in manufacturing industry in particular the drop was 25 per cent. There have also been changes in housing. The privately rented sector, which accommodated about nine households out of every ten at the turn of the century, contained less than half by 1971. Meanwhile council housing has grown: by 1971, most households were already council tenants in two Inner London boroughs, Tower Hamlets and Southwark. This trend is continuing, accompanied by a growth in owner-occupation for those who can afford it.

This 'polarisation' in housing has been paralleled by changes in the make-up of Inner London's work force. The proportion of skilled manual workers has fallen even more in Inner London than in London as a whole. With continuing population decline, will there be fewer still in the middle of the class spectrum (skilled manual workers and clerks) with more at the bottom (cleaners and kitchen porters) and the top (professional workers and executives)? Inner London has traditionally been the home of London's poorest and least privileged. The fear is that it may now become a permanent ghetto for the poor and the disadvantaged, while prosperity grows in the suburbs and the home counties.

This leads to another question; is Inner London's problem simply an historical legacy which will automatically right itself in time? Until such time, so long as there are poor people are they not inevitably condemned to live in the poorest environment? If, on the other hand, special efforts are needed, what kind of initiatives are required and who has to take them?

While the problems grow, the resources available to grapple with them diminish. Local authorities' revenues are falling as rates decline with industrial closures, and these losses are not being replaced by new industrial or commercial enterprises. Vandalism seems to be growing in the inner city, mugging and petty crime breaking out in formerly safe areas. Finally, racial friction has sporadically broken to the surface in areas where black and brown minorities are concentrated.

Taken together, these events offer a sinister caricature of the urban crises in the United States. The parallels are striking: are the inner areas of London, Glasgow, Liverpool, Manchester and Birmingham to go the same way as those of the USA? Is 'poverty in the midst of plenty', as President Johnson put it, also to be a chronic malaise of British urban society?

When we talk of London's inner area, what do we have in mind? There are various ways of defining Inner London. Our own broad definition is shown in Figure 1. While it contains all the problems discussed in this book, sporadic pockets of similar problems occur outside its boundary. We show separately the central area – the central business district – which has a predominantly metropolitan and national function. More than in any other British city, London's inner area contains relatively high status districts, such as Chelsea, Mayfair and St. John's Wood.

**Figure 1
Inner London**

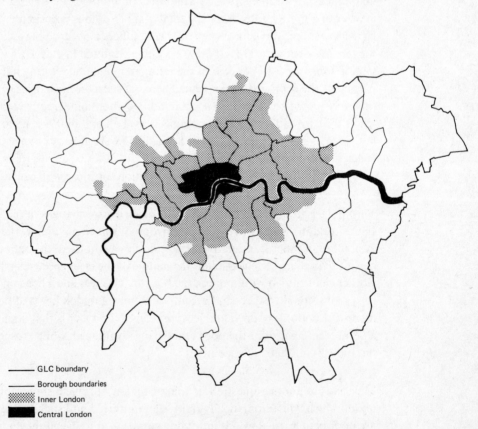

——— GLC boundary
——— Borough boundaries
▓▓▓ Inner London
█ Central London

2

This inner area covers 112 square miles, about a fifth of Greater London. Nearly three million people live here, at the highest densities in London, in the oldest properties. Broadly the area covers the flat lands of the Thames valley around medieval London, first developed in the late 19th century or earlier. It includes most of London's historic dock area, to which our conclusions clearly have some relevance and which has been studied separately.[1]

Nobody could say that the environmental problems of Inner London have been neglected since the end of the war. A great deal of urban renewal has taken place, and, taken as a whole, living and working conditions have improved over the last three decades. Yet something seems to have gone wrong, or rather many different things. Expectations may be higher, but for many they have not been fulfilled. The criticisms of 'the planners' by 'the planned' are more vocal than ever. Despite good intentions, many are dissatisfied with the results of 30 years of municipal planning and improvement.

Long established owner-occupiers and tenants in old terraced housing have fought bitterly, and with increasing success, to preserve their homes against demolition by local councils. Many people are fond of their locality and are vocal in their criticism of the dirt, mess and the shabby scene which often surrounds them. Many are also uneasy; so great have been the population changes that they do not know their new neighbours, some of whom are black.

These new doubts and queries did not arise overnight. The results of earlier policies took time to show themselves; the public reaction to immediate post-war measures, such as wholesale slum clearance, took more than a decade to make itself felt. The anxieties expressed by some people about trends in employment were not confirmed until statistical data about them became available some years later. All this suggested that the traditional remedies were no longer adequate. Would it not be wrong to pour more resources into the same policies, most of which appeared right at the time, but some of which could now be seen to have had powerful negative side effects? So the time was ripe for a fundamental re-appraisal of inner city problems and policies, in the light of post-war experience and new anxieties.

These anxieties can be summarised under three headings: economic, social and environmental. Symptoms of what is felt to be wrong could be grouped under one or other of these 'dimensions'; so could action to remedy them. But to look at any specific problem (such as wages, housing or child care) is to be sharply reminded of the interdependence of these three dimensions of urban life. Good 'one-dimensional' policies, even if in the right general direction, can produce lopsided effects. Economic policies can be anti-social, social policies can be prohibitively expensive and environmental programmes can be counter-productive on both scores – some highway schemes and slum clearance projects are obvious examples. So any specific study of one of these dimensions has to look over its shoulder at the other two; likewise with any proposed solutions.

(1) Docklands Joint Committee, *London Docklands: A Strategic Plan: A Draft for Public Consultation*. Full references to all works cited are given in Appendix 4.

These three dimensions coincide in Inner London, however its exact area is defined. The inner city problem could even be defined as one which analysis and observation show their coincidence and complementary nature. But one other vital aspect has to be added: these problems do not go away in times of prosperity. The greater resources that increased wealth can provide certainly makes redistribution in favour of inner areas easier. It does not ensure it will happen. If the experience of the United States teaches anything it is that it is not enough to be rich.

The impact of events in the ghettos and 'grey areas' of the great North American cities shocked observant British opinion. It might happen here. The initiatives in reform taken by various agencies in the USA might offer a suggestive parallel. The American programmes laid a new emphasis on the social aspects of inner city problems. In Britain too a broader view began to be taken of what was needed. Traditionally, the improvement of inner city life had been seen as a physical task; clearing slums, removing industry and other so-called 'non-conforming users' from residential areas, modernising the urban structure with new houses, schools, roads and other public services. But urban deprivation and poverty remained. Any studies of the inner city, and any policies that flowed from such studies, would have to take account not just of urban deprivation but also of the underlying causes.

Against this wider background, new questions could be asked. What new policies should replace the old ones? What adjustments to good policies should be made to see their benefits were received by those who need them most? What were the roles of public intervention, private enterprise and personal initiative? What new responses were needed from public officials and professionals? How best could the local community be involved and contribute to shaping their own environment? Were new political initiatives needed and, if so, in what directions? Similar questions have been asked of other British cities; together they represented a common set of issues, many of which were evident in acute form in Glasgow, Liverpool and Birmingham.

A new British initiative on the inner city came in 1972. Peter Walker, Secretary of State for the newly created Department of the Environment, announced during the Budget Debate[1] that he was launching six studies, three of which would be in industrial towns and three in the inner areas of major cities – Birmingham, Liverpool and London. The aim of the studies would be 'to formulate a comprehensive approach to urban inner area problems'.

> 'There is concern about a variety of growing problems in many of our inner city areas and a general feeling that not enough is being done about them. It may be that slum clearance, redevelopment and economic growth will remove them in the long run. But one cannot be sure. In any case, long-term solutions are not much help to the people living in inner areas now: the blighting effect of longer term plans may make life worse for them in the meantime. There is an urgent

(1) There had been earlier government-supported programmes in deprived areas for positive discrimination in education, for community development projects and for 'urban aid' projects. See, for instance, *National Community Development Project: Inter Project Report* and A. H. Halsey, *Educational Priority: Volume 1: E.P.A. Problems and Policies.*

need to discover what should be done in relation to the physical environment to help these areas, why it is not being done already, and what measures are needed; and to do this in a way which tries to see problems in the totality and how they relate, and not piecemeal.'[1]

The study in Lambeth

Lambeth was chosen as the venue for the London inner area study. The work continued under successive Ministers, with a change from a Conservative to a Labour administration in 1974.

Starting in November 1972, our study has passed through three stages: an initial exploration lasting four months to select an area for study within Lambeth and to propose a work programme; the main study (March 1973–April 1976); and the concluding phase, including writing this book and completing some action projects, during the remainder of 1976.

Our terms of reference were brief and very general (see Appendix 1). Thus it was up to us to interpret the commission in our own way. We had to explain what our approach and methods would be and then identify, separately, each task we would undertake. We had to formulate each proposal and cost it, seeking the authority of the Steering Committee as we went along. The Steering Committee, which took final responsibility for the study, was chaired by the Minister and included elected members from the London Borough of Lambeth, the Greater London Council (GLC) and, at a later stage, the Inner London Education Authority (ILEA). A Working Group, composed of officers and ourselves, considered reports and proposals a month before the Steering Committee met and made its recommendations to it.

The most novel aspect of the terms of reference was the emphasis on the 'total approach'. Most previous studies of urban problems had been partial, dealing with issues which, though complicated, remained discrete. We sought to develop a series of complementary studies which related to each other and which could lead to complementary policies and integrated action. For instance, meagre job opportunities, poor housing and low educational performance were inter-connected. But what policies could be devised which improved all of these in a co-ordinated fashion?

One extension of the idea of a total approach was to bear in mind that the problems of an area could in a sense be 'solved' by displacing its population. This is just what many redevelopment and rehabilitation projects had done. They had cleared the slums and replaced them with better homes, but at the cost of displacing some of the original residents, who took most of their problems with them to other areas. We sought instead to concentrate on the needs of the existing population, and either avoid moving them or ensure that their needs would be adequately met elsewhere.

(1) House of Commons, April 1972. See Appendix 1 for the full text.

We set out with certain initial assumptions. For instance, we would avoid proposing 'showpiece' solutions if they were likely to be so expensive that they could not be generally applied in the inner city as resources became available. We also took the view that the size of the problem was likely to require additional resources, but rejected the argument that nothing could be usefully done meanwhile. Our experience suggested the opposite. With hindsight, much public intervention in the past seemed to have been misdirected. With foresight and better understanding, we believed, it could be better directed, whatever the given level of resources available.

Our terms of reference also required 'a programme of study and experimental action, which should . . . provide a base for general conclusions on policies and actions'. Implicit in this was the view that research could inform policy and suggest action projects, that action projects could provide material for research and policy making, and that policy could be influenced by the lessons of projects in the field as well as by the findings of research. We thought these claims should be put to the test; that strong connections could be forged between the three sides of this triangle, even if much fell out on the way.

The programme we proposed was thus made up of two main elements: studies and action projects. Our first job, a household survey, was intended to provide a foundation for both. What should be the balance between study and action? A familiar viewpoint inside local authorities was that 'academic' research was unhelpful and unnecessary, since the people responsible, members and officers, knew what needed to be done. There was an opposite view, that we were all still so ignorant about the real nature of inner city problems that any programme involving immediate action would be a diversion, and would obscure a clearer understanding of the fundamental problems.

We concluded that, out of many different kinds of action projects, we could select some which could be started soon so that their results could be fed back quickly into the study and research programme. It was also important to establish the team's presence locally, not just through the household interviews for research investigation, but with a visible early involvement in helping change forward. Other projects would suggest themselves later when the household survey had revealed Lambeth residents' priorities for action and when the basic studies had yielded their first findings.

This was the pattern which we eventually followed. Certain of our proposals ran into difficulties. Most were approved, some were delayed, others took a different path from that originally intended and a few were rejected by the Steering Committee. We describe each of those undertaken in the relevant chapters of this book, and in Chapter 10 we describe those not approved. We do so not in an effort to justify ourselves, but to draw attention to failures which would otherwise escape notice. John Palmer, the Under Secretary responsible for the studies, has since defended this course.

'It will . . . be particularly important to look for negative lessons, that is to say, that the innovation being examined is not particularly effective or is not particularly practicable. Negative lessons, though suffering from limitations of the special case may in themselves be more compelling than positive ones which would need to be reinforced by other work . . . Negative conclusions may need some searching out . . . One can observe a natural tendency among those who have to consider the output of research but were not involved in mounting it to pick out the points which reinforce their current views. This is in itself no doubt useful. But it does mean that a systematic attention needs to be given to sifting out the points which are not picked up in this way.'[1]

Approaches to action and research

On action projects we looked at three possible approaches. We dubbed two of these 'Classical' and 'Liverpool' as distinct from the one we finally adopted. The 'Classical' approach would analyse basic research and known facts, propose a topic for a new policy investigation, set up a scheme to try it out and subsequently evaluate it. This seemed ideal, but involved the assumption that a lot of useful data and past experience were ready to hand (which they were not). It also required too long a time-scale and was, in any case, detached from a dialogue with local people.

The approach of our colleagues in Liverpool,[2] on the other hand, was to embark on a large number of action projects. These were either identified by the local authority at the outset or by the team, early in its work, in the expectation that the experience gained would lend itself to generalisation later. A similar procedure was followed in Birmingham.[3]

Our own approach was more cautious and selective. We did not propose any action project which did not have a prospect of generalised conclusions in view at the outset. As our time and resources would be limited, we deferred finalising a complete programme of action projects so as to concentrate on those which the residents' needs and our first studies would show to be of greatest priority.

Some problems of working method had to be tackled at the outset, if only to guide the selection of a study area. To what extent could a relatively small area be representative of Inner London as a whole? How much of the data that we needed could be collected from the study area, and what other kinds of information would we need from elsewhere? Should the study be directed to producing specific proposals for the study area or generalised proposals for Inner London?

(1) John Palmer, 'Using the results of action research in policy making'.

(2) Inner Area Study Liverpool, *Project Report* (IAS/LI/1) and *Study Review/Proposals for Action and Research* (IAS/LI/2).

(3) Inner Area Study Birmingham, *Project Report* (IAS/B/1) and *Progress Report: July 1973* (IAS/B/2).

In debating this we found it helpful to pose two alternative approaches; the 'strategic' and the 'tactical'. The 'strategic' approach would place little emphasis on the role of the study area, arguing that its problems were inextricably linked to dynamic processes at work over the whole city and metropolitan region. It would tend to dismiss proposals which emerged from examination of the study area as too specific, short term and palliative, whereas general, long term and fundamental solutions were called for.

The 'tactical' approach would concentrate on detailed investigation in the study area, in the hope that a properly handled analysis could be generalised to other areas in the inner city. In this way one might be more likely to get to the heart of the problem. So-called strategic and generalised investigations are often shallow and diffuse. They also have a habit of being invalidated or rendered out of date each time new data become available.

Our conclusion was that, knowing the faults of each, we had to combine the virtues of both approaches, and look at the area both from the outside in and inside out. The main thrust of the work should be directed at the study area, to help define the nature of deprivation and evolve proposals for relieving it. We did, though, see it as our job to try and relate our findings to the general problems of Inner London.

As a consequence of this we arrived at another important conclusion at the outset. While our findings on some topics would emerge from local area based studies, on others they would not. Data would be needed from different sources. We therefore proposed additional work on two non-area based topics; the labour market for study area residents, and changes in socio-economic structure in Inner London generally. These subjects turned out to be among the most important we tackled.

The household survey

Three kinds of investigation seemed to be needed: social, physical and economic. They had to be studied together and the multi-disciplinary team had to work out a multi-disciplinary approach. The first task, as already mentioned, was to carry out a household survey. This was carried out in the autumn of 1973; it provided information about a cross section of households and gathered the opinions of people in them aged 16 and over.[1] The survey aimed to provide a reasonably comprehensive data base for later investigations and to supplement the census material. Primarily designed to collect social and economic data, it was supplemented in a number of interviews by detailed physical observation of people's homes, using architects as well as interviewers to explore the relationships between the forms of dwellings and people's ways of living in them.

The other main purpose of our household survey was to examine residents' opinions and aspirations. We asked for their views on their homes and their neighbourhood,

(1) Details of the survey and its interpretation are given in Appendix 2.

on work and leisure, whether they would like to move or stay, and what they thought should be done to improve the area. This helped us complete our picture of the study area, rather than just catalogue its shortcomings. Finally, what people said helped us in selecting action projects.

We felt that it was essential to canvass the views of local residents, as well as those of officials and elected representatives, and we did this in a variety of ways. One way was to consult local community groups – neighbourhood councils, tenants' associations, residents' organisations and the like. At an early stage, we made contact with all such bodies as we could find in the area, and we tried to keep the lines of communication with them open throughout the course of the study.

Such groups provided us with useful information and ideas, but they do not by themselves represent local residents. They are not necessarily known to most people, and those who are active are usually only a minority of those who are members or who know about their existence. This is shown later to be true, in particular, of neighbourhood councils and our impression of other groups was that most of them were similarly run by a small and vocal minority. The household survey offered a means of collecting the views of the non-participating majority. Of course, most people are not able to suggest in detail what policies should be adopted, to know the resource implications of various alternatives, to balance one strategy as against another, to analyse the fundamental processes at work. But they can say where, for them, the shoe pinches. They can also express a view about the kinds of local change needed.

Selecting the area

As we have explained, one of our first tasks was to select an area for study within Lambeth. After detailed examination and discussion, we chose the area shown in Figures 2 and 3. It is bounded by Brixton Road, Harleyford Road, Wandsworth Road and the Brixton–Victoria Railway, with a population of about 50,000.

Our detailed criteria for selecting this area are described elsewhere.[1] As the main purpose of the study was to extract conclusions of general relevance, the area had to be reasonably representative of Inner London. Clearly, it would have been impossible to find somewhere that was an exact microcosm. Nor was this necessary. The main thing was to ensure that the chosen area contained the characteristic inner city problems and, to the extent that they could be usefully analysed, the main structural elements of Inner London – different housing types, social classes and so on. For similar reasons, it was important that the area should not be one dominated by a single characteristic, such as major redevelopment or an overwhelming proportion of immigrants, or by a unique feature, like Brixton town centre.

(1) Inner Area Study Lambeth, *Project Report* (IAS/LA/1). Appendix 1.

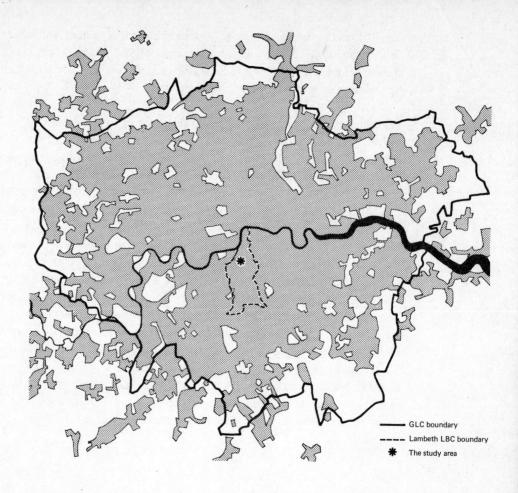

**Figure 2
The study area,
Lambeth and
Greater London**

GLC boundary
- - - Lambeth LBC boundary
✳ The study area

Thus, the chosen area contained all the dwelling types typical of Inner London
(Figure 4). Some parts had been redeveloped in the post-war period; others had
been improved or 'gentrified'; others again had been largely unaffected by these
processes. The population contained a mixture of social classes and ethnic groups.
One resident in every six had been born outside Britain and one in 20 in the
Caribbean. The immigrants were particularly concentrated in certain parts of the
area. There were several active residents' associations and local community groups
in the area, and this offered the prospect of useful community response.

The area contained concentrations of problems as identified by the statistics at our
disposal and the views of Lambeth people, particularly those in the Directorates of
Social Services and Health Services.[1]

Because of the non-correspondence, described in Chapter 9, between all the various
functional boundaries of local and central government, it would have been
impossible to define an area which matched all or even most of them. But the
selected area included almost all of one of the eight social service areas.

(1) This was before the reorganisation of the National Health Service in 1974, under which most of the
local authority's health functions were transferred to Area Health Authorities.

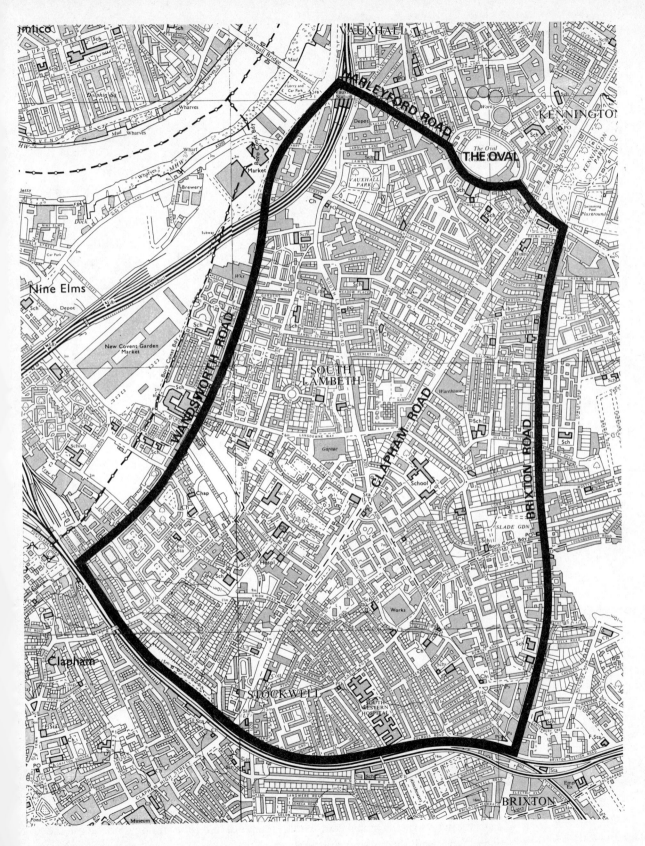

Figure 3   The study area

11

Figure 4
Housing types in
the study area

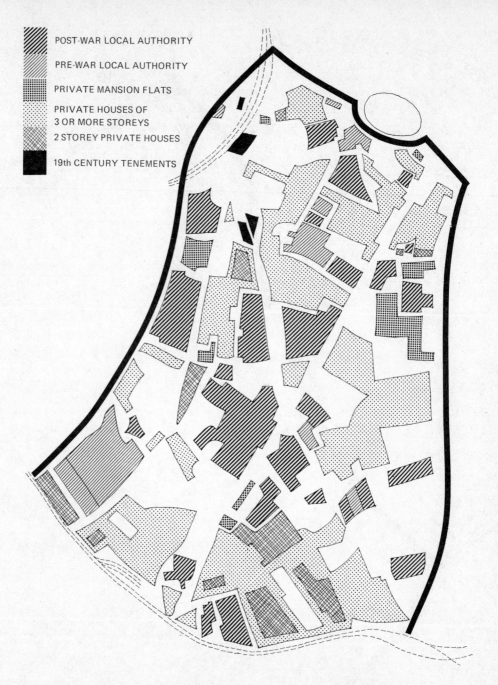

POST-WAR LOCAL AUTHORITY

PRE-WAR LOCAL AUTHORITY

PRIVATE MANSION FLATS

PRIVATE HOUSES OF
3 OR MORE STOREYS

2 STOREY PRIVATE HOUSES

19th CENTURY TENEMENTS

It conformed almost exactly with four district plan areas of the Directorate of
Development Services. It contained almost all of one neighbourhood council and
parts of two others.

Though the area is in many ways a mosaic of different localities, it has a centre
which many people recognise, and the name 'Stockwell' is used by local people to
describe the bulk of the area, although other place names such as 'Brixton' or
'Vauxhall' are current towards the fringes. It seemed right therefore to call the
district after its geographical centre, map reference and tube station, and we use the
name 'Stockwell' throughout this book.

12

Stockwell's past

Two hundred years ago Stockwell was a small village on the edge of London. It had a manor house, several houses of the lesser gentry grouped around the green, and perhaps two dozen workers' cottages. On every side there were open fields up to the edge of the city at Kennington. Slowly, the links with London grew. Georgian houses sprang up in terraces along the main roads to the metropolis. Many remain today, often converted for commerce – perhaps as a solicitor's office near to Brixton centre, but more commonly a general store, a newsagent's or a junk shop, with the sales area crammed into a single storey front extension built over the former front garden.

In the first half of the 19th century, several areas were laid out as small colonies for well-to-do refugees from the city. These were small groups of houses, usually 50 or so, arranged around some central feature – a small circus at Lansdowne Gardens, a crescent at Stockwell Park, a small park at Durand Gardens. The buildings had imposing entrances, large gardens and often rich architectural decoration. In short, they were 'houses of character' and, after a period of decline, many of them have now been converted back to their former glory. We call these little enclaves the 'oases'.

*Aerial view of an
'oasis':
Lansdowne Gardens.*

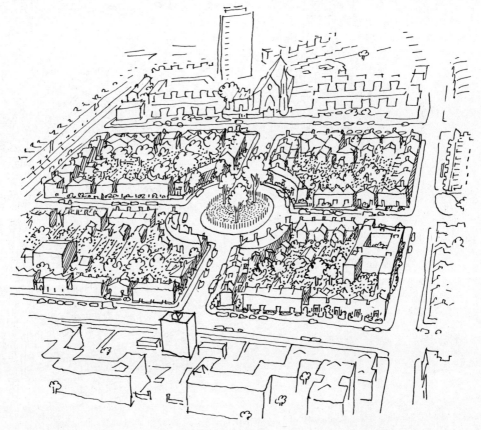

The rest of the area was rapidly built up at much higher densities over the next 60 years. By the outbreak of World War I a continuous sea of development joined Stockwell to Brixton, Clapham, Kennington and Camberwell. Save for the occasional small factory, shop or public building, most of this was housing, for even then the typical resident travelled into London to work. The houses themselves were usually poorer cousins of the buildings in the oases: typically a three-storey Victorian terrace with bay windows and small front gardens.

Their builders probably first expected them to be occupied as single-family houses by middle-class people, but it was not long before the area began to lose its

Two storey Victorian terraces: the Landor Road area.

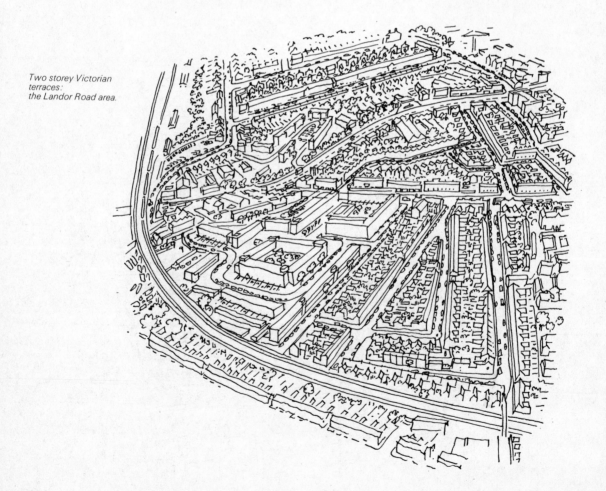

attraction for this part of the market, and most of them became multi-occupied with a separate working-class family on each floor. It is clear from the original plans that many were multi-occupied from the day they were completed. In a few places, as builders realised the changing nature of the market, they adapted their designs to suit the new form of demand, first, for example, by combining adjacent houses to economise on staircases and entrance doors, and ultimately by constructing separate flats behind what was still the facade of a single-family house. These were the ancestors of the so-called 'mansion' blocks which appeared at the end of the century.

Here and there, other types of housing made an appearance. These were usually various forms of purpose-built working-class accommodation. Several districts contained 'two-up–two-down' terraces, built right up to the pavement and without bathrooms or inside WCs. These were to become the first slums and most of them have now disappeared. At Vauxhall, the Railway Company built four tenement blocks – 'Coronation Buildings' – for its workers, and a number of 'mansion' blocks went up in the same area. However, the basic housing type remained that of the terraced house in multiple occupation. In some areas they were built in a smaller form as two-storey 'artisan villas', but even these often appear to have gone over to multiple occupation.

*The Springfield Estate,
built by the LCC
between the wars.*

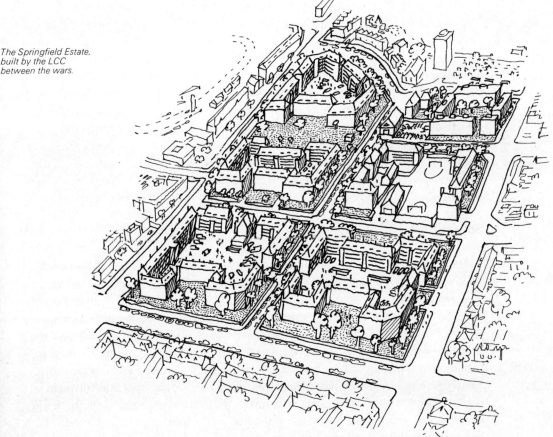

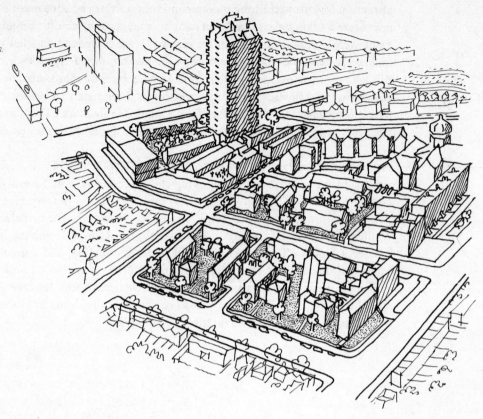

The disappearance of undeveloped land meant also the disappearance of the private developer. From then on, the requirement was for the redevelopment of older housing to provide cheap rented units. Then, as now, private enterprise could not do the job at an adequate profit, especially when there were much more lucrative opportunities in the suburbs. The role of the developer therefore passed to the local authority, first producing five-storey walkups in the slum clearance schemes of the inter-war period, and then, successively in the 1950s and 1960s, 'mixed development', 'slab blocks', 'point blocks' and 'high density low rise' schemes.

Stockwell today

By 1976 there were 17 major public housing estates, nearly half of all households were council tenants and some two-thirds of the land was in public ownership. Housing covered over three-quarters of the land. The next biggest land use was education, with four secondary schools and 11 primary. There is little open space, the only sizeable park being at Larkhall, a brave creation by the council over the past ten years. There are few factories and, with Brixton town centre on its edge, shopping in the study area is confined to a few minor parades and corner shops. Nearly nine out of ten employed residents work outside the area, half of them in Central London. It is not a quiet dormitory, for everywhere there is the bustle of people going about their business, of children's play and, in places, the roar of heavy lorries and commuter cars along the main roads that enclose and carve up the area.

16

A short walk around the area gives a range of impressions. In the east is one of our oases – centred on Stockwell Park Crescent but extending to Burney Road, Sidney Road and several other surrounding streets. In one short terrace of half a dozen houses live two senior civil servants and a departmental head of a local Polytechnic. But some of the older residents remain. An elderly man in the Crescent had his house bought up by the council for a proposed development. When this did not materialise, he stayed on as a council tenant. He viewed the changes with a mixture of pride and anxiety:

> 'The changes have been amazing in my life. When I moved in before the war, every house was going to the dogs. Now the place is full of lawyers and the houses are all bright and painted. It's got its problems, though. They're a tough lot over there and if you leave your car out you can come back home and find it bashed in or the tyres slashed. I used to go out for a walk round to the pub at night, but not now.'

The Crescent itself has large semi-detached houses with steps leading up to a classical portico around the front entrance. Most of the buildings have bright paintwork, polished brass door furniture and well tended gardens. But one gutted building, which remained in the same state for the three years of our study, is a reminder that the heyday of Stockwell's property boom is now over. The difference between the purchase price of an old house and its selling price in modernised form has narrowed too much to support the old rate of improvement, and local authority improvement grants do not make the same contribution as before.

Stockwell Park Crescent.

To the south is the Stockwell Park Estate, a recently completed Lambeth council scheme containing over 900 flats. It is designed in the low-rise high-density style, with no building over five storeys high and with access via a 'pedway' system running across the whole estate at second floor level. This is intended to keep pedestrians and vehicles apart, the latter being confined to a ground level garage and road system. There is a small shopping precinct, health centre, pub, play-group, and old people's day centre. High quality materials are used throughout and there are attractive touches of detail, such as large concrete window boxes to help compensate for the lack of garden space. But the marks of vandalism are everywhere. The glass screens along the pedways are shattered, walls covered with scrawled graffiti and the low level garages almost entirely derelict. Evidence of fire and other damage shows why people prefer to park their cars within view of the pavements and even on the landscaped areas. The ducks in the ornamental pond are, however, still alive, after 18 months.

Stockwell Road runs across the boundary of the estate, connecting the teeming shopping centre of Brixton with the much smaller centre at the crossroads by Stockwell tube station. Stockwell Road itself has a few small shops and four pubs, one of them noted for its jazz evenings. But its main claim to fame is as a centre of the motorcycle trade. A collection of stores sell what seems to be every model of motorcycle and every conceivable type of accessory. Most of them are owned by a single firm which has impressed its distinctive house style – red painted brickwork – on the townscape of the area. Leather-clad enthusiasts flock to the road from all parts of London, and often from abroad, to fit new parts to their bikes or compare the merits of new models.

On the other side of Stockwell Road is the Landor Road area: 50 acres of Victorian terraces and the scene of recent battles over rehabilitation versus redevelopment. The blight is now lifted from the area; immediate redevelopment plans have been dropped, two Housing Action Areas have been declared and the council has set up an office in an old chemists' shop to help with the improvement process. In the little streets that run south of Landor Road new front walls are being built, doors and windows painted, and worn out roofs repaired.

Like Stockwell Park estate, the Landor Road area has a large West Indian population, the product of a shift in the centre of gravity of the Caribbean community from its old nucleus on the other side of Brixton, parts of which have now been redeveloped. Many West Indians have bought themselves small houses, often, it seems, on high-interest finance company loans, which force them to take in lodgers to meet their repayments.

There are many people from other countries and the shops along Landor Road reflect this international community. There is a long established Italian drama school, the 'Italia Conti'. Further on, a West Indian grocers. Then a Chinese 'Pancake House', which somehow never seems to sell pancakes. Soon after, a traditional London egg and chips restaurant, of the kind which never has any name, simply a 'Cafe' sign alongside a Coca Cola symbol. Finally, at the end of the row, a

Above: Hargwyne Street from Pulross Road. Below: Arlesford Road from Landor Road.

photographer who specialises in pin-up photographs of local young people. The girls wear swimsuits, the boys boxing outfits. Both pose against Pacific island backcloths. The window display suggests a mixture of a beauty contest and the Olympic Games.

The area north of Landor Road has similar houses, but is somewhat smarter. From the three tower blocks in its centre – named after dramatists Beckett, Arden and Pinter – one can see the pattern of new roofs and other improvements.
Mr. Patterson[1] lives in Beckett House:

> 'They moved me here three years ago when my house in Clapham came down. It took a while getting used to this place, right at the top here. When the wind blows the whole block sways. You go into the bathroom and see the water sloshing around in the basin. And try putting screws into the walls. Bloody impossible – it's all solid concrete. Some of them don't like it here, but I don't mind. I've got the best view in London. Look, you could almost reach out and touch Big Ben down there.'

To the north is Stockwell Gardens, a fairly large estate of about 450 flats built for the London County Council (LCC) in the late 1950s and early 1960s. Now it belongs to Lambeth Council. The flats are mostly four-storey, built of red brick and grouped around small courtyards. This estate is better preserved than Stockwell Park. Apart from a few graffiti, there is hardly any sign of vandalism, and the little gardens along the Stockwell Road are well planted and looked after.

Constraints on the future

We have discussed the past and present physical states of Stockwell. Its future is in one sense the subject of the rest of the book, and Chapter 11 includes an explicit discussion of what it might be like at the turn of the century if our proposals were implemented. One point has to be made at the outset, since it has conditioned our thinking about what was possible: the physical structure of the study area seems unlikely to change fundamentally during the next few decades.

When we began this study, local government had a range of proposals for Stockwell which collectively seemed to offer the prospect of completely changing its physical face over a period of perhaps 20 years. We illustrate these proposals in Figure 5 and it will be instructive to recapitulate how much attitudes have changed on almost all fronts over the past three years.

On housing, by 1973 it had already begun to be recognised that much of the remaining 19th century stock was worth preserving, and proposals had been made for a network of Conservation Areas and General Improvement Areas covering most of what remained. Even so, a number of areas were earmarked for

(1) Here and later, we have used fictitious names for informants, in order to preserve confidentiality.

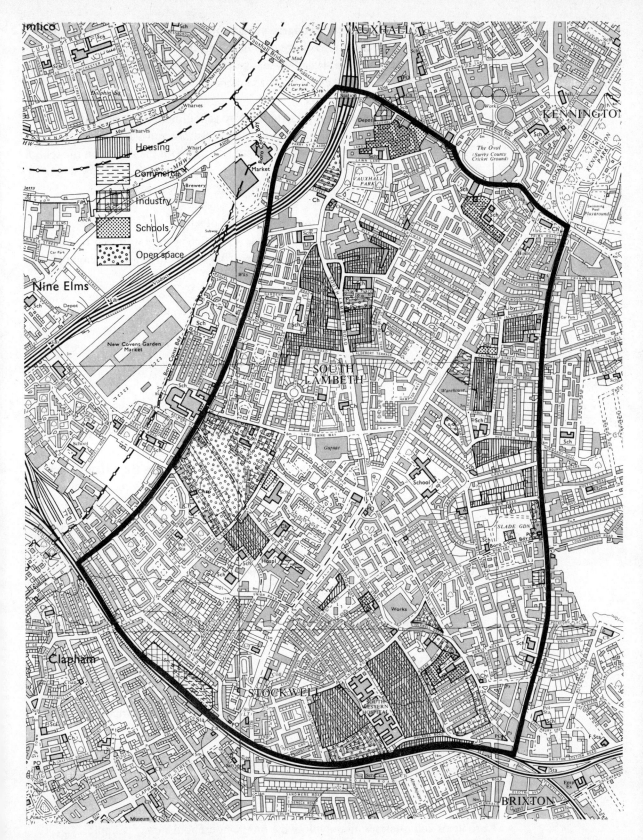

Figure 5   Development proposals in 1973

21

redevelopment, including the two large areas south of Landor Road. As we have pointed out, both of these areas have now been declared Housing Action Areas, with a 'guaranteed life' of at least 30 years and only those other redevelopments 'in the pipeline' by 1973 now seemed likely to go ahead.

Several sites had been reserved for extensions to school buildings, including two large ones near Archbishop Tennison's Grammar School and Vauxhall Manor Comprehensive School in the north of the study area. With the decline in the school population it seemed unlikely that either of these, or many of the primary school extensions, would be needed. But no decisions have yet been made.

Lambeth Council had also earmarked a number of sites for new public open spaces. Most of these were in the south of the area, where deficiencies were felt to be gravest. With the exception of Larkhall Park, now nearing completion, all of them appear to have been dropped.

In 1973 there were also extensive highway proposals affecting the area. The 'motorway box' was due to run along the southern edge and all of the existing main roads were scheduled for widening at some time in the future. The motorway box has now been deleted from the Greater London Development Plan and most of the road widening reservations have now been lifted.

On shopping and commercial development there were few sizeable proposals, since the whole of the study area lay very much in the commercial shadow of Brixton town centre where the major commercial proposals, including new shopping and offices, were concentrated. However, redevelopment proposals for Brixton itself are in jeopardy, since the developers previously associated with the Council have withdrawn their support. In any case, there is a strong school of thought that expensive redevelopment could destroy Brixton's function as a low cost shopping centre.

Finally, with the completion of the Clapham Goods Yard estate, there are no proposals for major new industrial premises.

In short, over a period of some three years, nearly all the major redevelopment proposals for Stockwell seem to have disappeared from view. This is not simply because of the current economic crisis; the present shortage of resources seems rather to have clinched the victory of those who argued that large scale redevelopment, whatever the purpose, was not the best use of resources even when they were available. We return to this theme in Chapter 8. Meanwhile, the limited scope for physical change has to be borne in mind.

□ The structure of the rest of this book is as follows. Chapter 2 describes the characteristics of the people of Stockwell and shows how they saw the place, its problems and qualities, mainly drawing on the household survey. Chapter 3 concentrates on poverty, its characteristics, causes and impact. Chapter 4 deals with jobs; this leads us into questions of unemployment, incomes, job opportunities, skills on offer, industrial decline and the need for training and retraining.

Chapter 5 describes the stresses in housing and the pressures on the present housing stock. In Chapter 6 we identify the 'housing trap' and in Chapter 7 we suggest ways of escape for those who wish to move out of Inner London. This analysis leads, in Chapter 8, to our specific suggestions for housing and planning policies inside Inner London.

Chapter 9 concentrates on personal and community services, and discusses problems of their delivery; it shows how better services could be provided through co-ordination. Chapter 10 reviews the role of studies of this kind and suggests what needs to be done if our programme is to be implemented. In the last chapter we list and summarise our policy proposals, identify where action has to be taken and by whom, and finally sketch a picture of what Stockwell could be like in the year 2000 ◻

2 The people and their views

Mrs. Simey lived about five minutes' walk from Stockwell Underground station. The Victorian terraced house had a basement and three more storeys. There were six steps up to the porch, punctuated by two pillars. The grandeur was undermined by the crumbling third step, the chips in the stucco and the peeling brown paint on the front door. Three other families lived there, but at the time of the first interview Mrs. Simey was the only person in apart from Mrs. Young, an 84-year-old widow living by herself in the basement. After the interview Mrs. Simey led the way down to Mrs. Young and made the introductions. 'Here's someone come to see you, dear', she shouted, 'It's about some survey'.

Mrs. Simey was aged 60; her husband, the only other member of her household, was 64 and worked as a labourer in a local factory. Plump, with a shining red face, and wearing a loose flowered dress, Mrs. Simey looked more like a farmer's wife than a Londoner. They had two rooms on the top floor and on the half landing a tiny kitchen, which contained an old blue and white gas stove on legs, a chipped shallow sink and three low cupboards with a working surface on the biggest. There was one WC in the house, shared by all the families. The Simeys had no bath (they went 'regularly to the public baths', as she carefully explained), no wash basin and no hot water. 'I know a lot of these young people are keen on having hot water from the tap,' she said, 'but it doesn't worry us. I just boil it up in the kettle'. Their rooms needed some repairing; the wallpaper was peeling away in places and electric sockets were hanging loose on the wall. But 'the landlord won't do anything'.

Despite these drawbacks, they did not want to leave their home, where they had been for 27 years. 'We've got a controlled rent of £1.20 a week. We've never had much money. My husband's never been in the £30 a week category. I don't know how we'd manage if we had a higher rent. I know it's a rubbishy old place here, but we're happy. It suits us all right. My husband loves it; he says he wants to spend his last days here.' Their 'one luxury' was colour television; 'I saved up for it and bought it for his birthday'.

No family is of course typical of those in Stockwell. We can, however, perhaps suggest something of the variety by portraying, more briefly, a few of the Simeys' neighbours.

One man was a Member of Parliament, living alone in a small flat. He explained that he was 'not really a resident'; his wife and, when not away at boarding school, his children lived in a manor house set in four acres in Wiltshire. 'I don't know much about the district, to be truthful. I'm a bird of passage. It's only a pied-a-terre – I just sleep here four nights week.' He knew enough, even so, to say that he was 'disturbed by the violence and vandalism you hear about round here. I'm not racially prejudiced, but it seems to be mainly the coloured youths who cause the trouble'. To him the main advantage of the area was its proximity to Westminster. 'I can get there in eight minutes.'

Mr. and Mrs. Roberts, who were from Jamaica, lived with their two children in a two-storey house in the Landor Road district described in the previous chapter. When we interviewed them the area was still due to be redeveloped by Lambeth Council. The front-window curtains were drawn all day, an outward sign that often distinguishes houses occupied by West Indians.[1] Inside, the house was clean and brightly painted, fitted with new cupboards and kitchen cabinets, and with central heating put in by Mr. Roberts himself. He was a skilled motor fitter; Mrs. Roberts worked part-time as a secretary. They had many relatives, his and hers, living nearby, and also many friends: 'We know them in the street, but there are others we meet when we're out shopping at Brixton Market'. Most of their friends were West Indians, 'but we say "Good morning" to the white people in the street; we get on quite well round here'. They did not want to move: 'We like the district. Our kids were born here', said Mrs. Roberts. Her husband laid more emphasis on the house itself: 'We've spent a fortune on this place so we want to keep it. We've had to pay a big mortgage; by moving we'd be in debt'. As things turned out, their house was reprieved when the Council reversed its policy and scheduled a Housing Action Area instead.

(1) All Stockwell's 'West Indians' are British citizens and many were born in this country; we use the term to refer to their cultural background in much the same way as one might describe people as 'Welsh' who were born in Wales or whose parents were born there.

Mr. Dawson, an advertising executive, lived with his wife and two children in an eight-roomed Georgian house. They had engaged an architect to restore and convert it, putting in two bathrooms and an open-plan kitchen/dining/day room in the semi-basement. The front garden was landscaped to take two cars – his Rover and her Mini. Mr. Dawson liked the district because 'it's convenient for my work. And it's much cheaper here. This house would cost much more in Chelsea'. He was also pleased that 'one is saving these lovely old houses'. They had, as well as the two cars and two bathrooms, a washing machine, dishwasher, fridge and freezer. But 'only black and white television; people like us don't have colour television'.

Mr. and Mrs. Donahue, in their thirties with two children, came from Northern Ireland. 'I am a Protestant and my wife is a Catholic. The pressures got too much. My little son was injured. We just had to get away.' They had sold their house in Belfast for £95 and now lived in three rooms paying £6 a week rent. 'The roof leaks. The flat is riddled with mice; we had to get a cat. There's no room for cooking, just a stove at the top of the stairs. There's no bathroom, no hot water. There's no privacy. The bedrooms are too small.' They hoped to move out to an expanding town: 'We've been to Andover. It's lovely there – all green fields, fresh air and everything's new and clean. It's quite different from this place. This is a rough area, not a nice place to bring up kids in, with lots of problem families and stereos blaring out all night.'

Mrs. Gordon was a wife living with her three young children on supplementary benefit; her husband would be in prison for the next six years. She was in two damp and draughty rooms; the wallpaper was peeling. The WC was shared and there was no bath in the house. The sink on her landing had no waste-pipe; the water simply splashed into a bucket which had to be regularly emptied down the WC. She said, 'It's so hard for the kiddies. They've nowhere to play. I wish we could get a place with a garden. I'd love to have a proper kitchen with a proper sink. I'd like to have hot water. I'd like to have electric plugs in the room.'

Household structure and age

Individual examples such as these can give no picture of the structure of Stockwell's population, or of how it differs from elsewhere. In trying to draw such a picture, we concentrate on four main issues. What kinds of household live in the district? What is the age structure of the residents? What about people's 'race' or colour? What is the structure of the population in terms of occupational status, and how has this been changing? Finally, by way of background to later chapters, what sorts of housing do these different kinds of people live in?

The main comparisons made are with Greater London and the country as a whole, drawing on the General Household Survey carried out nationally in 1973,[1] the year of our own survey in Stockwell, and also, to a more limited extent, on census data. Though the census is less up to date, it gives some information about changes over time as the survey does not.

Table 1 compares Stockwell with Greater London and Britain in terms of household types or stages in the household life cycle. The table shows three things. First, Stockwell contained a larger proportion of younger single-person households than Greater London generally, which in turn contained more than the average for the country. Census figures show independently that the concentration of single-person younger households in Stockwell and similar parts of London became more marked between 1961 and 1971. These findings no doubt reflect the features of Inner London – the bright lights of the West End, the special job opportunities, the range of entertainment and culture, the 'cosmopolitan' style of life – which exercise a continuing pull upon unattached young people from other parts of Britain and abroad.

Secondly, Stockwell contained a fairly large proportion of households with children – about the same as in Britain and more than in Greater London as a whole. In addition, though this is not shown in the table, Stockwell had a higher than average proportion of large families: 30 per cent of families with children under 16 had three or more, compared with 24 per cent in Britain. This difference is presumably explained mainly by two features of Stockwell's population discussed

(1) Office of Population Censuses and Surveys, *The General Household Survey 1973*. National and Greater London data for 1973 cited in this and subsequent chapters were either from this report or from analyses specially supplied by OPCS.

Table 1 Household types: Stockwell, Greater London and Great Britain

	Stockwell	Greater London	Great Britain
Younger one-person (aged 16–59)	12%	9%	5%
Younger two-person (aged 16–59)	15%	15%	14%
Household with children under 16	36%	32%	38%
Three or more people aged 16 or over	12%	13%	12%
Older two-person (one or both aged 60 or over)	12%	19%	17%
Older one-person (60 or over)	13%	13%	14%
Total %	100%	100%	100%
Number	1170 (weighted)[1]	1523	11,642

(1) In this and other tables the sample total in Stockwell is 'weighted'; an explanation is given in Appendix 2.

Sources: Stockwell Household Survey 1973, General Household Survey 1973.

later; it contained relatively large proportions of low-skill people and of black immigrants, both of whom have more children than other people.[1] Thirdly, Stockwell had relatively few old-person households, compared with Greater London and Britain.

Thus, as well as being particularly attractive to small younger households, Stockwell is a place with a high proportion of children compared to Greater London generally and with a low proportion of old people. These conclusions are confirmed by an analysis in terms of people rather than households (Table 2).

Table 2 Age structure of the population: Stockwell, Greater London and Great Britain

	Stockwell	Greater London	Great Britain
Age 15 or under	27%	23%	27%
Age 16 or over but under pension age (60 for women, 65 for men)	60%	58%	57%
Over pension age	13%	18%	16%
Total %	100%	100%	100%
Number	3186 (weighted)	4058	33,006

Sources: Stockwell Household Survey 1973, General Household Survey 1973.

Birthplace and colour

Since the mid-1950s Brixton has been one of the main settlements of West Indians in Britain, and Brixton Market, with reggae music beating out from the record shops and stalls piled high with green bananas and sweet potatoes, is a busy centre where West Indian culture mingles with that of native South Londoners. Many of our black respondents, and white for that matter, shopped there regularly and the West Indians in particular often stressed its importance as a place for meeting friends.

(1) See e.g. Ann Cartwright, *How Many Children?*, p. 101 and p. 139.

As the West Indian population has grown, its geographical span has extended too. There were in 1973 relatively high concentrations of West Indians in the south western part of our study area, and others living in other parts of Stockwell. The 1971 census showed that Stockwell, like Lambeth generally, had a higher than average proportion of black immigrants. Stockwell's proportion, 11 per cent, was nearly twice that of Greater London and nearly five times as great as that of the whole country. By the 1973 survey the proportion was 14 per cent, the overwhelming majority of whom had come from the West Indies. Another 6 per cent of Stockwell residents had been born in Eire, and a further 12 per cent from European countries, mainly Cyprus, Spain and Italy. The presence of the latter may be partly explained by Stockwell's proximity to the hotels and restaurants of the West End.

Whatever the explanation, it is clear that Stockwell's population was very mixed in terms of birthplace, with a total of nearly a third coming from outside the United Kingdom. Of the foreign-born people in Stockwell, however, 70 per cent had lived in Britain for more than ten years. In a sense, these were no longer immigrants, being more firmly established locally than some newcomers from other parts of Britain. Their settling-in was demonstrated by the increasing proportion of West Indians in council housing, reported later.

A person's birthplace is only one index of his ethnic background. Another is skin colour. Our survey followed the General Household Survey in asking interviewers to record the colour of the people they saw, including children as well as adults. They did this for all but 8 per cent of those living in the households interviewed. As many as 22 per cent proved to be 'coloured' (that is non-white), compared with 7 per cent in Greater London and 2 per cent in Britain. Their age structure was very different from that of whites in Stockwell: 46 per cent of blacks were children (aged 15 or under) as against 20 per cent of whites, and only 2 per cent were aged 60 or over as against 20 per cent.[1] These differences reflect two things. First, there were as yet few black people who were old, because most adults had moved to Britain relatively recently and were fairly young when they came. Secondly, on average blacks had more children than whites: among the families with children under 16 in our 1973 sample, 44 per cent of blacks had three or more compared with 22 per cent of whites.

At least among West Indians, family structures are apparently sometimes different from those standard in Britain. One West Indian pattern, reflecting that common in the Caribbean itself, is based not upon a stable relationship between husband and wife but on the tie between the mother and her children, often with different fathers. The women remain single and largely independent, though at any particular time she is likely to have a sexual relationship – including currently co-habiting – with 'her man', who may or may not be one of the fathers.

(1) These differences are broadly in line with those nationally. The 1973 General Household Survey found that in Great Britain 41 per cent of blacks were children compared with 25 per cent of whites, and 5 per cent as against 19 per cent were aged 60 or over.

We certainly came across families of this kind in connection with our day care action project, in which salaried childminders were attached to a local day nursery. As the report of that project shows,[1] most of the children requiring 'priority' day care (in the day nursery or from a childminder) were of West Indian parents, and most of the mothers were unmarried with a set of relationships like that just described (there were also a few 'unmarried fathers'). If we had gone by this evidence alone – admittedly drawn from a 'problem' minority of the West Indian population – we would have formed the impression that these fragile and ever-shifting co-habiting unions were indeed still the characteristic West Indian style. Such a family pattern would be consistent with the large families reported earlier.

In our survey there were rather more one-parent families among black households with children (22 per cent) than among whites (15 per cent). Though this difference was not large enough for chance to be ruled out as the explanation, it seems likely to reflect a real difference, since a recent national survey showed a similar variation.[2] However, some of the kinds of families we have described could not easily have been identified in an interview, since their 'men' might well have been living in the household at the time. In many interviews, there was little doubt that the relationships between the couples were like those of white husbands and wives in Stockwell; Mr. and Mrs. Roberts, cited earlier in the chapter, were one such example. But, since we did not ask the interviewers to record their impressions of the degree of stability or instability of unions, the survey results do not enable us to distinguish between marriage and co-habitation, between long-term 'husbands' and short-term. Thus it may well be that many more of the West Indian families than of others were based on relatively transitory partnerships. We naturally now wish we had explored this issue more fully in the survey.

Our own judgement is that there were indeed more temporary unions among West Indians than others in Stockwell, but that the majority of them had family patterns basically the same as those of their white neighbours. We would agree with Deakin's assessment in 1970: 'West Indians in Britain are increasingly following a family pattern which is typically British'.[3]

However, two characteristics of West Indian family life, which may be changing relatively slowly, affect the lives and opportunities of children and the attitudes of young people. The first is a rather detached attitude to young children on the part of parents, which is associated with the high proportion of West Indian mothers who work. We discuss this later. The second is the strict discipline often exercised in the home. As Banton has put it, young West Indians are often 'in conflict with their parents, for many of the older West Indians incline towards Victorian ideas of

(1) Phyllis Willmott and Linda Challis, *The Groveway Project* (IAS/LA/17).

(2) David J. Smith, *The Facts of Racial Disadvantage*, p. 173.

(3) Nicholas Deakin, *Colour, Citizenship and British Society*, p. 284. Sheila Allen, comparing family patterns in the West Indies and in Britain, says that 'many factors in the new environment led to placing greater emphasis on stable unions' (*New Minorities, Old Conflicts: Asian and West Indian Immigrants in Britain*, p. 83).

discipline'.[1] This inter-generational conflict helps to explain the apparent disaffection among black youths, which, as we show later, is reinforced by discrimination and by disappointments due to unrealistic aspirations.

Social class

Various indices of social class are used – income, education, family connections – but the most common is occupation. The jobs of Stockwell people are discussed in detail in Chapter 4. In this chapter, because we are using jobs as an index of social class, we describe how the occupational composition of the population compares with elsewhere, and how it has been changing.

We need to explain briefly how occupations have been classified into categories in this book. In general we have used broad combinations of 'socio-economic groups',[2] going into more detail (as in Chapter 4) where that seemed necessary. Table 3 illustrates the main broad categories used.

Table 3   Occupational classification mainly used in this report

Title	Socio-economic Groups	Examples of occupations
Professional	3 and 4	Architect, doctor, solicitor
Managerial	1, 2 and 13	Advertising executive, sales manager, works manager
Other non-manual	5 and 6	Clerk, shop assistant, teacher
Skilled manual (including foremen supervisors and own account non-professional workers)	8, 9, 12 and 14	Bricklayer, compositor, factory foreman
Semi-skilled manual (and personal service)	7, 10 and 15	Bus conductor, machine minder, waiter
Unskilled manual	11	Labourer, porter, office cleaner

Source: Office of Population Censuses and Surveys, *Classification of Occupations.*

Table 4 shows that, compared with Britain generally, Stockwell had a similar proportion of professional people, fewer managerial and rather more with limited skills. In other words, professional people apart, Stockwell had fewer households whose heads were in middle-class occupations and more in low-skill working-class ones.

Our survey confirmed the difference in occupational class by skin colour. As in the country generally, fewer blacks were in non-manual jobs and more in semi-skilled or unskilled. Thus in 1973 Stockwell was rather more 'working class' than Britain generally, and this was at least partly because there were more blacks than elsewhere and because blacks, as in other places, more often had lower-skill jobs.

(1) Michael Banton, *Racial Minorities*, p. 166.

(2) For an explanation of the two main official methods of classification, see Central Statistical Office, 'Social commentary: social class'.

Table 4 Occupational status of working and retired heads of households, Stockwell and Great Britain

	Stockwell	Great Britain
Professional	4%	4%
Managerial	6%	14%
Other non-manual	25%	20%
Skilled manual	31%	35%
Semi-skilled	22%	20%
Unskilled	12%	7%
Total %	100%	100%
Number	1169 (weighted)	11,342

Sources: Stockwell Household Survey 1973, General Household Survey 1973.

As we said in the previous chapter, a theme of recent debate about the inner city has been the supposed changes in its social class structure. Two main views of the trends have been expressed. One concentrates on what has been called 'gentrification'. The term was first coined by Glass, who used it to describe the process by which middle-class people invaded a formerly working-class district.[1] Despite the inaccuracy of the word (the people moving in can hardly be described as gentry), it is now so well established that it is probably best to continue to use it. The result of gentrification would be sizeable increases at the 'top' of the social scale in certain inner city districts.

The second suggestion is that what has been occurring is 'bi-polarisation', the argument being that the proportions have increased at the bottom as well as the top – at both poles – of the class structure.[2] The belief is that the inner city is increasingly becoming the preserve of the rich and the poor, with those in the middle – white-collar and skilled manual workers – squeezed out.

As part of our research we examined changes in the social class structure of Stockwell, in the context of trends within Greater London.[3] The subject is complicated, since one needs to take account of long-term changes in the occupational structure of the whole country: an increase in London or in parts of it among those in the higher socio-economic categories, or a decline say among skilled workers, does not indicate a specifically London or Inner London trend if it simply reflects what is happening generally. If, even allowing for this, there have been changes in some categories in some places, one does not know how much of the change has been due to migration – say to professional people moving in or skilled workers moving out – and how much to residents changing their jobs. Given the decline in the population of Greater London and of Inner London particularly,

(1) Ruth Glass, 'Introduction' in Centre for Urban Studies (editors), *London – Aspects of Change.*

(2) The 'polarisation' debate has been reviewed by Harris, who also discussed the terminology. If the change were an increase at one pole only, this would be described, in Harris's terms, as 'uni-polarisation'. See Margaret Harris, 'Some aspects of polarisation'.

(3) This study is reported in Inner Area Study Lambeth, *Changes in Socio-Economic Structure* (IAS/LA/2).

there is also the question of whether one is measuring absolute changes or proportionate ones.

With such difficulties as these, it is perhaps not surprising that different researchers have come to different conclusions. Our own view is first, that there has been some gentrification – larger-than-average increases, absolutely and proportionately, among professional and managerial people – in some parts of Inner London, including particular pockets in Stockwell. The scale of the change, in Stockwell as elsewhere, is quite small; its visibility – the repointed brickwork, the Habitat-painted front doors and the French blue house numbers – has given an exaggerated impression. What is more, it seems likely that market conditions, and arrangements for local authority improvement grants, were particularly favourable to the process before 1972; in Stockwell, as in Inner London generally, it seems to have slackened off since then.

Even if the process does resume its momentum, it does not seem to us that this should give any great cause for concern. Of course gentrification can be damaging if existing residents are over-persuaded or harassed out of their homes; as councils like Lambeth are increasingly aware, everything possible must be done to protect tenants against this. But there are also gains from gentrification. Older houses are repaired and improved. Partly because of the standards set by the improved houses and partly perhaps because of the local pressure exerted by the newcomers, the environment tends to get improved too. More important, as we argue in Chapter 4, one of Stockwell's major problems is the growing mis-match between jobs and residents. The proportion of non-manual jobs has been increasing but the residential pattern has followed suit only to a limited extent. As long as working-class residents who want to move out of Inner London have the chance to do so, and as long as those who remain have access to decent housing, there seems to us much to be said for a continuing process of gentrification in places like Stockwell.

Contrary to a commonly expressed view, many working-class residents seem to welcome the process. Mrs. Simey, who appeared earlier in this chapter, said: 'There are these young people moving into the old houses round here and doing them up. We like to see it. We prefer the old houses to these modern estates. We like to see them getting painted up. It cheers you up to see them.' She was speaking as a tenant. Mr. Roberts, a West Indian who was also mentioned earlier, put an owner-occupier's view: 'If richer people move in you obviously stand to gain by it, because the value of your house goes up.'

A more important trend than gentrification is the decline among skilled manual workers. Between 1961 and 1971 the proportion among working men fell by one in seven in Stockwell and one in eight in all Lambeth, compared with one in 17 in Greater London and no change in the country generally. Thus Stockwell and other inner city districts like it were losing proportionately more skilled men. The explanation presumably lies in two trends discussed more fully in later chapters, the changes in the industrial structure, with manufacturing industry moving out, and the changes in housing, particularly the continuing pull of the suburban style of life.

The proportion of semi-skilled and unskilled men remained fairly stable between 1961 and 1971, in Stockwell in particular and Inner London generally, against the background of a national decline. In this sense, Inner London's share of low-skill people increased. Given the increase among professional and managerial people at the 'top' over the same period, and the decline among skilled men in the 'middle', it seems to us indisputable that a degree of bi-polarisation was occurring in London's inner city over that decade.[1]

Our analysis of class changes also pointed up another trend, important but seldom discussed, taking place inside Inner London. The proportion of unskilled and semi-skilled men increased between 1961 and 1971 in the parts of Lambeth immediately to the south of Stockwell. We cannot tell how much of the increase was due to people changing to jobs of lower status and how much to migration. Nor, if people did move in, do we know where they moved from, but a likely explanation is that at least some of them came from districts like Stockwell itself.[2]

If this is so, it is extremely important for Lambeth and for inner city and metropolitan authorities more generally. It seems probable that changes in inner city areas have made it difficult, or perhaps just unpleasant, for some residents to stay. Searching for a home, they have moved slightly further 'out', where declining privately-rented property could be found. In consequence, their new areas have probably begun to take on some of the characteristics – and some of the problems – of the inner areas themselves. To oversimplify, it may be, ironically, that the more the inner city is improved by gentrification and council redevelopment, the further out it spreads. This underlines the arguments for considering inner areas as part of a larger whole, and it reinforces the need for policies which will take into account spill-over processes of this kind.

The main conclusion we would emphasise, however, is that the population structure of London's inner city, including both Stockwell and places slightly further from the centre, is being changed by a process of differential out-migration. Although some professional people have moved in, the general trend has been outward. Families in their thousands have moved to owner-occupied houses in the suburbs and beyond, or to new and expanding towns. The point is that the bulk of this movement has been by middle-class or skilled working-class people. The less skilled have had much less opportunity to go. One consequence has been the increase in Inner London's proportionate share of low-skill workers – the increasing polarisation towards the 'bottom' end of the class spectrum – together with, as we have noted, some degree of bi-polarisation.

(1) GLC researchers have come to different conclusions. Margaret Harris, op. cit.; Keith Dugmore (editor), *The Migration and Distribution of Socio-Economic Groups in Greater London: Evidence from the 1961, 1966 and 1971 Censuses.*

(2) A study in the London Borough of Enfield of changes between the censuses of 1961 and 1966 showed that this process was taking place there. People moving into the borough had mainly gone to inner wards containing older property, and most of them had moved from the immediately adjacent inner boroughs of Haringey, Hackney and Islington, *Report on the Changing Nature of Residential Areas.*

Families and their homes

In the previous chapter we described something of the housing of Stockwell and how it has been changing, and in this one we have already touched on the inter-relationships between the residents of the area and the kinds of housing available to them there. In looking more closely at who lives where, we examine housing in two ways: by the form of tenure and by the types of housing mentioned in the previous chapter.

Tenures in Stockwell in 1973 are compared, in Table 5, with those in Greater London and Britain. Stockwell had a smaller proportion of owner-occupiers, and a larger proportion of council tenants and private tenants. Council tenants accounted for nearly half the households in Stockwell. Of these, nearly two-thirds were tenants of Lambeth and the rest of the GLC. Despite the growth in council housing, relatively large proportions of people in Stockwell were still in furnished as well as unfurnished privately-rented property.

Table 5   Tenure of households, Stockwell, Greater London and Great Britain

	Stockwell	Greater London	Great Britain
Rented from local authority[1]	46%	25%	32%
Rented privately, unfurnished	28%	19%	12%
Rented privately, furnished	13%	8%	3%
Owner-occupied	11%	46%	59%
Other (mainly rented with job/business)	2%	2%	4%
Total %	100%	100%	100%
Number	1161 (weighted)	1511	11,553

(1) In Great Britain, this includes renting from new town development corporations.

Sources: Stockwell Household Survey 1973. General Household Survey 1973.

The relationship of tenure to housing types is straightforward. Owner-occupiers were mainly in the oases and in terraced houses. Private tenants were mainly in private flats and in older houses.

Households varied by tenure according to their stage in life. Owner-occupiers were mainly households with children, large childless households and younger couples. Unfurnished tenants, though they included households at all stages, were particularly common among older one and two-person households. Furnished tenancies, on the other hand, were concentrated among younger one and two-person households. Council tenants were mainly households with children, though there were rather more old people in the new local authority estates than in the old.

Social class, of course, strongly influenced people's housing. More professional and managerial people than others owned their homes but, looking at it the other way round, more than half of all owner-occupied houses belonged to manual workers. Council property was dominated by manual workers, but about half of clerical workers and the like were also council tenants. Manual people generally were dominant among private tenancies, the less-skilled in particular among furnished.

These findings, together with the fact that twice as many middle-class (non-manual) as working-class (manual) households lived in the oases, confirm the familiar general pattern, with housing opportunities broadly related to social class. The relationship between class and housing quality is, however, far from simple. Some younger professional people, for instance, were living in poorly-equipped furnished rooms, and a larger-than-average proportion of low-skill people were council tenants. So, though housing opportunities remain unequally distributed by class, the intervention of the local authorities has had some mitigating effect.

The next question is about the relationship between colour and housing (Table 6). The table includes other household members as well as heads. It shows that proportionately more blacks were owner-occupiers or furnished tenants, and proportionately fewer were unfurnished tenants. In the council sector, as other studies have found,[1] relatively more blacks were in the older, less preferred estates. This was presumably because their bargaining power was weaker than whites or because they were less well-informed.[2] Nevertheless, the proportion of black households, and people, was about the same as their proportion in the population, even in the newest council housing.

Table 6   Colour and tenure, households and all occupants

	Rent Council			Rent private un-furnished	Rent private furnished	Owner-occupied	All
	Old estates	New estates	Other property				
Percentage of heads of household in tenure category who were coloured	31%	15%	16%	6%	21%	26%	16%
Total number of heads of household (weighted)	110	347	55	288	137	123	1060
Percentage of all occupants (adults and children) in tenure category who were coloured	38%	22%	15%	6%	25%	36%	22%
Total number of occupants (adults and children) (weighted)	396	1005	141	689	255	373	2861

Source: Stockwell Household Survey 1973.

Population movement and community

We have already touched on some of the ways in which the population of Stockwell has been changing. It has been affected by migration from overseas, particularly from the West Indies. Gentrification, and the associated shrinking of the privately-rented sector, have contributed to changes in its class structure, as has the

(1) See e.g. Runnymede Trust, *Race and Council Housing in London*, 1975.

(2) The processes of allocation are discussed in David Smith and Anne Whalley, *Racial Minorities and Public Housing.*

movement out of skilled people. Council clearance and redevelopment have led many people to move their homes. What have been the consequences of all this for population stability?

There remained in 1973 a sizeable minority of established residents; about one household in six had, like Mr. and Mrs. Simey, been at the same address for 20 years or more. But as many as half of all households were relative newcomers, having been in their present home for less than five years. The comparable proportion in Greater London, as in Britain generally in 1973, was about a third.

Among households who had moved, those in Stockwell had moved more frequently; for example 12 per cent of them had moved three or more times, as against 5 per cent in Britain as a whole. An analysis of the frequent movers in Stockwell suggested that they were basically two kinds of people. The first were younger single people or couples, many of them middle class and many of whom had no strong desire to settle; they were just moving around within the bed-sitter land of Inner London. The second were families, desperately searching for a stable home, but shifting from one unsatisfactory stop-gap to another – living with parents, then in nominally furnished rooms, then squatting. Their problems are discussed in later chapters.

The relative instability of Stockwell's population would suggest that only a minority of people had relatives living nearby. Just under a third of adults turned out to have at least one within ten minutes' walk. Rather more people, about half, said they had at least one friend as near as this. We asked people about their contacts with these relatives and friends. Since the General Household Survey does not include questions on this, we could compare only with a survey by the Institute of Community Studies in the London Metropolitan Region in 1970.[1] The comparisons suggested that contacts with both friends and relatives were less common in Stockwell than elsewhere in the London Region. We could not compare directly with the earlier study in Bethnal Green,[2] but it is clear that kinship and community ties were much weaker in the Stockwell of 1973 than in the East End of 1955.

Such ties mattered, of course, to some people. A 28-year-old married man, a clerk, had a brother and mother-in-law nearby; with his wife, he saw his mother-in-law three times a week. A 29-year-old housewife had seen 'over 20' friends in the previous week: 'I know the whole district because I was living here as a child. I know nearly everybody.' Mr. and Mrs. Roberts, the West Indian couple quoted earlier, had relatives living in the district and saw them, and friends, often. Mrs. Roberts had met 15 friends in the previous week. But people like these were the exceptions.

A crucial issue is how the presence of a relatively large proportion of newcomers affected what might be called people's 'sense of community' – their feeling of

(1) Michael Young and Peter Willmott, *The Symmetrical Family: A Study of Work and Leisure in the London Region.*

(2) Michael Young and Peter Willmott, *Family and Kinship in East London.*

identification with the immediate locality and with their neighbours. We asked a question on this: 'Do you think there is an area around here that might be called your local neighbourhood – I mean the local area you live in or feel you belong to?' Only about a third (35 per cent) could recognise their local 'neighbourhood' in this way. This proportion was lower than in other places. In a survey in Hornsey (in the London Borough of Haringey), where the identical question was put, 75 per cent gave positive answers.[1] The proportion was 78 per cent in a national survey carried out for the Maud Commission,[2] and as high as 97 per cent and 99 per cent respectively in surveys in Ipswich and Northampton.[3]

The sense of neighbourhood varied inside Stockwell according to people's length of residence locally: one in six among those who had been there for less than six months as against nearly half – still low – among those who had lived there for 20 years or more or had been born there. This suggests that the relative mobility of the population, though it is likely to be part of the reason, cannot be the sole one. We can only speculate about the others. Perhaps the large-scale redevelopment and other physical changes have made the district less coherent physically than in the past. Perhaps the movements of population have made it seem less coherent socially even to those who have stayed.

People's recognition of neighbourhood also varied with class. Even though more professional and managerial people were newcomers, more of them recognised a neighbourhood – over half as against a third in other occupational groups. This confirms what other studies have suggested: middle-class people, presumably because they are more accustomed to moving home for job reasons, are more culturally adjusted to the process of settling in to new communities. Once in a new district, they find it relatively easy to identify with it, to 'feel at home'.[4] This process may have been helped in Stockwell by the distinctive and intimate character of the oases and similar areas to which such people had commonly moved.

We asked everybody, recognising a neighbourhood or not, if they could give a name to the area in which they lived. Just over half could do so; among these, as we have said earlier, the most common name was the one we ourselves have adopted. But this was given by only a minority, and a great variety of names were mentioned. A few people misunderstood the question (perhaps deliberately), and answered in terms of some feature that they disliked. Many spoke in terms of West Indians or other immigrants – 'Little Jamaica', 'Calcutta', 'The League of Nations', '57 Varieties'. The general impression from the answers to these questions is thus that Stockwell was, in the minds of most of its residents, not composed of a number of distinct and readily identifiable local communities, and that the sense of neighbourhood or community was not strong.

(1) Michael Young, 'A new voice for the neighbourhood'.

(2) Royal Commission on Local Government in England, *Community Attitudes Survey*.

(3) Shankland Cox and Associates, *Expansion of Ipswich*; Hugh Wilson and Lewis Womersley, *Expansion of Northampton*.

(4) See, for example, W. H. Whyte, *The Organisation Man* and Peter Willmott and Michael Young, *Family and Class in a London Suburb*.

One of the arguments for neighbourhood councils is that they may help to encourage this sense. Three neighbourhood councils between them covered about three-quarters of the area studied. When people were asked whether they had 'heard if there is a Neighbourhood Council for this area? (I don't mean the *Lambeth* Council)', only about one person in eight, in the districts with such councils, knew of their existence. The minority who did know were asked if they had ever attended meetings; only a fifth had.

These findings seem relevant not just to neighbourhood councils but more generally. We did not ask in our survey about tenants' associations or other kinds of community group. But, as we have said, our strong impression was that most such bodies were run by a small minority of residents and were not in close contact with the majority. We draw two conclusions about the role of such community groups. The first is that, in the absence of stability of population, they can do very little to foster a sense of community by organisational means. The second is that, though they can speak up for local interests, they cannot in any sense be regarded as representative of majority local opinion.

These are not, of course, the only ways to judge neighbourhood councils and community groups, and in other respects they have been strikingly successful. In Stockwell several such groups had brought pressure to bear – we think for the better – particularly on the two familiar themes of redevelopment and children's play provision. Some had proved their effectiveness in devising and implementing small-scale projects such as information shops or, again, adventure playgrounds. We later suggest ways in which such local groups could be helped to build on their strengths and participate more fully in the processes of urban improvement.

Seeking people's views

The household survey, our main source for people's opinions, gathered those of adults only. We were able to learn something about children's opinions through our 'schools project', carried out in association with the 11 primary schools and four secondary schools. Adults' views are reported in some detail in the separate report on the survey, and children's in that of the schools project.[1] Here we try to pull together the main threads of opinion and suggest the broad implications, as a framework for the discussion in later chapters.

The first impression from the interviews is of people's relative discontentment with Stockwell and their concern about current trends there. In answer to a question about what they 'liked' about the place, almost a third said 'nothing', whereas the proportion as dissatisfied as this in England as a whole was only a seventh.[2] Asked

(1) Inner Area Study Lambeth, *People, Housing and District* (IAS/LA/5) and Inner Area Study Lambeth, *Schools Project* (IAS/LA/13).

(2) This was an 'environmental survey' based on sample interviews carried out in 1972 by Social and Community Planning Research for the Department of the Environment. A report has not been published.

whether they found their area 'attractive' or 'unattractive' to look at, over half those in Stockwell, but again about a seventh nationally, thought it unattractive:

> 'Attractive? It's one of the worst slums in London.'

> 'The estates have spoiled it. It's all bleeding flats within a quarter of a mile from here. The tall blocks are the worst.'

> 'It's scruffy and dirty. Look at all the rubbish in the streets.'

Nearly half the Stockwell people, in answer to a question about whether they thought their district was 'improving or getting worse as a place to live in', said 'getting worse'; the proportion nationally was only about a quarter.

> 'Over the last few years the streets have got dirtier and there's been more vandalism and mugging.'

> 'The people aren't the same. There are all these coloureds and problem families and unmarried mothers moving in. It's definitely getting worse.'

The discontent was reflected in people's desire to move. 48 per cent of the respondents in Stockwell said they would 'prefer to move to another district'; in a sample survey in 1970 covering the whole London Metropolitan Region the proportion was 31 per cent. Though some of those in Stockwell who wanted to move said they would prefer to remain in Inner London, the majority sought the semi-detached houses and green spaces of suburbia,[1] which they contrasted in their own minds with the overcrowding, the unloved blocks of council flats, the dirt and litter, the resented newcomers, the crime and vandalism of the inner city. At least some of these views were echoed by children. When describing or drawing their 'dream house' they almost always portrayed detached houses with gardens, and they complained, for instance, about violence, the 'high crime rate' and 'tramps in the houses that are boarded up'.

But this is only part of the story. After all, over half the adults in the Stockwell sample did *not* think the area was in decline. Nearly a quarter actually thought it was improving, most of them citing housing rehabilitation and redevelopment as reasons. Similarly, over two-thirds of those in the sample said they 'liked' some aspect of life in Stockwell, usually its accessibility to Central London, to local shopping centres such as Brixton or to their work. A few (about one respondent in ten, compared with one in four nationally) extolled the 'friendliness' or 'niceness' of their neighbours. Among children, the younger ones often mentioned the 'friendly people' locally – the milkman, the policeman, the corner shopkeeper. And at least as many adults wanted to stay in the district as wanted to leave it.

The more positive attitudes were most common among two quite different kinds of men and women, both largely newcomers. The first were professional and managerial people of the kind who had moved into the oases and other areas of low-density housing. The second were West Indians. For example, the proportion of

(1) This desire to move out of Inner London is examined in Chapter 6.

professional and managerial people who said they liked 'nothing' about the district was lower than among other occupational classes. Conversely, more professional and managerial people than others thought the district was 'improving'. More blacks than whites also thought it was improving, and more found the district 'attractive'. Perhaps most striking of all, less blacks wanted to leave Stockwell and, of those who did, relatively few wanted to move out of the inner city altogether.

Thus more West Indians and, among whites, more professional and managerial people found Stockwell congenial. Their reasons are fairly obvious, though different for the two kinds of people. The middle-class residents who liked the place were largely those who had moved in as part of the process of gentrification discussed earlier in this chapter. As owner-occupiers, they had been able to exercise some freedom of choice over where they lived, and on the whole they had chosen the pleasantest parts of Stockwell. Some emphasised the proximity of their jobs in Victoria or Whitehall, the cultural centres of the South Bank, the theatres or restaurants of the West End. Some, like Mr. Dawson quoted earlier, pointed out how many thousands of pounds they had saved by buying in Stockwell instead of Chelsea or St. John's Wood. Some enthused about the 'friendliness' of their neighbours. As a manager's wife, living in a particularly pleasant oasis, put it: 'It's very much part of a community. It's got a village feeling'. Given attractions like these, why should such residents want to move?

As for the West Indians, their reasons are partly to do with the support of their local sub-cultures, built up over the previous 20 years or so. On the negative side, they are likely to feel less welcome, less at home, in other districts. On the positive side, many have friends and relatives nearby; there are shops and market stalls selling the kinds of things they want to buy; they can use their own clubs and call upon the support of their own ethnic organisations.

Themes of discontent

As we have said, the middle-classes and the West Indians were the exceptions. Among the other adults, what were the main themes of discontent?

They fell under two main headings – the social and the physical environment. First, many residents said they 'disliked' the presence of particular kinds of people whom they saw as different from themselves. About one person in ten in the sample complained in terms of other people's skin colour or nationality:

> 'Too many coloured people are coming into this area; there are far too many round here. They breed like rabbits.'

> 'This used to be a nice district but there are all nationalities here now – blacks and Greeks and I don't know what.'

A similar proportion, about one in ten, laid stress on what they saw as 'rough', low-status or 'problem' families:

42

'The class of people coming in. They are rough families, noisy and dirty. They are not well-behaved. They don't know how to live.'

'The council is filling up the estates with problem families. They're homeless families, people who can't pay their rent, people like that. The class of the district has definitely gone down.'

Another tenth or so of respondents complained about local children or teenagers:

'The children round here are rowdy and rough and abusive. They damage the cars in the streets. They throw bricks at the wall. They break milk bottles. Last week some of them lit a fire on the staircase in the flats opposite.'

'You get teenagers throwing bottles, stealing and smashing things up. They make a noise until one o'clock in the morning. The language they use is disgusting.'

As these remarks suggest, such criticisms of young people were often linked to complaints about vandalism and crime. These, again, were explicity referred to by about one person in ten.

'All the muggings that have started in the last two years. It's not safe to go out now.'

'There's terrible vandalism and hooliganism. They smash things up. A girl was raped in these flats last week. Old people get attacked and robbed. There's break-ins every other night.'

People were also asked what they thought was 'needed' in Stockwell. Nearly a quarter of the total adult sample suggested that facilities for children and young people – clubs, amenities, open spaces for play – needed to be improved.

'We need supervised playgrounds, lots of them. There are an incredible number of children round here. We need more facilities of all kinds. There is nothing round here – it breeds vandalism.'

'There ought to be more for the teenagers, a club or something like that – something to keep them off the streets.'

Schoolchildren of all ages also thought that more play facilities and clubs were needed, though they sometimes disagreed with the adults in their emphasis. For instance, whereas some adults complained about children playing near their homes or on their estate, many children resented 'always being told "No"': 'Angry ladies say "Go away and give us some peace"'; 'Sometimes we play football on the grass and the caretaker chases us off.' Though parents wanted safe places for children to play, at least some children apparently preferred more adventurous activities of the kind that irritated neighbours. 'We love the garages, climbing on the roof. Dads come and chase you off'; 'We can go up to the top floor in the lift and when the lady comes out we run down three floors.'

But the generations were agreed about some things, for instance the tarmac playgrounds on some estates: 'It's dangerous with bits of broken glass', said one child. Members of both generations likewise went beyond the need for play facilities to argue a more general case for more parks and open spaces locally. Children suggest 'swimming pools', a 'park with a duck pond', 'lakes', and 'more open-air acting places'. One adult in ten suggested that the district 'needed' more open spaces and trees:

> 'We could do with more green patches and tree planting. The outlook at present is just tatty bits and pieces. It could certainly be improved.'

> 'We need more parks and open spaces. There's not enough green spaces round here.'

The lack of such open space was something that a few adults mentioned among their 'dislikes'. In terms of the physical environment, the most common criticism was about the dirt and litter (also raised by older schoolchildren in particular). Dirt and litter were mentioned by one adult in eight in the Stockwell sample, compared with one in 50 in the national 'environmental survey' mentioned earlier. About one person in 12 in Stockwell complained about the council, and often these criticisms were in effect also about dirt. For example, the first two of the following people laid the emphasis on dirt and litter, while the last two focussed upon council shortcomings (and their answers were coded correspondingly):

> 'The most distressing thing, the minute you step out from your front door, is the dirt and litter. The people waiting in the bus queue throw their rubbish into the garden.'

> 'It's a filthy district, filthy roads. And the dogs mess on the pavements.'

> 'The cleaning – sweeping the roads and pavements. They don't do it properly. The street dustbins aren't emptied – they're full to overflowing.'

> 'The dustmen leave a trail of litter in the streets. After they've gone it's dirtier than before they came.'

People complained about the council (or rather the councils, since they did not usually distinguish between Lambeth and the GLC) on other grounds as well, notably the poor maintenance on council estates, which many said was due to the removal of resident caretakers. But as many as half of the criticisms addressed to the councils were about street cleaning and refuse disposal. If these complaints about the failure to clear dirt and litter were combined with those about their existence, the proportion of complainants on this score in Stockwell would be as high as one adult in six.

Apart from cleaning the streets and estates and providing more for children and young people, along with more open space generally, the question about what was needed drew a demand – again from one adult in six – for an improvement in the quality of the housing, both old houses and on council estates.

'So many of the older houses have been allowed to become derelict. Repair these and make them look nice. Paint them and clean them. Then the whole district would look better.'

'There's still some slummy housing round here that needs pulling down – they are dilapidated and overcrowded.'[1]

'They need to paint up the outside and the garages on these council estates round here. They need to keep the areas clean and tidy. They have deteriorated a lot since they were built. The estates should all be done up.'

To sum up, the answers to the various questions pointed to five main concerns, some primarily physical, some primarily social and some a mixture. These were:

1. Dislike of (mainly coloured) immigrants or of other kinds of newcomers considered 'rough' or 'problem families'.
2. Conflicts between adults and children, and the need for more play facilities, together with more open spaces generally.
3. Anxieties about vandalism and crime.
4. Dirt in the streets and estates, and the need to improve street cleaning and estate maintenance.
5. Poor housing, and the need to improve it.

The underlying question, of course, was why. Why were people apparently more discontented in the inner city area of Stockwell than in other kinds of district? And why was it that these particular aspects worried them so much?

Part of the answer is obvious enough. Of course much of the older housing needs attention; this is because of its age, the relatively poor design and construction of at least some of it and the neglect associated with the demise of the private landlord. Of course some of the pre-war council estates, being half a century old, need attention. Of course the area, for historical reasons, is relatively badly off for open space and provision for children's play. All these problems need to be tackled and we discuss in later chapters how this might be done.

But behind most of the other discontents were two main causes. The first was the relatively large concentrations of people, especially children, in some kinds of housing and in some of the local authority estates. The second was the high degree of mobility of the population, most of it not from choice, and the consequential lack of social ties. We look at these in turn.

(1) It is worth noting, however, that two questions asking whether people favoured 'knocking down' or 'doing up' old houses and pre-war council estates showed that the balance of local opinion was firmly behind the current emphasis on rehabilitation rather than wholesale redevelopment. (See Inner Area Study Lambeth, *People, Housing and District* (IAS/LA/5), Table 3.13 and Paragraphs 3.72 and 3.73.) Discussing the needs of the district, one man put it crisply: 'Less demolition, more renovation'.

Concentration of children

We compared the densities of different housing types and related these to the responses in the survey of people living in them. This analysis showed that, by and large, the kinds of housing where people were most discontented (as expressed, for example, in the proportion wanting to move) were those where population density, and particularly child density, were high[1] (see Figure 6).

We were able to take this kind of analysis further for local authority estates in particular.[2] We checked the validity of our survey, by comparing tenants' subjectively-expressed discontent, as shown in their answers to our questions, with the proportion of households on the same estate who had applied for transfers. The correlation between the data from the two sources was high. In others words, the unpopular estates, where large proportions had applied for transfer, were also those where most people complained.

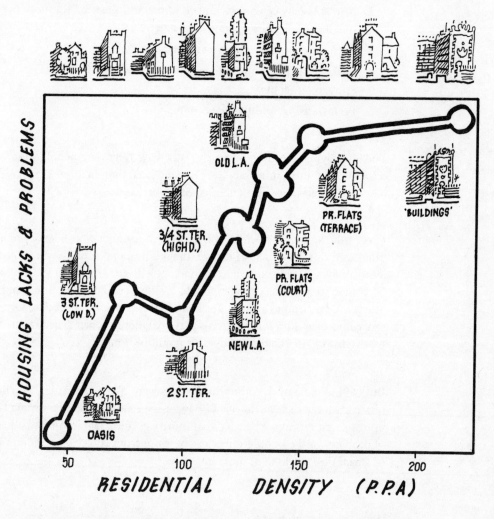

**Figure 6
Density and dissatisfaction**
Housing survey information on peoples' housing 'lacks' and 'problems' plotted against net residential density. Dissatisfaction with housing increases as density rises.

(1) See Inner Area Study Lambeth, *People, Housing and District* (IAS/LA/5), pp. 28–32.

(2) See the separate report on Inner Area Study Lambeth, *Housing Management and Design* (IAS/LA/18).

'OASES'   OLD TERRACES   PRIVATE FLATS   OLD ESTATES   NEW ESTATES   TOWERS

Number of children per acre.

In general we found a similar relationship between density and discontent in the comparison of estates as in that of broad housing types, but were able to confirm the findings in more detail. The estates where dissatisfaction was highest (and, for example, where vandalism was most in evidence, as well as most lamented) were also those with the highest child densities and the highest ratio of children to adults (see Figure 7). As a further check on our findings, we carried out a separate analysis of 40 GLC estates outside Lambeth. This analysis showed that child density and the ratio of children to adults were again major influences affecting people's satisfaction with their estate.[1]

The conclusion we draw is that a large number of children crammed on each acre and a high ratio of children to adults on the estate or in the street are key factors in helping to explain dissatisfaction of various kinds. By and large, the higher they are the greater the annoyance caused by children's play, the higher the level of vandalism,[2] the larger the quantity of litter generated, the scruffier the general appearance of the immediate environment. We would go further and argue that, because of the stresses on families, these factors are also related to the level of criticism directed against neighbours. When people are crowded up inside their homes and are surrounded by armies of children outside, the more disposed they probably are to criticise, not just the children but also, as an expression of a more general sense of stress, the 'coloureds' or 'roughs' among their neighbours. It is difficult to be entirely sure about this last point since, among GLC estates in particular, the densest – and the least popular – were exactly those where blacks and low-skill workers were most heavily concentrated.

(1) *Ibid*, Appendix

(2) This conclusion is supported by a study of vandalism carried out by the Home Office. See Sheena Wilson and Andrew Shurman, 'Vandalism'.

**Figure 7
Percentage of
children and
satisfaction**
The range of densities
on the estates shown
in this diagram was
quite narrow.
However,
dissatisfaction
increased with the
percentage which
children formed of the
total population on
each estate.

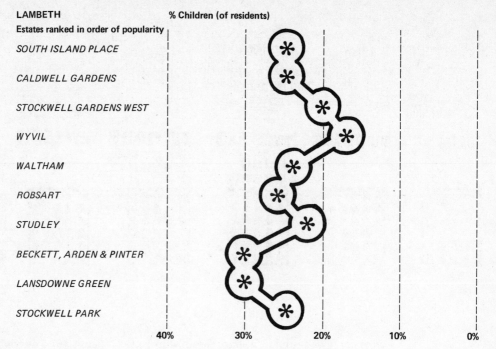

LAMBETH   % Children (of residents)
Estates ranked in order of popularity

SOUTH ISLAND PLACE

CALDWELL GARDENS

STOCKWELL GARDENS WEST

WYVIL

WALTHAM

ROBSART

STUDLEY

BECKETT, ARDEN & PINTER

LANSDOWNE GREEN

STOCKWELL PARK

40%   30%   20%   10%   0%

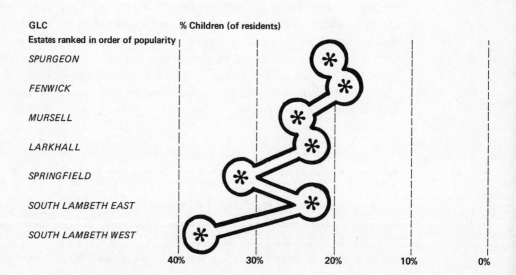

GLC   % Children (of residents)
Estates ranked in order of popularity

SPURGEON

FENWICK

MURSELL

LARKHALL

SPRINGFIELD

SOUTH LAMBETH EAST

SOUTH LAMBETH WEST

40%   30%   20%   10%   0%

As well as the crucial link between satisfaction and density, especially child density,
satisfaction is affected by management and initial building standards. If the building
quality is minimal and management poor, the tolerable level of density is low. If
investment is high and management good, then higher densities are acceptable. As
expenditure on both building fabric and management is likely to be restricted in the
foreseeable future, it is essential that new schemes do not make heavy demands on
management services. This implies fewer elaborate services, such as lifts or refuse
systems. But it also implies lower densities, and low child densities in particular.

48

Thus one objective of policy should be to reduce the concentrations of children, so as to relieve the stress. Some councils are already trying to do this. Lambeth, for example, will let dwellings on certain estates only to single people or to couples without children, and its policy is not to house families with children under 12 years old above the fifth floor in high-rise blocks, and the GLC has similar policies. But we think that more officially-sponsored migration of tenants from Inner London is needed to reduce the pressure. Since as we show later, many people, particularly many families with children, want to move out of Inner London, such a policy would suit them as much as it would those who stayed. And since low-skill and low-income families, though living more often in the crowded parts of the district, have largely been denied the opportunity, priority should be given to helping them to go if they want to, as we argue in Chapter 6. As we show in Chapter 4, this suggestion makes sense in terms of job opportunities, since many of the low-skill jobs for which local residents are currently equipped are increasingly available outside rather than inside the inner city.

Breakdown of community

We have noted the relatively high mobility of households in Stockwell. Over the past quarter of a century, there have been major upheavals in Stockwell and inner city areas like it. The explanation is two-fold. First, large-scale clearance and redevelopment. In 1951, the proportion of council tenants in Stockwell was less than one household in four; by 1973 it was about one in every two. People have had to move out of the old terraced streets as the bulldozers moved in. (Actually, they usually moved several years earlier; this long-term 'blighting' effect of large-scale redevelopment, itself a major source of discontent, has contributed to the population instability. As one man, formerly in a clearance area, put it 'For years nobody knew where they were.') Some of those displaced have been rehoused near their former homes, but it seems clear that most have not. In estates in Stockwell, for example, we met people rehoused under clearance schemes from Peckham, Kennington and South Clapham. Half of those in our survey who had moved to their present home during the previous five years had come from somewhere else in Lambeth and most of the rest from elsewhere in Inner London. Thus the actions of the councils, for the best of motives and despite the efforts made to meet people's wishes over choice of district, have had the general effect of displacing families and breaking up established communities.

The process has been reinforced by trends in the private sector. Controls on private landlords, and in particular over the rents they charge, have worked against mobility. It is true that people with protected, low-rent housing have had a strong motive for staying put. But the same policy has, over time, worked in the opposite direction. Tenants have sometimes been persuaded or pressured to move, so as to enable the landlord to sell the house, realise his capital and help on the process of gentrification. Even if sitting tenants do not move, they eventually die. When that happens the landlord obviously tries to sell rather than allow the tenancy to pass to a married son or daughter of the former tenant, as commonly happened in the past.

For these various reasons, continuity from one generation to the next, and over a person's own lifetime, have become more and more difficult in inner city areas. In the early 1970s fewer Stockwell residents than in earlier decades were people who had been born or grown up there.

A high degree of population movement almost inevitably works against other things that people value, like neighbourliness, local social contacts, mutual aid and a sense of community.[1] We have already noted that there are exceptions to this rule, particularly among the professional and managerial middle-class. But most Stockwell residents are not of that class; most of them have not apparently found it easy to strike up friendships with the strangers around them or to feel at their ease among them. The process has not been helped by the fact that so many of those neighbours have different coloured skins. As a 52-year-old clerk put it: 'There's a suspicious atmosphere. It applies to both coloured and white.' Nor has it been helped, in some of the older estates, by the suspicion that the newcomers were families with different, usually 'lower', standards than their own. 'The sense of pride has gone on this estate', said one tenant, 'With the smell of urine on the stairs, you can't ask friends round like you used to'.

We do not want to exaggerate. Most people learn to get along with those around them, and some of those we interviewed, as we have reported, spoke positively about the 'friendliness' of others, while a few emphasised that in their view Stockwell worked well as a 'mixed' community. Nor do we imply that the majority, whose responses suggested that they had little sense of community with their neighbours, were themselves at fault. Some no doubt were, being racially prejudiced or unthinkingly hostile towards newcomers. But most were simply the victims of circumstances. They were critical of others, distant towards them, lacked a sense of community identity, not because of themselves but because of the kinds of changes we have described.

We are thus arguing that population instability lies at the root of many of the complaints about other people, and of the conflicts between neighbours, including those over children's play. We also think that the relative anonymity, and the consequential lack of informal control by familiar neighbours, partly explain the vandalism and crime which upset so many people. It follows from this analysis that we think that one objective should be to encourage greater population stability. This will depend on planning policies and also on housing allocation and management, both of which we discuss more fully later.

Our two main suggestions – that people should be encouraged to move if they want to move, as a means of reducing child density where it is too high, but to stay if they want to stay – may seem paradoxical. How, it might be asked, can we reconcile our demand for measures to promote further mobility out of Inner London with our case for population stability? The contradiction is, however, more apparent than real, since different people want different things. Our two-pronged proposals, apart

(1) A well-known American documents this conclusion: Peter Rossi, *Why Families Move*.

from their contribution to the two major problems of high child densities (in some areas) and community breakdown, are essentially based on the argument for giving people more choice over their lives.

☐ This chapter has been about two things – the kinds of people living in Stockwell, and their own views about what needs to be done. On the first, the main conclusions are about change: the district is becoming increasingly attractive to younger small households and it is losing skilled workers rather than semi-skilled or unskilled. On the second, we have identified two major themes – the need to reduce child density, particularly by helping the outward movement of less skilled people and their families, and at the same time to encourage stability within the district among those who do not wish to leave. We have also identified other issues that cause local concern: improving older housing, creating more small open spaces, providing for the recreation and play of children and young people, improving street cleaning and estate maintenance, and reducing vandalism.

Most of the implications for policy that follow from this are explored more fully in later chapters. But we can sum up in general terms the main policy conclusions so far. First, child densities should be reduced by allocation and management policies, particularly in areas where they are associated with other problems. This will be helped by a determined programme to build housing for rent in Outer London or beyond, offering the choice of suburban life to those to whom it is at present denied. In general, people should be given more choice than at present over their housing and the district they live in, and local authority housing management and allocation should be made more sensitive to people's wishes. These measures should strengthen local community by making it easier for people to stay in the area if they want to.

Finally, more should be done to improve the appearance of small areas in the district, to provide more small open spaces, to improve facilities for recreation and children's play and to meet people's complaints about the standards of street cleaning and estate management. If the specific proposals we put forward in later chapters can offer ways of dealing with these issues, they will be responding to Stockwell's needs as perceived by the people who live there ☐

3 Poverty and deprivation

An important question was left out of the previous chapter. It is commonly believed that inner areas like Stockwell contain large proportions of families in poverty or with social problems of other kinds. As we have shown, this is exactly what was suggested by some of the people we interviewed. But to what extent is it true?

This chapter first examines whether Stockwell does contain a higher than average proportion of poor people and people with other kinds of problem. It then considers the degree to which the same households suffer from a number of problems at the same time, in other words the scale of multiple deprivation, and its causes. Next, it looks at the circumstances of coloured immigrants and their children. Finally, it looks at explanations and possible remedies for such deprivation, multiple or not, as exists in places like Stockwell.

The extent of poverty

In order to compare with the country generally in terms of poverty, we had to start by deciding how it was to be measured. Inevitably, we treated the concept as a relative one. There is little point in asking how many people are in poverty compared with a century or a quarter-century ago, or compared with contemporary India. The only sensible comparison is with the standards – in income, housing and the like – that apply among the population generally in contemporary Britain.

Income poverty is as good an example as any. As average incomes rise, so should the 'poverty line'. Following other studies,[1] we used the official supplementary benefit scale to determine this line. It is generally recognised that one needs to add something to the scale to make some allowance, first for the higher rates and discretionary payments to which some claimants are entitled and secondly for 'disregards' – the additional income, for instance, from a small part-time job or from relatives, not taken into account when eligibility is being calculated by the Supplementary Benefits Commission (SBC). We decided to add 20 per cent to allow for these. Thus we judged a family to be in poverty if it had an income of less than 120 per cent of its basic supplementary benefit entitlement.

We have already used the term 'family' rather than 'household', which is the basis of most other analyses in this book. By household we mean (following the census) any group of people who live and eat together in a single dwelling; this is obviously the right unit to consider when discussing housing, the possession of household durables

(1) See e.g. Peter Townsend and Brian Abel-Smith, *The Poor and the Poorest*; Department of Health and Social Security, *Two-Parent Families*; Michael Young (editor), *Poverty Report 1974*.

or of a car. By family we mean (following the Department of Health and Social Security) those who commonly pool their money.[1]

In December 1973 the proportion of families in Britain in poverty, measured in the way described, was 20 per cent. That in Stockwell in October/November 1973, the date of our survey, was 23 per cent. Given the sample size in Stockwell and this relatively small difference in percentages, we cannot on this basis say with any confidence that more families in Stockwell were below the poverty line, but only that it looks as if more might have been.

We continue in later analyses to use this standard 'poverty line' as an index for Stockwell as for the whole country, but there is one sense in which the comparison may be misleading. It is generally agreed that the cost of living in London is higher than elsewhere, though this is not reflected in SBC scales. We decided to try to take account of this, drawing upon the official report on 'London weighting'[2] and comparing the recommended additional weighting with average earnings at the nearest available date. We concluded that the cost of living was about 7 per cent higher in London. On this basis the proportion in poverty in Stockwell would have

**Figure 8
Composition of
families in poverty:
Stockwell and Great
Britain**
Of all those in poverty,
families with children
formed a higher
proportion in
Stockwell.

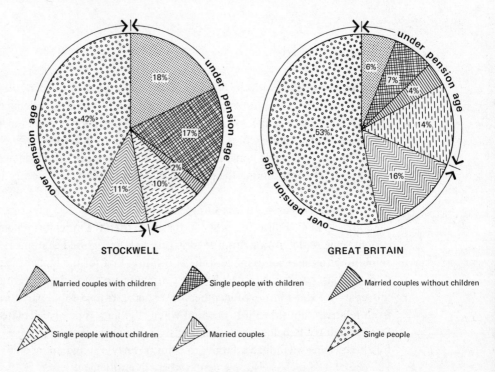

Source: Stockwell Household Survey 1973, Department of Health and Social Security (special analysis)

(1) A family, for this purpose, is a person living alone, a married couple, or a couple or single parent plus any dependent children (that is, children below the minimum school-leaving age or continuing in full-time education). This has been the basic unit in terms of people's legal responsibility to maintain each other since the National Assistance Act 1948 abolished the Poor Law responsibility of wider relatives to support each other, and is therefore the basis on which supplementary benefit entitlement is calculated.

(2) Pay Board, *Advisory Report on London Weighting*.

56

been 27 per cent; if we had allowed for the extra cost of housing, which is certainly borne by some poor people, the proportion in poverty would have been about 29 per cent. These figures are obviously higher than the national average at the same date.

In some ways, the composition of those in poverty is more important than the comparative percentages below the poverty line. Which kinds of families were poor in Stockwell as compared with the rest of the country? Figure 8 shows that there was a different pattern in Stockwell: more of those in poverty were families with children – both couples and single-parent families – and less were in other types of family, particularly pensioners.

These variations might be because the distribution of family types was different from that in Britain generally, or because more families of some particular kinds were poor. The explanation is in fact a bit of both. Stockwell contained less old people, as we showed in the previous chapter, and the lower proportions of the poor who were old reflect that. The area also contained a higher than average proportion of single-parent families (one-parent families accounted for 7 per cent of all families, compared with 3 per cent in Britain in 1973); the higher proportion of single-parent families among the poor in Stockwell reflects this difference.

But there were some kinds of family which were more often poor in Stockwell than in the rest of the country. This is clear in Figure 9 which shows those in poverty as a proportion of each family type. The diagram indicates that, among those who were over pension age, the proportions in poverty were large – and broadly similar – in Stockwell and in Britain, and likewise among single-parent families. Old people and one-parent families are vulnerable wherever they live. It looks as if rather less of those under pension age without children were in poverty in the study area than in Britain (though London's higher cost of living should again be borne in mind). But, most important of all, three times as many married couples with children were poor in the inner city district as in the country as a whole.

What about other dimensions of deprivation? We have already indicated that, despite the high proportion of local authority property, much of Stockwell's housing is of a poor standard. In 1973 the proportion of households with more than one person per room was 15 per cent; the proportion in Great Britain (and, for that matter, in Greater London) was 4 per cent.[1] The proportions lacking the basic amenities were also higher. 24 per cent of households lacked or shared a bath, compared with 12 per cent in Britain generally, and 15 per cent shared a WC, compared with 5 per cent. Less households in the study area had central heating: 24 per cent as against 39 per cent in Britain as a whole.

If we look at Stockwell in terms of the characteristics of people rather than of their housing or their family income, the picture is more mixed. We have already noted that in 1973 it contained about double the national average of one-parent families. But the proportion of people in our sample with a chronic sickness or disability

(1) Again, our source for these and other national figures is *The General Household Survey 1973*.

Figure 9
Proportion of each family type who were in poverty
A large proportion of pensioners and single parent families were in poverty. The proportions were broadly similar for Stockwell and Great Britain. But married couples with children were more likely to be poor in Stockwell.

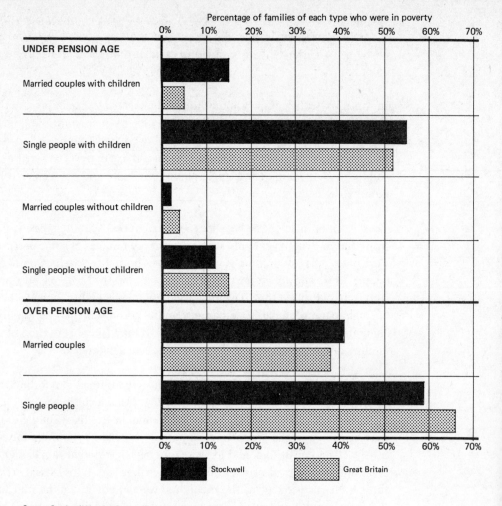

Percentage of families of each type who were in poverty

Source: Stockwell Housing Survey 1973, Department of Health and Social Security (special analysis)

which limited their activity (12 per cent) was about the same as in Britain. Similarly, the proportion of unemployed people in our survey was about the same as in the nationwide survey in 1973. This particular comparison, however, gives a false impression. Compared with later years, 1973 was a time of relative boom; as the next chapter shows, the study area was more affected than other places by the subsequent economic decline. It looks as if, though Stockwell did not have markedly more unemployed in 1973, it did in 1974 and 1975. Its working population, in other words, proved to be particularly vulnerable to unemployment; the reasons are discussed later.

We cannot be sure whether the district contained large proportions of vulnerable people of other kinds. There are limitations to our data on this, since some such people are the kinds most likely to be missed in a household survey. The homeless, the meths drinkers, the rootless young are less likely than others to be contacted and more likely to refuse to participate if they are. What are usually called 'problem families' might similarly be less likely to participate. What is more, it is not easy with a survey such as ours to be sure that one has accurately identified such families,

58

though we later identify multiple-deprived families – not quite the same thing – and make some attempt to assess the proportion of 'problem families' among those we re-interviewed.

To sum up, a larger-than-average proportion of families with children in Stockwell were in poverty, the district had a relatively large proportion of single-parent families, housing deprivations of various kinds were relatively common and what happened in 1974 and 1975 suggests that people were, more than elsewhere, vulnerable to unemployment.

Who are the poor?

We have already said something about the characteristics of those who were poor. Figure 10 confirms that poverty is as closely related to people's stage in the life cycle as it was when Rowntree studied it in York in the 1930s.[1] In Stockwell, in York and elsewhere, the poor continue to be concentrated among children and old people. Out of all those in poverty, the overwhelming majority were either old-person households or families with dependent children: 88 per cent of all the poor families in Stockwell and 82 per cent in Britain were people over retirement age or with dependent children.

Figure 10
The life cycle of poverty
In Stockwell, as in York in the 1930s, poverty was concentrated amongst the elderly and families with children.

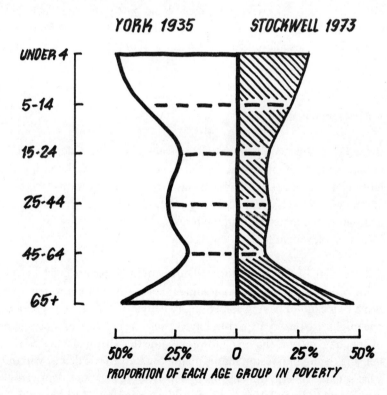

(1) The study in York in 1936 (B.S. Rowntree, *Poverty and Progress*) was a repeat of his pioneering research on poverty at the turn of the century (B.S. Rowntree, *Poverty: a study of Town Life*) which first showed the pattern of life cycle poverty.

Among families with children, as we have noted, the number of parents made a difference, more single-parent families being poor. So did the number of children; among families with one or two children, 21 per cent were in poverty; among those with three or more, 29 per cent. Particularly where there are children, another crucial influence is whether the wife works outside the home. Among couples with children, the proportions in poverty were: wife working full-time, none; working part-time, 4 per cent; not working, 24 per cent. Thus, if the wife goes out to work, this in itself lifts the family, almost automatically, above the poverty line. We met examples among some of the families we re-interviewed for the study of multiple deprivation discussed later in this chapter. At the first interview with one family, in 1973, the youngest child, a daughter, was three years old and the wife was not working. Eighteen months later, the daughter was attending a nursery class every morning, and the wife had re-started work as a secretary in a firm near Vauxhall. 'It's only part-time', she said, 'but it's made a lot of difference to us. I don't need to scrimp and save so much. I can afford to get clothes for the children when they need them, and I can buy things for the home. I want to get a washing machine.'

Of course, other factors as well as family structure and stage in the life cycle played a part. One example is social class, measured once more by the occupational status of the head of household. Contrary to the common view, there was, however, no difference in terms of the skin colour of the head of household; no more blacks than whites were in poverty. This seemed to be partly because their age structure was different – few blacks were pensioners – and partly because black mothers worked outside the home more often than their white counterparts. Among married couples with at least one child under five, 46 per cent of the black wives worked compared with 11 per cent of the white.

Is deprivation multiple?

Being below the income poverty line is only one form of deprivation, even if arguably the most important. We also examined so-called multiple deprivation, looking at the extent to which various forms of deprivation clustered together and among which kinds of family.[1] Two methods were used in combination: statistical analyses of the material from the household survey and a series of re-interviews with 59 households identified as deprived in that survey.

The meaning of the term 'multiple deprivation' is not self-evident. 'Deprivation' literally means having had something taken away, but in ordinary usage it has also come to mean not having something (whether or not one has previously had it) that one might reasonably expect to have. Thus one can talk of a person being deprived of adequate income (having a lower income than he or she 'needs') or decent housing (being in housing that is dilapidated, overcrowded or without amenities). If a list is made of such dimensions of deprivation, someone deprived of two or more can be said to be suffering from multiple deprivation. Although the importance of

(1) This work has been described more fully in two reports: Inner Area Study Lambeth, *Poverty and Multiple Deprivation* (IAS/LA/10) and *Second Report on Multiple Deprivation* (IAS/LA/15).

different deprivations in any list is bound to vary, and vary in different ways for different kinds of household, it seems reasonable to assume that in general having three deprivations is worse than having two, having four worse than having three, and so on.

This was the basis we used to study the subject, described more fully in the separate reports. We chose a set of six main indices of deprivation: income poverty, overcrowding, lack of housing amenities, absence of car and telephone, disability and job instability. One problem about this list is that of cause and effect. Disability, for example, can be both a cause of job instability and, either alone or in conjunction with that, also a cause of low income. Likewise, income poverty, whether caused by disability, retirement, low earning capacity or the presence of children, is itself partly a cause of other deprivations such as the lack of a car or telephone. But each of the six could be an important deprivation in itself independent of the others, and we thought it right, after our preliminary analyses, to settle on them. With each, we had to choose a suitable 'cut-off' point below which the household would be judged deprived. We have already explained what we did about income. Overcrowding was defined as more than one person per room; and households were regarded as deprived of housing amenities if they had less than four out of a basic list. Similar thresholds were defined for the other deprivations, the idea being, as far as possible, to strike a level for each which would identify the fifth or so of households who were worst off.

Table 7   Percentages of households with different numbers of deprivations

None	28%	} 59%
1	31%	
2		27%
3	11%	
4	3%	} 14%
5	1	
Total 100%		
Number (weighted)	1170	

(1) Less than 0·5%.
Source: Stockwell Household Survey 1973.

The proportions of households suffering from different numbers of deprivations are shown in Table 7.[1] On the most literal interpretation, it could be said that the 41 per cent of households with two or more were multiple-deprived. But we would judge that a more realistic measure would be suffering from three deprivations or more. On this definition about one household in seven living in Stockwell was multiple-deprived.

We were able to compare the Stockwell material on multiple deprivation with data from surveys in two other inner areas: Small Heath, Birmingham (where a survey

---

(1) This is based upon adding together each household's deprivations and counting each as one. It would be possible to use a more elaborate form of summary, in which different deprivations were given different 'weights' based for instance on some judgement of their importance or on a statistical procedure such as principal component analyses. This issue is discussed in Appendix 1 of our *Second Report on Multiple Deprivation*, where we also explain why we decided to retain the straightforward system of unitary weights.

was carried out by Social and Community Planning Research as part of the companion Inner Area Study there)[1] and Camden, London (where the survey was done by the Institute of Community Studies for the Department of Health and Social Security).[2] In Small Heath the proportion of multiple-deprived households was similar to that in Stockwell. That in Camden was lower – one in eleven. Given its more middle-class composition, a difference of this order might have been expected between Camden and the other two areas.

We set out to answer three questions about the patterning of deprivations. First, to what extent were deprivations concentrated among a small minority of households? Secondly, what kinds of deprivations went together? Thirdly, what kinds of households most often suffered from multiple deprivation?

Concentration and clustering of deprivations

On the first question, the extent to which deprivations were concentrated among relatively few families, we can perhaps explain what we mean in terms of two extremes. One extreme would be a very high degree of concentration. Most households would suffer from none, and such deprivations as there were would be clustered among a minority of households; there would be quite a lot of households with four, five or six deprivations. At the other extreme, deprivations would be dispersed fairly randomly among many households; most would have no deprivations or just one.

We have, in one sense, already given the answer: the pattern in Stockwell was more like the second extreme than the first. A minority of households – one in seven – suffered from three deprivations or more. Very few suffered from four, even fewer from five and none from six. Apart from those suffering no deprivations, most of the rest suffered from one or two. On the face of it, deprivations were distributed fairly widely rather than being greatly concentrated among an identifiable minority.

As a check on this, we calculated the proportion of households likely to have been multiple-deprived if deprivations had been distributed by chance among all households in the sample. The analysis showed that the number likely to have three or more deprivations was 3 per cent below those who actually had them. Thus, in terms of the particular deprivations we had selected, defined in the ways we defined them, the degree of concentration was not very marked. The general picture was much the same in Small Heath and Camden.

It is obvious from other research that some deprivations are linked, particularly between one generation and the next. For example, the educational achievement of children is closely related to parental background,[3] and children from deprived

(1) Inner Area Study Birmingham, *A Social Survey* (IAS/B/5).

(2) Lucy Syson and Michael Young, 'The Camden Survey'.

(3) See e.g. J. W. B. Douglas, *The Home and the School* and Michael Young, *Innovation and Research in Education*, Chapter IV.

homes do much less well than others on a whole range of measures.[1] But the findings from our study, concentrating as it does on one generation alone and using the particular set of selected indices, do not show a very high degree of multiple deprivation in Stockwell or the other two districts.

Our second question was about the clustering of deprivations. Were there distinct patterns, with the same three or four deprivations commonly being found together, or was there a greater spread? The answer is that, though there were some patterns, they were not all that marked. The largest number of households with any three deprivations amounted to only 5 per cent of the total.

But some such clusters were evident. One was disability, job instability and low income. Disabled people often had a record of instability in their work: they either had a lot of time off work or they had needed to give their jobs up and thus changed fairly frequently. In any case, they were more vulnerable to unemployment than other people and generally worked in lower-paid jobs. One unmarried man, for instance, had a vascular disease and in consequence had, in the previous four years, been off sick three times for long periods – six months, eight months and five months. Another man, married and with three children, had a slipped disc. He had been working in the building trade when he first suffered from it; he was off work for nine months – 'We were very badly affected then; we were really hard up' – and had since had to take a lighter and lower-paid job.

Another characteristic pattern was among old people. They generally had low incomes and many of them, because of their age, had disabilities or health problems. They suffered, for example, from chronic arthritis, bronchitis, heart disease or high blood pressure, or sometimes a combination of these; one widower had chronic bronchitis and was deaf and partly blind. Some old people had housing problems as well. None were overcrowded, but relatively more of them than younger people lacked amenities such as bathrooms and hot water.

In an attempt to measure statistically this kind of clustering, we carried out a special computer analysis; it was designed to identify, among all the households in our sample taken together, which of the six deprivations most often went with each other. This analysis confirmed that low income, disability and job instability went together in one group, and showed that being overcrowded, lacking housing amenities and lacking car and telephone went together in a second.

This finding has to be interpreted against the background of what we said earlier about clustering. The associations between the different deprivations in each of the two clusters were not very strong, and the general pattern of overlap between deprivations was complex and scattered. It was, for example, not common for households which were overcrowded also to lack or share housing amenities. Some households were both in income poverty and in bad housing. But, insofar as there was a tendency for the six deprivations to go together at all, it was broadly into the two sets that could be labelled 'income' and 'housing'.

(1) See Peter Wedge and Hilary Prosser, *Born to Fail?*

This conclusion is one of the most striking that came out of our study. It calls into question one of the stock ideas about the so-called 'cycle of deprivation'. In the characteristic diagrams portraying this cycle, the assumption is made that low income usually leads to households living in bad housing.[1] Our study suggests that, on the contrary, income poverty and housing deprivation are not strongly associated with each other.

We need to be cautious in generalising from Stockwell's experience in this. After all, the study area was well endowed with local authority housing; nearly half the households there were council tenants, as we have said, compared for instance with a third in Camden and a quarter in Small Heath. When we repeated the analyses for those two districts, though the pattern in Camden proved to be broadly similar to that in Stockwell, that in Small Heath was different. In Small Heath income poverty did go with housing deprivation. This finding is in line with the conclusions drawn by the Birmingham inner area study team.[2]

In Stockwell, although there were of course some households suffering from both income poverty and housing deprivation, in general the link has been greatly weakened compared with what must have happened in the past. This must be mainly the result of public intervention into the housing market. The conclusion is an encouraging one. It suggests that three-quarters of a century of municipal socialism has had an important effect.

Who is multiple-deprived?

In examining which kinds of households suffered most from multiple deprivation, we used several different forms of statistical analysis. These all involved dividing up households in terms of various characteristics likely to be related to deprivation and then seeing which of these made the greatest difference to the household's deprivation 'score'.

The main influences on deprivation, as suggested by our analyses, could be summed up under four headings. The first is a household's basic social class position. Secondly, there are the demographic variables, reflecting a household's stage in the life cycle: whether people have children, whether they are over pension age and the number of earners. Thirdly, there is housing tenure. The fourth is the skin colour of the head of household. The influence of the last of these is discussed more fully later.

There is little mystery about the way in which social class influences a household's propensity to multiple deprivation. Skills and education affect the kinds of jobs people can get, and their job largely determines their level of income, which in turn

(1) South East Joint Planning Team, *Strategic Plan for the South East, Studies Volume 2: Social and Environmental Aspects*; SNAP, *Another Chance for Cities?*

(2) See Inner Area Study Birmingham, *New Housing Policies for the Inner City* (IAS/B/11); this argues that low income was associated with poor housing, all the examples cited being in the private sector, rented or owner-occupied.

largely determines their capacity to buy a car or household durables. As for stage in the life cycle, it clearly influences the number of dependants in a household and the capacity of its members to earn.

The influence of housing tenure is more complex. Owner-occupation was associated with low deprivation scores. The same was true of council tenure, largely because council tenants were virtually never deprived in terms of housing amenities and were seldom overcrowded. Council tenure is partly a matter of chance (perhaps one's parents were council tenants or one happened to live in a redevelopment area) and partly the result of a response by the local authority to a need (one had high priority or one was homeless). So, in some instances at least, being a council tenant had resulted from something deliberately done to help reduce a household's deprivation. It is in this sense that the policy clearly has had some success.

As for owner-occupation, are we to consider it as something that actually reduces deprivation or as something made possible for example by wealth or social class? The second explanation must obviously be the main one. About a quarter of professional and managerial household heads were owner-occupiers in our survey, but only one in ten in other socio-economic categories. Yet some low-skill manual households were owner-occupiers and were also less deprived on our combined measure than others of similar occupational status. Such households had, despite the obstacles, been able to become owners, either by saving hard at a time when houses cost less or by good fortune (for example, being offered a house as a sitting tenant). As owner-occupiers they were unlikely to be overcrowded and unlikely to lack amenities. It seems clear that owner-occupation, once achieved, can under certain conditions have a reinforcing effect in reducing deprivation.

There are several reasons why this might be so. First, given inflation and the present tax arrangements, it is usually a clear financial advantage to a household to get into owner-occupation. In real terms, the cost to the household of buying a home usually falls over time, while the rents paid by tenants rise. On top of such financial benefits, owner-occupiers are likely to feel a sense of personal pride in their home and contrive somehow or other to put into it, by way of modernisation and improvement, more investment than most tenants consider reasonable. Some owner-occupiers, as we know, are overcrowded (having had to fill the house to pay the mortgage), but in general the standards of home improvement and of equipment are much higher than in privately-rented houses of comparable age, even when the tenants have similar levels of income.

The experience of deprivation

Before we try to bring together our findings in an attempt to identify the causes of multiple deprivation, we need to mention various additional points from the re-interviews with deprived families. Some of the findings are to do with the influence of the life cycle. Deprivation can be affected by the age at which couples get married and the spacing of their children's births. The following example is an exception to the general point made earlier about income and housing; the family was both poor and badly housed.

> Mr. and Mrs. Darwin married when he was 19 and she was 18. By the time of the first interview, when he was 21 and she was 20, they had three children – twins aged 20 months and a baby aged one week. Apart from what had been given by relatives, they had no furniture or household equipment when they started, and they had been buying some on hire purchase. The cost of that, together with the £150 they had to pay as 'key money' to get into their present privately-rented three rooms and the expense of redecoration, meant they had got into debt. Mr. Darwin said in the re-interview, 'We had the children too soon, and it was bad luck we had the twins to start with'. His wife added, 'It would have been better if we'd had a year with both of us working first. As it is, we never catch up with ourselves'.

This couple, like several others with young children, had married in their teens (with some it had been because of a premarital pregnancy). They had not been able to build up savings or consumer durables for their home, and their multiple deprivation was mainly due to the absence of such resources. The problem was usually compounded, as for Mrs. Darwin, by the wife being tied to the home because of the children and thus unable to supplement the family income by working. We have earlier shown how crucial is the wife's ability to earn.

Other examples also illustrated the point that, as well as the longer-term life cycle of poverty, there are shorter-term changes. A married man with three children had been unemployed when first interviewed. When we saw him again he explained, 'The unemployment money was a bare minimum. We could pay the rent but we had to allocate the rest, what was left over. We couldn't buy clothes or shoes for the children or ourselves.' Now he had a job again and they were no longer below the poverty line: 'It took us about six months to recover.' Another husband, with two children, had in November 1973 been receiving £18 a week while being trained by his firm to convert gas stoves and other equipment to natural gas. He had completed the training and when interviewed a year later was earning £51 a week. With his new job, the household had moved out of income poverty and he had bought a car. Among ordinary families with children (though certainly not among the elderly nor the severely disabled) there is clearly quite a lot of this kind of movement in and out of poverty.[1]

Among men of working age who were interviewed, there were examples of the importance of education and job skills. Of course some men in the main household survey had, despite lacking skills or training, managed through intelligence, energy or good luck to find their way into work that, even if nominally semi-skilled, was

---

(1) This has been noted in other studies. Fried, whose research was based on interviews with housewives aged 20 to 64 in an inner area of Boston (USA), noted that 61 per cent of those below the poverty line at one date had moved above it three years later. (Marc Fried, *The World of the Urban Working Class*, p. 159.) For Britain, the Department of Employment's New Earnings Survey (dealing with individual earnings rather than household income) showed that 'less than half of those who were in the lowest tenth of the distribution in April 1970 were still in the lowest tenth in both April 1971 and April 1972' (A. R. Thatcher, 'The New Earnings Survey and the distribution of earnings').

secure and well-paid enough to keep them out of deprivation. But, among the deprived families, men without basic skills explained that it was difficult for them to find stable jobs providing a high enough income. The choice was either to continue in a low-paid steady job or to try new jobs 'for the money', only to find that the hours were too long, the work too tiring, the overtime reduced or the job terminated. Mr. Baker had left school at 15 and was now in his late 20s:

> 'I never had the chance to learn a trade. My father died when I was at school. There were five of us and my mother wanted me to go for a job with good money as soon as I left school. I don't blame her; the family needed the money. But that's why I've kept changing jobs. I've always been looking for more money and then something always seems to go wrong. I earned big wages when I worked as a casual labourer in the building, but that didn't last long. I found it difficult to get jobs in between. I was doing all right in my next job as a car salesman until the petrol shortage came along and I had to give that up. Now I'm a builder's labourer again. I'd really like to learn a trade; I'd like to take a course in bricklaying.'

The interviews also confirmed the split between housing problems and income poverty. Although there were some families, like Mr. and Mrs. Darwin cited earlier, who were poor in income and were also in bad housing, it was frequently clear that a particular household's difficulties could be identified as 'primarily housing' or 'primarily income'.

Close study of the circumstances of the families interviewed also showed that these two factors – low income and poor housing – were usually the most fundamental to a family's well-being, and were thus the keys to tackling deprivation. If a household's income were substantially raised or its housing improved, its deprivation would be radically reduced as a result. Another examination of the potential or actual help from services for deprived families interviewed by us in Stockwell, showed that, although a wide range of services and other forms of support – such as meals on wheels, free school meals or free prescriptions – could do something to relieve deprivation, they were fairly marginal in their effects compared with what would be achieved by improving their housing, substantially raising their income, or both.[1]

A final point suggested by the interviews was about what are sometimes called 'problem families'. The term is difficult to define; it is usually intended to suggest families with multiple difficulties which are compounded by behavioural or psychological handicaps. By way of illustration:

> Mr. and Mrs. Murdoch and their two children were apparently well known to their neighbours. As the interviewer walked away from their council flat, the caretaker remarked to her, 'That's a nice family you've been to see. Oh dear, dear, dear. Are you from the social security?' Mr. Murdoch said he had a 'sprained back'. He was unemployed when interviewed in October 1973 and, though in a job, was off sick when seen again in June 1974. He had changed

(1) Phyllis Willmott, 'Gains and losses in health and welfare'.

jobs four times in five years. He had recently been in trouble because, frustrated by his waiting at the Supplementary Benefits Commission office, he had, despite his bad back, assaulted the counter clerk. He had a history of violence, and had been in prison two years earlier for assault. The family, though they had recently started renting a new colour television set, were in arrears with their rent and their electricity bill (the electricity board was threatening to cut off the supply).

How many such families are there in inner city districts like Stockwell? We have suggested that something like one household in seven was multiple-deprived on our definition. But, although virtually all 'problem families' are multiple-deprived, it is certainly not true that most families with multiple difficulties are 'problem families'. We tried to assess, on the basis of the interview reports, how many of the multiple-deprived households interviewed were 'problem families' in the sense used here. We came to the conclusion that, even on the widest interpretation, no more than about one in six or seven of those interviewed could be so described. This suggests that such households amounted to fewer than one in 40 in Stockwell.

Though such families are very much in a minority, they may well be conspicuous and therefore a source of irritation to their neighbours. They can also create difficulties for the authorities, including the local authority housing and social services departments. Clearly, they need special help. This minority of families, and some others with multiple problems, need concentrated support, for example with household budgeting, in addition to any other action taken to help with income or housing. In districts where they are relatively numerous, like Stockwell, they clearly impose extra demands on such services.

Explanations for deprivation

To propose remedies, one needs to understand causes. In trying to explore the causes of deprivation, we draw upon the various sets of material from Stockwell already reported in this chapter, and on a sizeable body of work done elsewhere.

A number of alternative explanations have been put forward. For instance, the Community Development Projects, funded by the Home Office, have concentrated on 'structural' interpretations. The CDP Information and Intelligence Unit has summed up in this way the common theme emerging from these projects: 'Poverty and associated problems were argued to be social consequences of structural economic processes.'[1] In more general discussion about the influence of 'structure', there seem to be two main arguments: poverty and deprivation are firstly due to the inegalitarian social class structure of 'capitalist' societies like Britain, and secondly to structural changes in the economy, usually where technological developments have 'left behind' a region or a district so that it is no longer capable of meeting economic demands and generating employment.

(1) *Centre for Environmental Studies: Ninth Annual Report*, p. 66. See also e.g. *National Community Development Project: Inter-Project Report*.

By contrast Sir Keith Joseph, for example, has laid more emphasis on the effects of child-rearing practices and of parental inadequacy.[1] Our own view is that any explanation has to be a multiple one; clearly there is something in both the views mentioned, and there are other contributory causes. Perhaps the most useful approach is in terms of various levels of explanation.

We start with social class. Britain obviously is a society in which people's life-chances – their opportunities and the resources available to them to live a full life – are largely constrained by the social class into which they are born, whether that is defined by the wealth, income or occupational status of their parents.[2] This kind of stratification is a feature not only of 'capitalist' or 'mixed-economy' societies but of virtually all that have been studied, though the degree of inequality – the gap between 'top' and 'bottom' – varies from one society to another, as does the relative ease or difficulty of movement from one stratum to another by, for example, educational achievement or occupational promotion.[3]

Whatever the differences between societies, it is plain that in Britain people born into working-class families, particularly the poorest and those in which the parents lack occupational skills, start off more vulnerable than others. This vulnerability is clearly reinforced if they themselves, as well as lacking economic support from their family, have limited educational success or fail to acquire job skills.

Such people, whom one could describe as 'structurally disadvantaged' in the social class system, are of course likely to be the first to suffer from the kinds of structural changes in the economy mentioned earlier – those with geographical, as against class, origins. The two structural aspects are related, since people without skills are in general more subject than others to unemployment in a national recession, and they are even more so if they live in a region such as Clydeside or, in a London context, Stockwell when affected by changes in the structure of industry and employment.

Thus these two inter-related types of 'structural' explanation – in terms of the social class structure and of the economic/geographical structure – are fundamental to an understanding of poverty and deprivation. At the next level of explanation, demographic factors come into play. The most vulnerable stages in life are when there are children and after retirement. Among families with dependent children, some are more at risk than others. Their predisposition to deprivation depends on the number of children, the number of parents, the stage at which the first child is born and whether the wife is able to supplement the household income by working.

(1) Sir Keith Joseph, 'The cycle of deprivation'.

(2) This is shown in studies of education (e.g. J. W. B. Douglas, *op. cit.*, and Michael Young, *op. cit.*), of social mobility between generations (e.g. D. V. Glass and J. R. Hall, 'Social mobility in Britain: a study of intergeneration changes in status') and of other aspects of life (e.g. Frank Field, *Unequal Britain: a Report on the Cycle of Inequality*).

(3) There has been some discussion about differences in class structure (e.g. John H. Goldthorpe, 'Social stratification in industrial societies') and about the variations in the extent of occupational mobility in different societies (e.g. S. M. Miller, 'Comparative social mobility').

The third level is that of the family or individual. It is clear enough that, within the general framework of social class, families exert great influence on their members. If parents suffer from behavioural or emotional handicaps, these predispose their families towards deprivation, particularly within the social strata which are relatively deprived to start with. Such handicapped families can, through the transmission of their attitudes and values, contribute to the disadvantages of children who grow up in them. In such ways, 'problem families' can be perpetuated over successive generations. Even without such familial transmission, people who themselves suffer from physical or mental handicaps are more susceptible than others to multiple deprivation.

The influence of colour

What, in our series of explanations for deprivation, is the influence of skin colour? Our study area, as we showed in the previous chapter, contains a relatively large proportion of people with black or brown skins, most of them from the West Indies or with parents from there. We should therefore be able to make some kind of judgement about the relationship between colour and deprivation.

The question has been given particular point by the writings of Peter Walker, the (Conservative) former Secretary of State for Environment who, as noted in Chapter 1, launched the inner area studies. Looking back to that time, Walker has recently written:

> 'I was deeply concerned that there were concentrated in a number of our inner-city areas a coloured population suffering from considerable multi-deprivation. A combination of bad housing, bad education and racial prejudice meant that they were destined to be the unemployed and the perpetual poor. The true facts were not available and to obtain the facts was one of the purposes of my instigating the three Inner-City Studies in Liverpool, Birmingham and Lambeth – all three in districts with a substantial immigrant population.'[1]

In the same article, Walker gave some evidence, most of it impressionistic, to explain his continuing anxiety. Of West Indians in particular he wrote, 'I believe that two-thirds of them are either badly-housed or are suffering from unemployment and the majority of them have a much lower standard of literacy and numeracy than the nation as a whole. . . . We have districts in which in every street there are West Indian families in overcrowded and deplorable housing conditions. Every other teenager is unemployed or playing truant from school; low incomes and numerous one-parent families; and above all, no hope.'

We have touched on some of these issues in this and the previous chapter. We now review the evidence and attempt a summing-up on the extent of deprivation among West Indians and other blacks in Stockwell.

We start with housing. The main issue is about access to council property. As we have shown, the story is complicated. As they were proportionately represented in

(1) Peter Walker, 'Race and the inner city: an open letter to the Prime Minister'.

council housing, old and new, they were not deprived on this score. Yet in another sense they were deprived, since more of those who were in council property lived in the older and less desirable estates. Furthermore, when living in private property, rented or owner-occupied, they were more deprived than whites in that they more often lacked or shared amenities. In both public and private housing they were more overcrowded, this being at least partly a function of their larger families. Thus in housing they were in general worse off than whites, though council housing had gone quite a way to redress the balance.

As for income, that depends on various things. We pointed out in the previous chapter that blacks were more often in low-skill jobs. We report, in the next chapter, that our survey showed that earnings were lower among blacks than whites. Job for job, they got paid less. As we also show, they had more often experienced recent unemployment, particularly long-term. We also show in the next chapter that unemployment was particularly high among teenage blacks.

Yet we said earlier in this chapter that, in terms of overall percentages, no more blacks were below the poverty line than whites. As we pointed out there, this was partly because few were pensioners and partly because family incomes were more often supplemented by wives working. These two factors masked the problem of poverty among blacks. The conclusion must be that in general they were worse off, because of discrimination, because they lacked education or training, or because of these in combination.[1]

What about the suggestion that more blacks were multiple-deprived? Our analyses showed that the skin colour of the head of the household made some difference to the household's deprivation 'score'. Though black households had higher multiple deprivation scores on average, skin colour was by no means the most important of the factors influencing these scores. Renting instead of owning, having low occupational status, being a pensioner, having children, not having multiple earners, not being a council tenant – all these had a stronger influence towards multiple deprivation. The question we were trying to answer was about the independent effect of skin colour. The statistical analyses showed that, other things equal, being black in itself went with a higher deprivation 'score'; a black household with children and low occupational status, for instance, was likely to be somewhat more deprived than a white one similarly placed. Thus colour did have an independent influence, even if not a dramatic one.

There is little doubt that education plays some part. Evidence about the relationship of skin colour to educational achievement is hard to discover, in the area of the Inner London Education Authority as elsewhere. But certainly much disquiet was expressed to us, by employers, teachers and residents, about the poor educational

(1) The PEP research, already referred to, showed that 'the level of formal education and academic qualifications is substantially lower among both Asians and West Indians than among white men', David J. Smith, *op. cit.*, p. 174. As Smith also reports, a series of controlled tests showed that 'Asian and West Indian applicants for semi-skilled and unskilled jobs face racial discrimination in one third of cases', *ibid.* p. 176; see also David J. Smith, *The Extent of Racial Discrimination*.

record of many black children and the apparent failure of the schools to provide curricula that hold their interest.

It seems that the difficulties are at least partly explained by differences in the early childhood experiences of West Indians in particular, as compared with whites. This suggestion comes from a study carried out in Brixton in 1967–1968 by Margaret Pollak, a local general practitioner.[1] She compared three groups of local children when they were aged three – those born to British parents, those born to West Indian parents, and others. The central interest was in the comparisons between the first two categories, families having been matched in terms of occupational status and the father's weekly earnings. The study concentrated on a series of 'development tests', covering 'motor development', 'personal-social development', 'adaptive behaviour' and 'language development'.

The main finding was that West Indian children did less well than white on these sets of tests, except for 'motor development'. The author concluded that the explanation was to be found in the different 'family culture' of West Indians compared with whites. The distinctive traditional West Indian pattern of family life, described in the previous chapter, is consistent with this, as is the higher proportion of West Indian mothers working outside the home. Pollak shows that, by the age of three, 71 per cent of West Indian children, as against 18 per cent of white, had been looked after by unregistered child-minders, and that, of these, half the West Indian children but none of the white had already had three or more minders. She sums up that the West Indian child:

> '. . . is not made to feel that he is a human being in his own right, precious to his parents and with all the dignity that a human being possesses. Due to the meagreness of his contact between him and his parents, he is deprived of many of the advantages which a greater degree of personal contact can offer. As a result, he develops a weak sense of his own identity. He is deprived of the environmental stimulation which encourages the building up of the schemata and skills which are so necessary for cognitive growth.'[2]

Pollak argues that this limited development may lead West Indian children to be incorrectly assessed as backward or educationally sub-normal.[3] Such a family background gives them the worst possible start at school, and, having started badly, they are unlikely to find it easy to make up the ground later.

Pollak's study was done several years ago, and was in any case on quite a small scale. Our salaried childminding project suggested that her findings still apply. If they do, the different attitude to the family and to children on the part of at least some West Indian parents is a contributory explanation for their apparent educational difficulties.

(1) Margaret Pollak, *Today's Three-Year-Olds in London.*

(2) *Ibid.* p. 143.

(3) Pollak cites an ILEA report which showed that the proportion of 'immigrant children in educationally sub-normal schools are about double their proportion in normal schools'.

There is of course more to it than that. Black children, experiencing prejudice and discrimination in the wider society and even at school, may easily become discouraged and disaffected. Once started, such a process feeds on itself: children who are labelled 'backward' or 'difficult' often respond by being more rebellious or staying away from school altogether. It may in any case be very difficult for West Indian boys to sustain an interest in education when they see their older brothers doing so badly in the job market.

To sum up, though it looks on the evidence from Stockwell as if Peter Walker somewhat exaggerated the case, it is clear that being black is in itself a handicap, and is associated with various forms of deprivation. The main explanations seem to be discrimination on the part of the host society, together with cultural patterns among West Indians and a sense of disaffection among young men in particular, both of which inhibit educational advance. The explanations for poverty presented earlier thus need to be modified to take account of discrimination and of the cultural patterns of minorities, both of which can intervene in such a way as to increase a household's deprivation.

Implications for policy

We have argued that the two most crucial forms of deprivation are income poverty and poor housing. Raising the real incomes of the poor and improving the housing of the badly-housed would end the bulk of deprivation. Housing is discussed in later chapters. In general, the most effective form of income maintenance is through paid work, the subject of the next chapter. Although we have not carried out a special study of education in Stockwell, what we have just said about West Indian disadvantage underlines the relevance to employment opportunities of education and training, a term that should be interpreted as covering everything from day care for under-fives to training for young people and retraining for those in middle age.

In discussing policies we concentrate in this chapter on income support and on the limits and possibilities of local measures to combat poverty. The importance of the first cannot be understated. It is clear to us, from what we have seen of the daily grind of poverty in the lives of some residents of Stockwell, that most of them simply need more money if they are to begin to live a decent life. Employment, as already stated, is crucial. But there also needs to be a new national scheme for income maintenance, to give more generous support to those who cannot earn or whose earnings have to be supplemented.

Such a scheme, since it would involve a redistribution of resources to the poor, would inevitably be costly, and there is little prospect of an immediate reform of this kind in a period when public expenditure is being held down and when, because of the pressure on living standards generally, public support is unlikely to be forthcoming. But, as Britain's economy starts to grow once more, a redistribution in favour of the poor should become more acceptable than it is now.

There is general recognition that something is wrong with the present set of arrangements for benefits, allowances and income tax. On the one hand, they fail to provide adequate help to many who need it; on the other, they lead to 'poverty traps' which make people worse off when they earn more and thus discourage incentives. There are some major technical problems to be overcome, and the opportunity should now be seized to examine the whole subject and prepare what would constitute a 'post-Beveridge' scheme for the 1980s.

The main criteria for a new scheme are clear enough. Since poverty is concentrated among the retired and among families with children, there need to be higher pensions and higher children's benefits. The new child benefit scheme is obviously a step in the right direction, at least for one of these vulnerable sections of the population. Higher benefits are also needed for people at other stages in life who are in need, such as the disabled, the long-term sick and the lone parents. The allowances and benefits need to be paid automatically, thus avoiding problems of take-up, and to be related to levels of taxation, so as to avoid any disincentive effects. Since we have not studied the subject in detail, we have not worked out how to resolve the various technical difficulties, the best method of financing a new scheme or whether the right method of distribution would be some form of general tax credit scheme or a series of separate schemes for the various categories of household in need.

A programme of this kind has to be a national one, because almost every district contains some poor families. In this sense, inner city poverty is no different from poverty elsewhere. Not only are there people living in arcadian suburbs who are as poor and deprived as those in Stockwell or Small Heath; numerically there are actually more outside inner areas than in them. The feature of the inner areas is that such people are more concentrated in other kinds of area, in the sense that they represent a higher proportion of the local population. They are, of course, also more concentrated in the sense that densities are higher.

Thus there is a specific inner city dimension to deprivation. The concentration of deprived people, not in all of Stockwell but in particular pockets of it, adds to their deprivation. The immediate environment – it may be a street of decaying Victorian houses or an inter-war housing estate – is often neglected and dreary, cluttered with decomposing mattresses and dumped cars, and lacking trees and open space. We showed in the previous chapter that local people care about such things, and area-specific measures, addressed to the physical improvement of housing and immediate environment, can obviously ease 'deprivations' of some kinds. Likewise, the concentration of disadvantaged people puts additional burdens on welfare services, and area-based measures are needed to help with these. We thus favour 'positive discrimination' of these two forms in deprived inner areas, though there are major problems in deciding how large such areas should be and on the criteria for selecting them.

Co-ordinating existing family and community services more effectively can do something to help deprived people, and others, to make fuller use of them, within the framework of existing resources; this issue is the subject of Chapter 9. Though the present period is, again, not one in which additional resources will easily be found, it seems clear that such concentrations of deprivation do require additional resources both for physical improvement and for welfare services. One modest measure needed is a more intensive form of support, including advice with budgeting, to help the minority of 'problem families' and others with multiple problems.

There is a final point. As we noted in the previous chapter, our research has shown that there is a general tendency, as conditions improve in the inner city, for the physical and social problems to 'spill over' to adjacent areas further 'out' from the centre. While housing standards rise in inner areas as a result of renewal or rehabilitation, the housing in these adjacent areas may deteriorate. In response to the physical changes, the concentrations of deprived people decline in inner areas and increase in those somewhat further out. Thus the process is a dynamic one, and the local authorities need to monitor changes so that they can, as needed, switch resources for physical and welfare services to new 'problem areas'.

□ Many of the conclusions from this chapter are taken up elsewhere. Housing and environmental improvement are discussed in Chapter 8. Chapter 9 looks at the organisation of some local services. The more specific policy suggestions from the present chapter are as follows:

1. A new comprehensive national scheme for income maintenance, to ensure in particular higher pensions for old people and higher children's benefits. Such a scheme should redistribute to those who are poor, by a method which is automatic (avoiding low take-up) and preserves the incentive to work.

2. Area-based initiatives are needed to direct resources for both physical improvement and welfare support into districts where concentrations of poverty have produced physical decline and have generated particularly heavy demands on services. Study will be needed to determine the most appropriate size of area for help of these kinds, and the criteria for selection.

3. Changes in the physical fabric and in the population structure of areas adjacent to the inner city need to be monitored so that resources can be switched to these areas as needed □

4 The job market

We have, in the previous chapter, given one reason why employment is so crucial; it is the most effective means of keeping out of poverty. But it is obviously also fundamental to the prosperity of the people and the area. Its importance in the Inner London context is now, as we write, more widely recognised than when we started our study in Stockwell. Our work on this subject has been described in two separate reports.[1]

We have already noted that the district, like much of Inner London, has a population characterised by relatively low occupational status, low incomes and, by London standards, high unemployment. Our studies sought to explain this pattern in terms of a number of factors. The main problem with any such attempt is to sort out causes from effects: do people have particular characteristics (such as low skill, low pay, unemployment) because they live in Stockwell or do they live in Stockwell because they have those characteristics? Much of our work has been aimed at untangling this particular conundrum.

The jobs held by the people of Stockwell collectively represent the economic base of the area. The fewer at work and the lower their pay, the lower the income of the population and the more people dependent upon welfare services. Low disposable income will ultimately be reflected in low expenditure on housing, leading for example to overcrowding, poor standards and inadequate maintenance. Local services in the private sector, such as retailing, will suffer from a lack of local spending power. Services in the public sector, provided primarily by local authorities, will be overloaded and there will be less money from the rates to pay for them.

These problems, stemming from employment decline since the mid-sixties, have given rise to a new debate in planning circles about the general direction of planning for London. This debate came out in a rather confused form in the Inquiry on the Greater London Development Plan (GLDP) and has continued in relation to such issues as the proposed housing strategy, regional economic policy, Docklands and the role of the New and Expanding Towns. There is no longer the clear consensus in favour of reducing London's population and employment as a means of reducing congestion and improving housing and the general environment. Instead, major conflicts seem to be emerging between, on the one hand, fiscal and social arguments for bolstering the economic base and, on the other, arguments for continuing to reduce pressure, density and congestion.[2] We examine this issue directly in Chapter 7, but the evidence on employment is relevant to the debate, showing for

(1) Inner Area Study Lambeth, *Labour Market Study* (IAS/LA/4) and *Local Employers' Study* (IAS/LA/16).

(2) See, for example, David Eversley, 'Old cities, declining population and rising costs'.

example the relationships between employment decline, unemployment and low incomes, and the conflicts and contraints involved in trying to maintain or develop industrial activity in the inner city.

The previous chapter examined the incidence and characteristics of poverty and deprivation in Stockwell. The job market is clearly the most important single influence determining whether people are deprived. Unemployment is a serious deprivation in itself, and job instability generally can give rise to other kinds of deprivation. So can low income.

One of the area's most acute and distinctive social problems is unemployment among young blacks. The unemployment rate among young black males is higher than that for anybody else. Homelessness and street crime are also common among them. A major part of any attempt to tackle their multiple problems must be to ensure that they are adequately equipped to compete in the job market and that there are enough suitable local job opportunities.

How much unemployment?

A first question was whether Stockwell had an especially serious unemployment problem. The exact figures for unemployment rates vary considerably according to the sources of data, the area boundaries used and the exact point in time. But the general conclusion is that this area has experienced somewhat higher unemployment rates than the country as a whole, and markedly higher rates than those prevailing in London and the South East. The Brixton employment exchange area (covering most of the borough) was one of four in London to have registered male unemployment rates consistently more than double the regional average between 1971 and 1975.[1]

Unemployment rates have tended to be high in Inner London and low in Outer London. These and other comparisons are shown in Figure 11. In 1971, males seeking employment were 5·0 per cent of the economically active in Inner London and 2·7 per cent in Outer London, and the 13 worse boroughs were all inner ones. Lambeth was the third worst borough on this index, following Tower Hamlets and Kensington and Chelsea. Apart from this inner/outer contrast, there has also been a general tendency for rates to be higher on the eastern side of London, with the Brixton area's high unemployment an exception to this.[2]

The size of area chosen for analyses affects the figures, so that sharper variations emerged when exchange areas were used rather than boroughs, and there was considerable variation at the very local level. A special count of registered unemployment by street in the study area in 1973 showed concentrations in the Vauxhall and Brixton corners, with rather lower rates in the middle. Variations at

(1) GLC, *Employment in Greater London and the Rest of the South-East Region.*

(2) *Ibid.*

78

**Figure 11
Relative
unemployment
rates for men, 1971**
Unemployment in
Lambeth and
Stockwell was higher
than in Inner London
as a whole, though
rather lower than in
the East End.

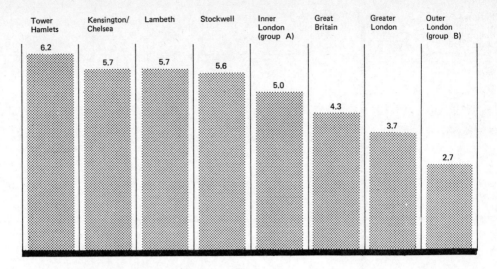

Sources: Census 1971
County Report for Greater London, Part I, Table 18
E.D. sheets (Stockwell)
1% Summary Table 13 (Great Britain)

Note: These figures are males out of employment, excluding the sick, as a percentage of economically active males aged 15
and over.

this level must be explained mainly by the different types of people living in different
types and tenures of housing.

Our studies showed not only that the area was among London's worst for
unemployment, but also that there had been a relative deterioration between 1966
and 1971 compared with the rest of Britain. Figures for the wider Inner South
London area suggest that its relative disadvantage had persisted to 1975 (Figure 12).
This was against a background of much higher national unemployment rates in the
1970s than in the mid-1960s, and also considerable cyclical fluctuations. The latter
have affected the study area as much as anywhere, with high unemployment in 1972
and even higher rates in 1975. Unemployment halved in the 1972–73 boom, which
explains why the rates recorded in our household survey and the special count were
relatively low, around 3 per cent for men. However, the survey also showed that
9 per cent of male workers and 8 per cent of female workers had experienced some
unemployment in the preceding 12 months. Seasonal variations were also evident,
averaging about 20 per cent, but were clearly less marked than the national
economic recessions.

Unemployment struck at men more than women. According to the 1971 census,
male rates were worse than female rates both absolutely (5·6 per cent against
4·1 per cent) and relative to GLC averages. Perhaps more striking was the finding
that a high proportion of married women were at work, even by London standards
(Table 8).

Taken together with our evidence on earnings and on trends in labour demand and
supply, these findings led us to concentrate our attention on the job market for men.
There appeared to be an imbalance in Stockwell, even more than nationally, which

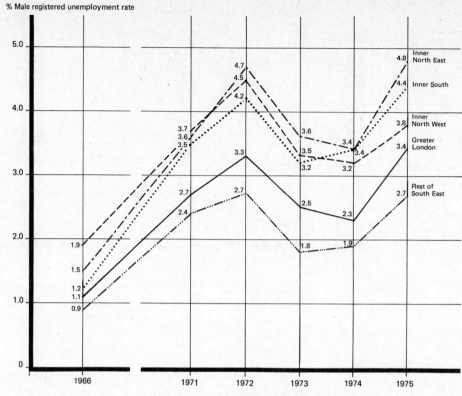

**Figure 12
Trends in male
unemployment
since 1966**
Unemployment in
Inner London became
relatively worse
between 1966 and
1975.

% Male registered unemployment rate

Inner North East 4.8
Inner South 4.4
Inner North West 3.8
Greater London 3.4
Rest of South East 2.7

Source: G.L.C. (1975) op. cit. Table 6; Registered unemployed males aged 18+ in April of each year as percentage of estimated resident, economically active males aged 15 and over; central area omitted; Inner South = Lambeth, Southwark, Wandsworth and Lewisham.

Table 8 Married women working as a percentage of each age group: Stockwell, Greater London and Great Britain

Age	Stockwell	Greater London	Great Britain
25–34	52%	44%	40%
35–44	65%	62%	58%
45–54	72%	64%	57%
55–59	67%	55%	47%

Sources: Census 1971, General Household Survey 1971.

put men at a disadvantage in the job market. Indeed it could be argued that the female workers' problem was the opposite. Available job opportunities made it possible for more women to work, and in many families the necessity arose because of the inadequate earnings of husbands or because mothers were unsupported. With inadequate day care provision, there was a resulting social problem of large-scale unregulated childminding. The importance of wives working was confirmed by our study of poverty and was one reason for our day care action project.[1]

Other distinctive features of Stockwell's unemployment problem began to emerge when we looked at the age distribution of the unemployed, which was distinctly biased towards the younger age groups (Figure 13). Although unemployment is traditionally associated with older workers, who undoubtedly find it more difficult

(1) Phyllis Willmott and Linda Challis, *The Groveway Project* (IAS/LA/17).

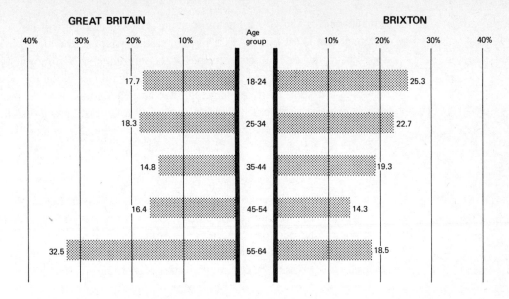

Figure 13
Age distribution of unemployment
Unemployment in the Brixton area was concentrated amongst the younger age groups. Even though the 18-24 band was smaller than the others, it accounted for the highest percentage of unemployed.

GREAT BRITAIN   BRIXTON

| 40% | 30% | 20% | 10% | Age group | 10% | 20% | 30% | 40% |

17.7 — 18-24 — 25.3
18.3 — 25-34 — 22.7
14.8 — 35-44 — 19.3
16.4 — 45-54 — 14.3
32.5 — 55-64 — 18.5

Sources: Brixton E.F.A. from E.D.S.82A sheets courtesy of D.E. Regional Office; Great Britain: sample survey of unemployed
register, from D.E. Gazette, March 1974. c.f. 1 AS/LA/4 Tables 3.3.1 — 3.3.3.

and take longer to obtain work after redundancy, there has been a growing problem nationally for the under-25s since about 1967,[1] culminating in the present crisis facing school-leavers. However, this problem has been more marked locally than elsewhere. Between 1961 and 1972, registered unemployed men in Brixton trebled in number, but the number of boys on the register multiplied eight times. Things appear to have further deteriorated since then.

Apart from raising the general question of why the young are increasingly liable to unemployment, this evidence can be related to two more specific characteristics of the local unemployment problem. First, in common with much of London the area's unemployment tended to be of shorter duration than the national average, and this can be explained by age, since average time on the register varies, for example from around six weeks for 18–24 year olds to around 25 weeks for 60–64 year olds. Age for age, average time on the register was somewhat higher in Inner South London than in the rest of London, and the weekly rate of registration was higher than the London level for the under-25s and lower for the over-50s.[2] In other words, Stockwell has had more frequent short bursts of unemployment among young people.

Secondly, as noted earlier, the area's most striking unemployment problem was that of West Indian youths. Statistics on this are less than adequate[3] but the 1971 Census showed that it was a national problem, though obviously concentrated in areas of high West Indian settlement like Brixton. Thus, in Great Britain in 1971, 16 per cent of West Indian boys available for work aged 15 to 19 were out of work, compared with 8 per cent of all boys in that age group. This suggests that a major part of the

(1) S. Mukherjee, *There's Work to be Done*.

(2) GLC, *op.cit*

(3) See for example Community Relations Commission, *Unemployment and Homelessness: A Report*.

explanation for the youth unemployment problem in Lambeth lies in the sizeable proportion of West Indians in the younger age groups of the local workforce. It was apparent from our contacts with the local community and from other studies that black youths suffer from a combination of disadvantages in the job market, including problems with language, literacy and education, problems with families and homelessness, unrealistic expectations and, of course, racial discrimination. Initial failure resulting from these and from lack of local manual jobs would naturally reinforce tendencies to a sense of alienation, job instability, and resort to crime.

The household survey enabled us to look more generally at the employment patterns among coloured and immigrant groups. Coloured men were more likely to have experienced unemployment, particularly longer-term unemployment, in the preceding 12 months than were white men. In terms of country of birth, unemployment was more common among West Indians, Africans and Indians than among males born in Britain, but less common among the Irish and 'others' (mainly southern European). We also found that the sharpest difference between coloured and white males was in skilled manual jobs. This suggests that discrimination is more severe in skilled trades, an unfortunate fact in view of the concentration of blacks in skilled manual occupations and the apparent preference of young blacks for this kind of work. Our survey of local employers suggested a similar pattern; a number of firms, though having a large number of skilled jobs, employed few black workers in these jobs.

For blacks and whites together, however, unemployment was generally higher among manual than non-manual workers, and higher in the less skilled than in the skilled occupations. This conclusion was consistent with other studies,[1] and it can be argued that the high overall unemployment in areas like Stockwell is largely explained by their higher proportion of less skilled residents.[2] While there is some truth in this proposition, it is not a sufficient explanation. Within almost all occupational groups except the junior non-manual, local unemployment was higher than London or South Eastern averages as can be seen in Tables 9 and 10.

Table 9   Unemployment rates by socio-economic groups: Stockwell, Lambeth and Greater London (males and females, 1971)

Socio-economic groups	Stockwell	Lambeth	Greater London
Professional and managerial	2·6%	2·1%	1·9%
Intermediate non-manual	4·7%	3·1%	2·8%
Junior non-manual	1·6%	2·2%	2·0%
Personal service	2·2%	3·4%	2·6%
Supervisory and skilled workers	3·9%	5·2%	3·4%
Semi-skilled manual	7·0%	6·0%	3·5%
Unskilled manual	5·5%	6·1%	5·5%
Own account workers	5·7%	8·1%	4·5%
Unclassified	53·1%	45·8%	46·5%
All	6·3%	6·1%	4·6%

Source: Census 1971, 10% analysis.

(1) See for example GLC, op.cit.

(2) See for example D. Metcalf and R. Richardson, Unemployment in London.

Table 10   Male registered unemployment rates by socio-economic groups: Brixton Employment Exchange Area and South East (March 1974)

Socio-economic groups	Brixton	South East
Professional and managerial	2·5%	0·9%
Other non-manual	0·8%	1·9%
Supervisory and skilled manual	5·8%	1·7%
Service and semi-skilled manual	3·9%	1·4%
Unskilled manual	16·3%	11·2%
Total	4·8%	2·0%

Source: GLC, *Employment in Greater London and the Rest of the South East Region.*

Incomes

The main conclusion from the 1973 household survey was that median male earnings in Stockwell were lower than in Great Britain generally, by about 17 per cent or £7 per week. There were fewer highly-paid workers and about double the national proportion of men earning less than £24 a week. Women, by contrast, earned slightly more than the national average; despite this and the fact that more of them worked, average household income in Stockwell was still about 12 per cent below the national average.

Regional comparisons of male earnings showed that the study area was worse off than most parts of the country (Figure 14) including high unemployment areas like Merseyside and Glasgow, as well as traditional low-wage areas like Manchester and East Anglia. Such comparisons are perhaps unfair, insofar as comparable small areas within these regions might well have been worse off. Perhaps more significant was the large discrepancy between men living in Stockwell and the average for men working in Greater London. This point was underlined by recent estimates for individual London boroughs[1] which showed that jobs in Lambeth and neighbouring boroughs did not have unduly low average earnings. In other words, although men living in Stockwell had low pay, those working in and around the area did not. This suggests that residents' low earnings could not simply be blamed on the low pay in local jobs. Instead it seems that lower paid workers tended to live in areas like Stockwell or, to put it another way, that Stockwell residents were unable to obtain the better paid jobs on offer.

This handicap is partly explained by the lower occupational status of Stockwell's residents. Low pay was particularly concentrated among unskilled workers and service workers: 30 per cent of the former and 46 per cent of the latter earned less than £24 per week. But, within every socio-economic group, men in Stockwell earned less on average than those elsewhere. The main reasons for this additional variation seem to be the type of industry and the type of firm found locally. Some industries pay less than others for any particular level of skill because of factors such as national wage agreements, capital intensity and the degree of competition. Some firms, as we saw among those we studied, pay less because they offer limited opportunities for overtime or shiftwork, or because trade union influence in them is

(1) *D.E. Gazette*, January 1975, p. 28.

**Figure 14
Earnings of full
time workers in
1974:
some comparisons**
Male earnings in
Stockwell were lower
than in most other
parts of the country.

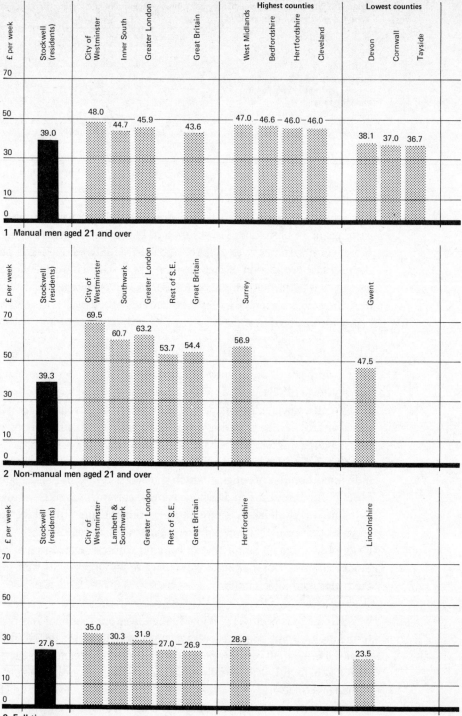

1 Manual men aged 21 and over

2 Non-manual men aged 21 and over

3 Full-time women

Sources: Stockwell household survey (by of residence) adjusted for 6 months inflation; other areas — New Earnings Survey
(1974) in D.E. Gazette, January 1975, p. 28-35 (by area of workplace).

weak. In other words, local earnings in Stockwell are due to a mixture of the low skills of many residents and the characteristics of local industry and of local firms.

Finally, low pay was slightly more prevalent among coloured men, 21 per cent of them earning less than £24 per week compared with 17 per cent of whites. As with unemployment, the really striking difference was in the skilled manual category, with 23 per cent of skilled coloured men earning less than £24 per week compared with only 9 per cent of skilled whites.

The geography of the job market

Labour market analysis is difficult in a big city like London, because one cannot easily define the geographical boundaries of the market. Most workers living in a particular place cannot reasonably be expected to seek work in all parts of the conurbation, but it is not clear exactly how local the relevant area is. To throw some light on this and hence be able to evaluate local job opportunities, we analysed the evidence on three questions. First, we asked which parts of London were accessible to Stockwell residents within certain time and cost constraints. Second, we looked at where residents worked and how this had changed. Third, we asked local employers where their workers lived.

Only a third of Stockwell's households had cars and less than one in every seven workers used a car to get to work. We therefore concentrated on public transport services, particularly tubes and buses, and mapped out contours of accessibility in terms of both time and cost. These suggested that the area which was reasonably accessible to most Stockwell residents was Inner South London – Lambeth, Southwark and Wandsworth boroughs – and most of Central London. Radial journeys into Central London were relatively easy, but access to other parts of London was restricted by the slowness and unreliability of bus services. When analysing job opportunities, we therefore concentrated on two labour market areas. The first was Inner South London, made up of the boroughs of Lambeth, Southwark and Wandsworth. The second was a wider zone which also included the City, Westminster, Camden, Hammersmith, Kensington and Chelsea, and Merton (Figure 15).

The evidence on people's journeys to work confirmed that these zones were sensibly chosen. In 1966, 44 per cent of Stockwell's workers had jobs in Inner South London, and 87 per cent in the broader area. There has apparently been a trend since 1966 to somewhat longer work journeys, with fewer residents working in Lambeth and more in Central London and the outer boroughs in the south. By 1973, for example, nearly half of all Stockwell workers worked in the central area. This could imply that people had been forced to make longer journeys by the decline of local job opportunities, but there was a general trend in London for people to travel further to their work and the opening of the Victoria Line extension in 1971 improved access to the West End. The household survey evidence on work journey times did not suggest major problems: 71 per cent took less than 30 minutes whilst only 3 per cent took more than an hour.

Figure 15
Labour market
areas
The smaller area
covered the London
Boroughs of Lambeth,
Wandsworth and
Southwark. The wider
area also included
Kensington and
Chelsea, Merton,
Camden,
Hammersmith,
Westminster and the
City of London.

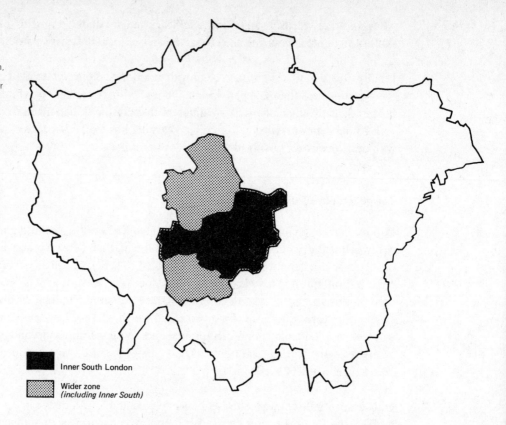

■ Inner South London

▨ Wider zone
(including Inner South)

There were differences in the work journeys of different kinds of people in Stockwell. Women more often worked in the central area than men (60 per cent compared with 40 per cent) presumably because of the predominance of office and service jobs there. Men, particularly those in skilled manual jobs, more often worked further afield, in other parts of London or even outside it. This reflected their greater mobility and the geographical scatter of industrial jobs. Income was strongly related to where men worked; those working inside Lambeth earned less on average than those working further afield.

Many people who worked in Lambeth's industries and services were not local residents, but commuted from other areas, mainly further out. In interviewing local employers we confirmed this, and were also able to distinguish between the patterns for different kinds of job. In most firms it appeared that management, professional and other senior staff were rarely local residents while, at the other extreme, most unskilled workers did live locally.

By far the biggest concentration of jobs, particularly service jobs, in London is in the central area. It includes the City, Whitehall and the headquarters offices of major concerns, together with entertainment, tourism, the law and higher education. In 1971 about 1¼ million people worked there. We have said that this was where as many as half of Stockwell residents with jobs worked in 1973. The proportion was much the same for residents of Inner London generally and, as well as half of Inner Londoners working in the central area, about half of those working there were Inner

86

London residents, and of the rest just under two-thirds lived in Outer London and the remainder outside London altogether.

There are other, though smaller, concentrations of jobs in London. But, unlike the central area, most of the major concentrations of manufacturing industry are not very accessible from Stockwell, apart from an industrial belt along the south of the Thames and up the Wandle Valley. Inner South London, as shown later, has fewer jobs than resident workers in most occupation groups. Though accessibility is a problem for many Stockwell residents, there seems to be limited scope for improving it. Cars offer greater mobility but their availability and use is bound to remain limited by income levels, by petrol prices, by congestion, parking problems, and policies of restraint. There is unlikely to be major investment in public transport in this part of South London or other changes which would improve the pattern of accessibility.

Job opportunities

We wanted to find out whether accessible job opportunities were inadequate for particular groups living in Stockwell, and whether lack of demand could explain high unemployment rates and low earnings. Also whether trends over time were having an adverse effect, and to what extent the decline of industry could be blamed for this.

To avoid a circular argument, we had to find indices of labour demand other than the traditional measure – the unemployment rate. Notified vacancies expressed as a percentage of total jobs in the area provided an index of this kind, although not an entirely satisfactory one. From the census we could measure the ratio of jobs to resident workers in a particular area and the rate of decline (or growth) in jobs as compared with resident workers. Finally, a more subjective source was the response of local employers to questions about how easy or difficult it was to recruit labour.

As each of the main occupational groups forms a largely separate labour market, we calculated separate indices for them. Among men, local demand was relatively strong for professional, managerial, intermediate non-manual and skilled manual workers, and very weak for the unskilled.[1] There was a moderate level of demand for junior non-manual, personal service and semi-skilled workers. The evidence from the employers' survey was consistent with this; the main difficulties were in recruiting skilled men, and few firms found it hard to get unskilled workers.

Job opportunities were very limited in Inner South London, as is shown in Appendix 3. Things were rather better in the wider area, including Central London, for people with certain sorts of skills, for instance in transport, clerical and service jobs. But even in the wider area labour demand was weaker than in most other parts of the South East Region. This last point underlines the need for a policy to help low-skill workers to move out of Inner London.

(1) These and other relevant findings are shown in Tables 19 to 22, Appendix 3.

Mismatch of jobs and workers: the skills possessed by local residents did not match the jobs available to them.

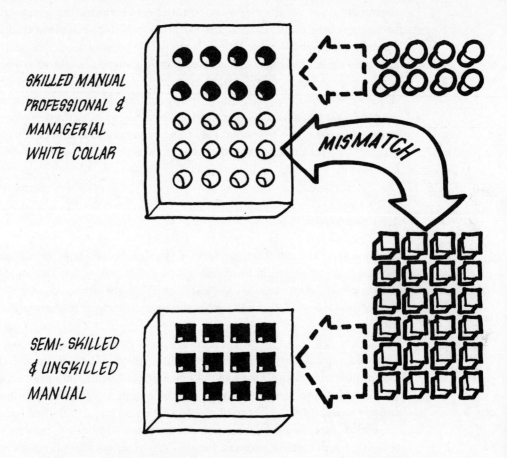

SKILLED MANUAL
PROFESSIONAL &
MANAGERIAL
WHITE COLLAR

MISMATCH

SEMI-SKILLED
& UNSKILLED
MANUAL

The evidence on the pattern of local job opportunities tended to confirm our hypothesis that there was an imbalance or mismatch between supply and demand in the local labour market, and that unemployment was, in large measure, a consequence of this. The imbalance had two elements: geographical and occupational. Local job opportunities were poor and employment trends unfavourable, while certain occupational groups, mainly the less skilled males, suffered most. The combination of these two elements produced acute unemployment in Lambeth, which was greatly exacerbated by the recent recessions. The other side of the imbalance was a relative shortage of more skilled workers, particularly in the economic upswing of 1973.

The immediate causes of this growing imbalance seemed fairly clear. On the geographical side, there had been an accelerating decline in many local industries since 1966, while population dispersal had mainly involved non-manual and skilled manual workers. The lower paid and unskilled tended to be trapped in the area by the housing system. This housing trap, and the need for policies for more balanced dispersal, are discussed in Chapters 6 and 7.

The occupational aspects of mismatch were rather more complex. Only part of the loss in semi-skilled and unskilled jobs in Inner South London could be explained by the fall in jobs generally, with manufacturing probably accounting for about a third of this. Equally important were major permanent job losses in railways, road transport, gas, electricity, water, distribution and certain other private sector services, together with the recession in construction. More important than these industrial declines was a marked shift within most industries and services in the kinds of labour they employed, with less reliance on low-skill workers and more on professional, technical and administrative staff. Much of the responsibility for this shift may rest with the major public sector services, which accounted for a large and growing proportion of total employment. By 1971, about a third of jobs in Inner South London, compared with a quarter in Greater London, were in this sector. Most of Lambeth Council's employment growth after 1967 consisted of salaried staff.

On the other hand, among the private firms we interviewed, relocation and other changes seemed to have had the effect of reducing non-manual and skilled jobs more than unskilled. This could have been because firms were to some extent adjusting their labour force to use the skills available.

The failure of labour supply to adapt to changing demand is associated with two main factors in addition to the housing trap. First, vocational training is the logical way to prepare people without skills for new kinds of job. The trouble is that training provision in Britain – and in Stockwell in particular – is in many respects quite inadequate compared with that in other countries. Secondly, many young entrants to the local labour market were apparently leaving school with minimal educational qualifications. This, taken together with the loss of less skilled manual jobs, provides a plausible explanation for the area's abnormally high unemployment among young people. Both these issues are discussed later.

There are other causes of unemployment in Inner London. One commonly invoked is the high proportion of people with characteristics which make for vulnerability to unemployment, regardless of the availability of jobs. But vulnerability is not the same thing as unemployment; it only becomes so when the demand for labour falls. In other words, vulnerable groups like the young, the old, the blacks, and the disabled, are more likely to suffer from either a national recession or a local job shortage, but they can usually obtain work when and where demand is high.[1] This is an important part of the social case for full employment policies. And the independent measures of labour demand discussed earlier showed that job opportunities were inadequate in the area around Stockwell, at least for the less skilled.

Job decline

We have discussed the effect of employment decline and the changing structure of job opportunities. (By way of general background Figure 16 shows the structure of

(1) See for example, M. J. Hill *et al.*, *Men Out of Work*.

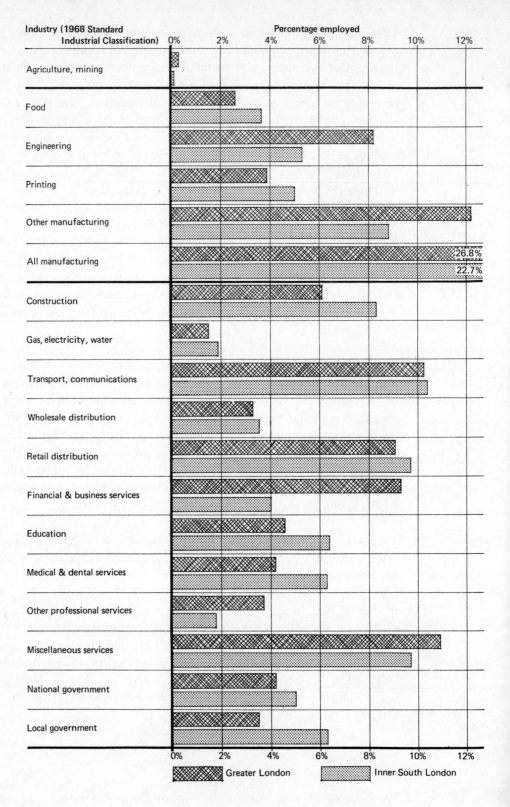

**Figure 16
Employment
structure of Inner
South London**
Compared with
Greater London as a
whole it was heavily
biased towards
services.

Industry (1968 Standard Industrial Classification)

Percentage employed

All manufacturing: 26.8% / 22.7%

| Greater London | Inner South London |

Source: Census 1971 — Economic Activity County Leaflet : Greater London

employment in Inner South London in 1971 and Appendix 3 shows the main changes.) Are these trends harmful? Can they be reversed? In trying to answer these questions we draw mainly on evidence from our survey of local employers, but we need first to say something about the general pattern of employment in the area.

We decided to focus our survey on a fairly narrow sector of employment, for various reasons. The large public sector was excluded because it behaves differently from the private sector, because much of it had not declined and because more was known about it anyway. Small employers (with under 30 employees) were excluded for technical reasons and to keep down the number of interviews. Purely local services like retailing were excluded, and it was felt that the construction industry would have required a separate survey. Our sample was reasonably representative of local manufacturing, which was our main interest, but more limited and impressionistic in terms of services. In all, 39 firms were interviewed in depth and limited information was obtained about a number of others – mainly non-responders, movers and closures. Interviews took place between July and November 1975; this was unfortunately a period of severe recession, but we tried to allow for that in the questionnaire.

There were a number of reasons for our concentrating on manufacturing, despite the fact that its decline was not the only or the major cause of unemployment. First, manufacturing is a basic industry in the sense that jobs in local services depend to some extent upon it, directly or indirectly. Secondly, manufacturing provides well-paid manual jobs, and hence the incomes of people in Stockwell are likely to suffer if it continues to decline. Thirdly, it provides semi-skilled and skilled manual jobs and some of the corresponding avenues for training. Fourthly, it does provide many jobs locally for black people. Fifthly, thinking on Britain's overall economic strategy currently lays emphasis upon shifting resources back into manufacturing industry.

There was a final reason for our emphasis. Manufacturing industry had declined more sharply in Inner South London, as in London generally, than in the rest of the country. This decline was not because local manufacturing industry had a particularly vulnerable structure; it was not biased towards those industries declining most rapidly elsewhere. Instead the causes seemed to be connected with the characteristics of individual firms or with the problems of operating in the area.[1] What were these causes?

We looked at four aspects of employment decline:
1. What was the quantitative effect on employment of openings, closures, relocations?
2. Why had firms closed or moved?
3. How many and which firms were vulnerable to future closure, rationalisation or relocation?
4. How and why had employment changed within firms still operating in the area?

(1) See for example GLC, *op.cit*.

A Department of Industry analysis for London and the South East covering the years 1966–74[1] showed that new manufacturing openings were quite plentiful in London, suggesting that the city continued to perform its traditional 'seedbed' function for industry. It also found substantial movement out of London but negligible movement inwards. (This was consistent with our finding that none of our firms had moved into London, whilst a number had moved outwards from the centre.) Of Greater London's total manufacturing job loss – 383,400 during the period studied – the Department of Industry attributed 27 per cent to movement, 51 per cent to closures (less openings) and 21 per cent to losses within plants which remained. Patterns were similar in Inner and Outer London. Our own estimate on the basis of our survey of employers, referring to Inner South London between 1970 and 1975[2], was 58 per cent to movement, 23 per cent to closures and 19 per cent to losses within remaining firms.

The closures, of course, represented some form of economic failure, although the reasons were often complex. Of the four firms in our survey which had closed, technological change causing a shift in demand to competing products was the major factor in two, and the need for economies of scale featured in a third. Static or declining demand affected three of the four firms, though in one this was partly due to a failure to compete internationally. Labour shortage and obsolete premises were contributory influences. Finally, in one firm rigidities had been introduced by trade union agreements, resulting in closure instead of what might otherwise have been a more gradual rundown.

Within the overall sample we had a number of examples of relocation, including complete and partial moves, and actual, probable and possible ones. These all throw light on the reasons for outward movement, which turned out to be very diverse. There was no single universal factor. Shortage of space and labour supply were the two most important general reasons. Space constraints are normal in a densely built-up area; in addition, premises were often old and inconvenient. The escape to sites where a growing firm could expand usually meant a move away from Inner London unless there was a particular local tie. The most important tie was access to markets, particularly in Central London and particularly for service sector firms. Proximity to suppliers was rarely important.

On the other hand, Inner London's disadvantages as an industrial location emerged in many comments. Apart from inadequate premises and labour supply problems, these covered a whole range of environmental difficulties including inadequate parking, road access, public transport and amenities and the incidence of vandalism and crime. Taken together, these factors did not make Inner London seem an attractive or cheap location when a choice arose.

(1) Department of Industry, *The Decline of Manufacturing Industry in London.*

(2) This is not directly comparable with the Department of Industry figure and much more tentative. If there is any dispute it centres on the definition, and hence the extent, of 'relocation'. We found in the survey considerable evidence of partial or gradual relocation of production (and hence employment) away from Inner London to firms' other plants elsewhere, and often this process would not be accompanied by any official openings or closures.

It may seem paradoxical that labour shortage was a problem at all for firms, given what we have reported earlier about unemployment. The key to the paradox lay in the mismatch, confirmed in the interviews with employers, between the skills that were available and those the firms actually needed. Some of these skills were scarce nationally, electrical engineers being an example; others, such as clothing machinists, were local. Some firms had labour problems because they paid low wages; others because their factories were inaccessible, insalubrious or in areas that were run-down or lacking facilities such as lunch-time eating places.

Whether most of the labour force lived locally or not affected some firms' attitudes to moving. Several firms where workers did not live locally seemed to be more disposed to move, their destination being influenced by where their workers lived. Some firms with a predominantly local labour force, on the other hand, were disinclined to move for fear of losing their workers.

Central and local government policies were much less important reasons for moving than those so far mentioned. No moves had been explained by refusal of Industrial Development Certificates and only one firm had been refused an Office Development Permit. There was, however, some evidence these restrictions had been a hindrance to firms seeking to expand. Planning refusals by local authorities had also been a problem, but a major overt reason for moving in only two instances. Short of demolishing the surrounding property, there was little that planners could do to allow firms to expand when their premises were hemmed in. Redevelopment proposals threatened four firms, creating considerable uncertainty. Clearly this problem has been more widespread and serious for small firms, not included in the survey. Likewise, planning constraints must have inhibited the growth of new firms. Finally, there were some cases where the possibility of redeveloping the existing site for more profitable use such as offices may have been a contributory factor.

Although moving firms or new branches often went to new towns or assisted areas,[1] it seems likely that the incentives and opportunities presented in such areas steered their choice of location rather than caused their initial decision to move. The main implication is that London could probably retain more of its industry, or attract new, if it could compete on comparable terms with new towns and the like. As we argue later, the removal of IDCs and of planning constraints, though necessary, will not in themselves be enough.

Likely future changes

From the answers to specific questions and from the general comments made by employers, it was possible to get an impression of how secure a firm's future was. An optimistic interpretation of the evidence suggested that about a quarter of the firms (both manufacturing and service) and about a quarter of their total labour force seemed vulnerable to closure or being moved away from the area. Under more

(1) See also Department of Industry, *op.cit.*

pessimistic assumptions, though most of the remaining service firms appeared secure, rather more than half of the manufacturing sector could conceivably be lost. Thus, the adverse trends of the recent past seemed likely to continue, unless there was intervention to arrest them. This is clearly a disturbing conclusion from the interviews.

We compared 'vulnerable' with safe firms to see what the consequences of further decline would be. The two types were similar in terms of size, the spread of their labour force, and various other characteristics. But average earnings among 'safe' firms were rather lower; this means that continuing decline will further reduce local earnings. On the other hand, safe firms employed more blacks and unskilled workers, so on this score at least, further decline will not hit at vulnerable people in particular.

Employment changes within firms which remain can affect local job opportunities as much as moves and closures. Such changes might reflect a range of factors, including demand, productivity, investment, and constraints, all of which might vary from firm to firm. We asked employers about the reasons for employment changes between 1970–75, and the constraints they faced. Their answers are shown in Table 11.

Table 11   Circumstances of firms, 1970–75

		Number of firms		
		Manufacturing	Service	All
1.	Demand declining, employment falling	5	1	6
2.	Demand, productivity and employment static	2	2	4
3.	Productivity outstripping demand, employment falling	3	2	5
4.	Productivity offsets demand, employment static	1	1	2
5.	Demand outstripping productivity, employment rising	5	3	8
6.	As 4, but subject to constraints	5	2	7
7.	As 5, but subject to contraints	5	2	7
	Total	26	13	39

Source: Local employers' study 1975.

The table shows that 'structural' reasons for employment decline – that is, where demand was declining or being outstripped by productivity – applied to only a minority of firms, and even then were exaggerated by the recession. Equally important were the firms whose potential growth was constrained, the main problems again being space and labour supply. This evidence reinforced our conclusion – from the statistical data on industrial structure[1] – that the area's

(1) GLC, *op.cit.* Table 18; Department of Industry, *op.cit.*; Inner Area Study Lambeth, *Local Employers Study* (IAS/LA/16), paragraph 5.23.

employment decline could not be attributed in the main to a preponderance of declining industries. On the contrary, many of the firms were in a good economic position, but were frustrated by constraints associated with operating locally. Together with the evidence on relocation, this pointed to a need to formulate policies aimed at helping firms to overcome their constraints, particularly space and labour skills, *within* London.

Policies for industry

The employers' survey, which we have just been reporting, was concerned with the problems of existing firms, and we have shown that policies are needed to help them to remain in the inner city. We have, however, noted earlier that a major component of the loss of manufacturing jobs has been the 'deaths' of firms as distinct from movement. This means that measures are also needed to enable existing firms to survive and, even more important, help new ones to be born. The proposals which follow contain all these elements.

Before we outline these proposals, we need to say something about how the prospects for local employment are likely to be affected by a future up-turn in the national economy. The pressures will be very different in a period of economic growth than in one of recession, and the consequences of growth will be different as between existing firms and potential new ones.

For existing firms, the results of growth are likely to be mixed. Those in a weak position, suffering from declining demand, are obviously more likely to survive in an improved economic climate. But those that are already doing well are more likely to want to move out of Inner London, since they will feel the pinch of space and labour shortages even more sharply. As we have already pointed out, these stronger firms are in a majority. Thus on balance, unless effective measures are taken to overcome the constraints, Inner London may well lose out in terms of existing firms.

As for the prospects for the development of new firms, it is highly unlikely that Inner London will maintain its share of these unless there are some radical changes. Under present conditions, as a location for new industry, Inner London labours under heavy disadvantages compared with green-field sites in new towns or development areas, particularly for larger plants. Suitable sites and new buildings are not available, land costs are high, parking inadequate and accessibility poor. So deliberate intervention will be needed if Inner London is to be able to compete on anything like equal terms with other potential locations for new enterprises, or provide for the growth of recently established enterprises.

The first step is to change the climate of official opinion in favour of industrial development. The policies of the past 30 years have left industrialists with the impression that their future lies elsewhere. The symbolic deterrent effect of existing policies is just as important as their direct effect.

The most obvious example is Industrial Development Certificates (IDCs). They are not being very effective in directing industry to the development areas, but at the same time they undoubtedly contribute to the general weakening of industrial renewal and replacement in London. We can see no point in maintaining them. But it is clear that any move to abandon IDC controls will run into opposition from the representatives of the development areas. Other measures will also involve difficult choices. Local planning policies could be made less harsh towards so-called 'non-conforming' industry and redevelopment schemes could be redrawn to allow pockets of industry to survive.[1] More land could be provided for industry, to allow for new factories or expansions of existing building, and local authorities could themselves build some premises for letting to new firms. Our survey evidence indicated that sensible planning should allow for lower overall employment densities.

But it is only in a few parts of Inner London that suitable space can be found on any scale. Around Stockwell, there is little land available for any form of development and most of it is intended for housing or other non-industrial uses. Even in Docklands, current plans only provide for a small proportion of the available land to be used for industry – well below the amount thought to be necessary for the needs of East London. In Docklands, as elsewhere, most of what land is available has been earmarked for housing or related uses and space for industry can only be provided by sacrificing such objectives. Although as much land as possible should be made available for industry in Inner London, there are clearly severe restraints. Most people will not be prepared to countenance the wholesale displacement of housing and other uses. Another difficulty is land prices. The powers made available by the Community Land Act will help local authorities to assemble industrial sites, but they will not solve this problem. If the price of industrial land in Inner London is to be brought down to levels comparable with outer areas, then some form of direct subsidy will be needed.[2]

A final requirement is improved access. Industry needs transport to collect its workers, raw materials and other inputs, and to take away its products. But there is little hope of providing new roads in most parts of Inner London. And current proposals for traffic restraint – in particular the GLC's plans to restrict goods traffic – may only make industrial prospects bleaker. Again, any measures to improve things for industry will tend to work against local environmental conditions. Finally, there is much that local authorities could do to provide information and advice to industry. In particular, they could keep registers of available sites and offer advice to firms on relocation possibilities.

Most of these policies are, at the time of writing, being considered seriously by a number of London authorities. Some commentators have, however, suggested that

(1) Such policy changes have recently been made in a number of London boroughs. In Lambeth, for example, following the recommendation of the Working Party on Unemployment, policies towards non-conforming industry have been tempered and the principle has been adopted that redevelopment schemes should not involve a net loss of employment.

(2) This might involve the 'writing down' of industrial land values generally or direct financial assistance to selected firms. See, for example, South East Joint Planning Team, *Strategy for the South East: 1976 Review*.

they do not reach the heart of the problem and that more radical approaches are called for. In particular, the need for greater public control over industrial investment decisions is often emphasised, whether through national channels such as the National Enterprise Board or at the local level. The economic and political issues raised are too broad to be treated adequately here, but our evidence on the immediate causes of employment decline raises doubts about such proposals. Labour and space constraints, technological changes and conflicting pressures on the local environment are all real problems which industry has to face in London, regardless of who owns or controls it.

Training

Measures to strengthen local industry are one way to overcome the problems of mismatch. Another approach is to find ways of enabling the population to adapt to the jobs which are available. First of all, this will involve training of existing workers and better preparation of new entrants into the labour force.

There would not be such a problem if young people entering employment had the necessary skills. Increasingly the opportunities are in non-manual and service occupations, particularly higher-grade non-manual jobs. It is particularly disturbing that levels of academic attainment of local school leavers are relatively low. Employers we interviewed tended to confirm that young recruits were often inadequately educated for even simple tasks. They often made unfavourable comparisons with other areas or with the past.

This problem is not confined to Stockwell or Inner London, nor is it just a criticism of schools. Home background and cultural attitudes do affect educational performance. Immigrants, as we have shown, can have special educational problems. As our study did not incorporate any special inquiry into education, we are only in a position to point to a need rather than propose ways of meeting it. But it is clear that more priority needs to be placed on the achievement of basic standards of literacy and numeracy, and on more vocational preparation for less able secondary school pupils.

The need for better vocational training figured in the comments firms made to us about the employment of school leavers and young people. Few firms recruited many young people, for diverse reasons. Many firms pleaded a lack of suitable opportunities, though we thought that some of them could have created more openings. Employers were sceptical about spending money on training if they thought they were going to lose the newly trained workers. Some firms said they could not recruit or keep young people even if they tried, and many made adverse comments on lack of motivation and interest, absenteeism, unreliability, irresponsibility, indiscipline and the like, as well as poor education. Problems with workers' unwillingness to train were confined mainly to younger workers.

All this adds up to a picture of young people leaving school inadequately prepared for the realities of work, with little idea of how to obtain jobs or make the most of them, and likely to drift from one to another. The high level of unemployment among young people was not, therefore, wholly attributable to a lack of jobs. Part of any solution should include more and better guidance and preparation in schools, including realistic information on the choices available, the value of education and training, and how to set about finding and securing a job.

Training and recruitment

There were many gaps in vocational training from the point of view both of employers and workers. For example, if someone failed to start on apprenticeship or traineeship on leaving school, second chances were difficult to find. The Training Opportunities Scheme is only available to those over 19. Many courses are over-subscribed, whilst the nearest skill centres to Stockwell are at Poplar and Croydon apart from a small annexe in Sydenham. Many boys would probably like to take an apprenticeship or course, but lack the more elementary skills needed to gain entry. Most firms do not meet all their skill requirements by internal training, which gives rise to a vicious circle of poaching and wastage. It was particularly noticeable that where firms employed moderate numbers of craft-level skills they did not provide this kind of training.

The first responsibility for training rests with the government or its agents such as the Manpower Services Commission. They should, to a large extent, financially underwrite firms' training programmes, since an individual employer cannot guarantee to benefit from any investment in training for easily marketable skills. New ways of financing on-the-job training by employers must be found.[1] Secondly, more attention should be given to less able young people and hence to jobs below craft level. Perhaps the biggest need is for a new form of course to ease the transition from school to work, which would have an industrial setting and would be a form of broad induction leading towards semi-skilled work, of the kind likely to be available and with the option to move on to courses for higher skills.[2] The existing Training Opportunities Scheme, largely geared to adult re-training could be expanded in a selective way, with new skill centres in areas of need like Lambeth. Finally, the large public sector employers could be required to act as training agents on a large scale.

Education and training, though important, are not the only barriers to job mobility. The recruitment practices of firms and the job information networks also pose problems for some people. Although the number of less skilled jobs was limited and declining, labour turnover in them was high. Turnover in skilled jobs was lower. This, and the unwillingness of many firms to promote workers made it difficult for people to move from unskilled to skilled jobs.

(1) We strongly support the kind of initiative proposed in Department of Employment/Manpower Services Commission, *Training for Vital Skills*.

(2) For example the proposed 'gateway courses' described in Training Services Agency, *Vocational Preparation for Young People*.

The most common methods of recruitment from outside were newspaper advertisements, through existing staff, the Department of Employment (DE) for un-skilled workers and agencies for secretarial staff. The first two methods were the preferred ones. The DE (now of course the Employment Services Agency) and private agencies came in for a lot of criticism, mainly for being insufficiently selective, with the added complaint that the DE sent applicants who were considered of poor quality. The two main policy implications seemed to be, first, that vocational preparation in schools, and subsequent counselling and guidance, should indicate to clients the way unofficial channels (newspapers, personal contacts) could be used. Secondly, the ESA should try to play a broader agency role, not just for the unemployed, and should take more care in matching applicants to the reasonable requirements of employers.

Promoting residential mobility

It must be recognised that what can be done to arrest the decline of jobs in Inner London is limited, and that even a sizeable expansion in training will not in itself overcome the mismatch of jobs and skills. There must therefore be far more effective measures to help the less skilled and less affluent to move, if they wish to do so, to Outer London and beyond, where there are more jobs for them. This would make it easier for those with skills in demand in Inner London to find housing there. The extent of demand by low-skill workers for migration out of Inner London, and the measures needed to facilitate it, are discussed in Chapters 6 and 7.

It may be that one of the causes of unemployment, under-employment and job immobility is that information and advice about available opportunities are inadequate. Our proposals, apparently in line with current government thinking at the national scale, are aimed at increasing job mobility. It may therefore be appropriate to experiment with new methods in the official employment service. We propose an experimental counselling service, with case-workers visiting unemployed people in their homes and trying to sort out all their job-related problems. The objective would be to discuss with each client questions such as re-training, the availability of jobs elsewhere in the South East or in other regions, housing possibilities if he decided to move to take a new job, and arrangements for children to change schools or for relatives to move together. Such a service would be particularly valuable in inner city areas. It would need to be tied with the proposed multi-service team suggested in Chapter 9.

□ Proposals for improving the employment prospects of Inner Londoners fall under three broad headings:

1. Measures to arrest the decline of manufacturing industry and promote the development of new firms (Chapter 11, Proposals 4 to 12).

2. Better facilities for education, training and re-training. These would enable existing workers to adjust their skills, and new entrants to the labour force to start with the necessary skills (Chapter 11, Proposals 13 and 14).

3. Increased residential mobility, to enable those whose skills are in greater demand elsewhere to move out, and to some degree those whose skills are in higher demand to move in (Chapter 11, Proposals 15 to 19)

As a background to the discussion of helping people to move out of Inner London, we review in the next chapter the main housing problems of Stockwell residents ☐

5 Stresses in housing

We have already shown some of the inter-relationships between where people live and the kind of jobs they do, and have discussed some of the resulting employment problems. Now we focus instead on housing and in particular on the housing difficulties of inner city residents. The subject, therefore, is what has become known as 'housing stress'.

The term can cover a variety of ills. First, stresses may arise from badly designed housing, such as the old back to backs of northern industrial towns which have poor natural lighting and ventilation, no bathrooms and only a couple of outside WCs for a whole terrace. Secondly, originally sound housing may have fallen into disrepair, with leaking roofs, rotting timberwork and faulty damp proof courses. Thirdly, housing which is basically sound and well equipped may suffer serious problems if there is not enough of it, and people are forced to live in overcrowded conditions, without the basic essentials of privacy and often at high rents. In other words, certain kinds of stress arise when housing is deficient in quality, and other kinds when it is deficient in quantity. But most districts with 'housing stress' suffer from a combination of these factors.

One particular combination is that of the 'slum', a term freely used in common parlance but with a specific legal meaning. To be so scheduled by a local housing authority, a dwelling must have defects in its structure, layout or equipment so serious as to make it 'unfit for human habitation'. In practice the application of this definition has been known to vary widely from one housing authority to another, but in Lambeth – which is known for its firmness in applying housing standards – relatively few dwellings still justify this label. In 1976, only 634 properties remained to be demolished in the slum clearance programme.[1]

This is not to say that the physical condition of Lambeth's housing presents no problems. Many of the privately rented dwellings need extensive repair, and in the public sector tenants are becoming increasingly dissatisfied with their homes and surroundings, especially in the old inter-war estates. However, the overriding problem is one of scarcity. There are too many people chasing too few dwellings and if this pressure could be reduced it would also be easier to tackle the problem of poor quality. Apart from the strains that the pressure imposes on families, it also makes it difficult to modernise and repair older houses. If it could be reduced, there would be more elbow room to carry out renovation or replacement and, because fewer bathrooms and WCs would be needed, the costs would be lower than at present.

(1) London Borough of Lambeth, *Community Plan 1976, Volume 3: Housing Programme Area.*

Late Victorian terraced houses in multiple occupation. Candidates for conversion?

Symptoms of current scarcity and pressure are extensive multi-occupation, high rents, an enormous waiting list for council housing, widespread homelessness and squatting. We discuss each of these in turn.

Multi-occupation

Little of the remaining housing in Stockwell is the jerry-built, low standard, working class accommodation which elsewhere has been the main target of 20th century slum clearance programmes. Instead, most of the older housing was originally middle class or quasi-middle class: 19th century terraced housing which all over London has proved extremely durable and adaptable, either for single-family occupation, multiple occupation, or more recently for conversion into self-contained flats. By 1973 about four out of every ten Stockwell residents lived in such buildings.

In 1973 one third of these terraced houses were in single-family occupation.[1] Some

(1) Measurement of the extent of multi-occupation is complicated by the fact that the census definition of a 'dwelling' was changed in 1971 to embrace all units which do not share circulation space between living rooms. Under this definition the top floor of what most people, including ourselves would regard as a multi-occupied house, will often be identified in the census as a separate dwelling. A household occupying such accommodation will not be identified as a 'sharing' household. For our purposes, therefore, the 1971 census over-estimates the number of separate dwellings and under-estimates the number of multi-occupying households. The figures given here are taken from our household survey.

of the others had been converted into self-contained flats, for rent by the councils or by housing associations, or in the 'oases' and other more favoured areas, for sale by private developers. The remaining multi-occupied houses contained a disproportionate number of households. In 1973 around two-thirds of the households living in terraces shared their house with one or more other households and a similar proportion lacked or shared one or other of the basic amenities – hot water, inside WC and a fixed bath or shower.

Multi-occupation can take various forms. Sometimes a household occupies one or more complete floors, sometimes a single room. It may rent under a 'controlled', 'regulated' or 'furnished' tenancy, with varying degrees of security of tenure and of government control over the rent paid. About half of Stockwell's multi-occupying tenants share the house with the landlord. As well as affecting relationships between occupants, this is now important for the tenants' legal rights. The broad pattern is currently as follows:

1. All private tenancies which were 'unfurnished' before the 1974 Rent Act remain 'protected' by the Rent Acts. This means that tenants cannot be evicted unless the landlord has extremely powerful reasons. Most rents are fixed by the local rent officer, at a level which 'ignores scarcity' and is therefore well below the free market level. These are known as 'fair' rents. A minority of tenants have 'controlled' tenancies, with rents fixed at an even lower level.

2. Private tenants who were 'furnished' before 1974 obtained similar rights if their landlord did not live on the premises.

3. If the landlord lives on the premises, then not only his old 'furnished' tenancies, but also any tenancy created after August 1974 – with or without furniture – is 'unprotected' by the Rent Acts. Such tenants are not entirely defenceless. Their rents can be decided by the local rent tribunal which normally fixes rents well above the levels set by the rent officer, but often somewhat below the free market level. The rent tribunal can also delay an application for an eviction order, but only for limited periods.

The distinction between resident and non-resident landlords has, therefore, largely replaced the old distinction between furnished and unfurnished tenancies. Because of the prominence of resident landlords in Stockwell, this has important implications for housing improvement policy.

It would, however, be unwise to over-estimate the extent to which tenants make use of their rights under law. In the Borough's first Housing Action Area, which contained over 100 eligible tenancies at the end of 1975, only one 'fair' rent had been fixed by the rent officer. Of the tenancies in Stockwell covered by our household survey only 27 per cent of those eligible had had 'fair' rents fixed. The reason for their low response was sometimes that the tenant felt the rent officer would not make much difference or would even increase the rent: about a fifth of them said they thought their existing rent was reasonable. There were other less comforting reasons: another fifth of the eligible tenants did not know of the existence of 'fair' rents and this lack of knowledge extended to other facilities available to private

Smaller terraced houses with varying degrees of embellishment. The two above are currently being demolished. The one below left narrowly escaped this fate.

tenants. This is shown in Table 12. We pointed out in Chapter 3 that only a minority of households below the poverty line, who might be assumed to have been eligible for help, were getting benefits. Table 12 includes not just poor, but all private tenants, with furnished distinguished from unfurnished; it should be made clear that many would not have had low enough incomes to qualify for rent allowances, though all could have applied to the rent officer or rent tribunal. The conclusion is that this range of aids has not helped the majority of private tenants.

Living in multi-occupied housing does not necessarily involve hardship. Some people, especially the young and the single, may appreciate the cameraderie of shared facilities. However, as we emphasise later, the markets within which inner city people find their homes do not always match dwellings to the kinds of people best suited to them. A third of the household survey sample living in terraced housing complained about having to share a bathroom, or having to use an inadequate bathroom. One in six said they needed more rooms. The reluctance of private landlords to carry out repairs is another problem: 22 per cent of tenants complained about poor repairs and decorations and a further 15 per cent said they suffered from damp in one form or other. Overcrowding is also concentrated in this kind of housing, with 9 per cent of housholds living at over $1\frac{1}{2}$ persons per room in 1971 compared with 5 per cent in other housing.

Table 12 Response by private tenants to various forms of assistance

	Unfurnished tenants		Furnished tenants	
	Rent allowances	Fair rent registrations	Rent allowances	Use of the rent tribunal
Have received	6%	27%	1%	4%
Have applied for, but was refused	2%	0%	0%	0%
Know about fair rents but don't know whether one has been registered	—	25%	—	—
Know about, and have either applied or are considering applying	9%	0%	8%	0%
Didn't know about existence	31%	19%	60%	30%
Other reason (already satisfied, didn't want trouble, etc.)	52%	29%	31%	66%
Total %	100%	100%	100%	100%
Number	316	313	140	142

Source: Stockwell Household Survey 1973.

Prices and rents

The concentration of poor people in inner city areas is often explained in terms of the availability of cheap, older housing. Is this assumption correct? At the end of

1973 we tried to answer this question by comparing housing costs in Stockwell with those in other areas of the London Region.

There were basically two kinds of property for sale – whole houses varying greatly in size and condition, and self-contained flat conversions with two to four rooms and the basic facilities. Apart from a few small flat conversions at around £9,000, the lowest prices in Stockwell were around £12,500 and at least £15,000 would have been needed to buy a terrace house in reasonable condition.

It was not difficult to find cheaper property further out in South London or elsewhere. For example, there were plenty of pre-1914 terrace houses available in the Croydon/Carshalton/Sutton area in the £10,500 to £12,500 range, with an average price about £2,500 less than in the study area, and prices were lower still outside London. Post-war terraced houses could be had from about £9,500 in Crawley and even less in Basildon. Three bedroom semis of the inter-war period cost from £12,000 in Croydon and £11,500 in Redhill. New purpose-built flats and maisonettes were available in these areas at an average price of around £11,500. Thus, in terms of the amount and quality of housing available at a given price, Stockwell offered quite poor value for money. Clearly, there was a high premium attached to accessibility.

In rented accommodation, only the furnished sector, up to the 1974 Rent Act, offered ready availability in a relatively free market. A study of classified advertisements and flat agencies suggested that average rent per room was around £7.50 a week; for a self-contained flat with two or more rooms the rent was likely to be between £15 and £30 a week and few Stockwell residents could have afforded this much. The difference in rents between Inner and Outer South London was small, so that in this respect Stockwell was no more expensive than elsewhere. In practice, however, this apparent lack of disadvantage was of little benefit to anyone in Stockwell, since very little furnished accommodation was actually available locally; most of the advertised places were further out.

Finally, at the time of our household survey council rents (before rebates) in Stockwell ranged from £3.50 for a two-bedroom flat in the Springfield estate to £9.70 for a similar sized flat in the Stockwell Park estate, with an average of £6.90 for all council dwellings. The average rent charged by Croydon council in 1973 was £4.78, by Sutton £5.16 and by Kingston £5.52.

To sum up, though these comparisons present a mixed picture, it is clear that on balance housing costs in Stockwell (and, by extension, similar areas in Inner London) are much the same or are higher than in areas further out. There does not seem much truth in the proposition that Inner London housing is cheap. One exception is that the inner city does contain rather more small units of accommodation in older houses and tenement blocks. Their tenants pay relatively low rents, though they do not get very good value for money, and constitute only a minority of local residents.

106

Though prices and rents have changed since 1973, there is no reason for thinking that the pattern has altered since then. So the general conclusion is that few local people have low housing costs. If anything, they pay rather more for what they get, in terms of size and quality of accommodation.

The council waiting lists

Within Stockwell, value for money in housing varies widely from one sector of the market to another. At the extremes, a 'furnished' tenant can pay as much for a poorly furnished room as a council tenant pays for a newly built two-bedroom flat. Table 13 measures average rents per room paid by council tenants, regulated tenants and furnished tenants at the time of the household survey.

Table 13　Average rent per room by tenure

	Lambeth and GLC tenants	Regulated private tenants	Furnished private tenants
Median rent	£6.90	£5.10	£6.40
Average number of rooms	3·9	3·5	2·2
Average rent per room	£1.74	£1.41	£3.59
Number	542	316	140

Source: Stockwell Household Survey 1973.

The average room was twice as expensive in the furnished sector as in the council sector, with the regulated sector being cheapest of all. We could not take account of the quality of accommodation in this analysis, but if this were done council tenants would probably stand out as the most favoured. A room, for a council tenant, is normally a room in a self-contained flat, while for a private tenant it often involves sharing a bathroom, or even a kitchen, in a poorly maintained building.

Council accommodation therefore offers relatively high value for money, a result of the subsidies provided by the exchequer and the rate fund. At the same time, the supply of privately rented housing has almost dried up, with the demolition of large parts of the stock and the passing of successive Rent Acts which have encouraged existing tenants to stay put and deterred landlords from re-letting vacant dwellings. A new household looking for its first home in Stockwell, or an existing household looking for better accommodation, will therefore now normally turn to the council.

The conventional means of access to the council sector is the waiting list. In Lambeth, this is open to anyone who has lived in the Greater London area for at least five years, of which at least one year must be in Lambeth itself. In 1976 the list, with 17,000 households, was the longest in London.[1] It is not getting any shorter, since most years the number of new registrations is greater than the number of waiting list households that are rehoused (Table 14).

(1) We do not wish to suggest that the size of a council's waiting list is a sensitive social indicator. This would clearly be foolish since the constraints on registration vary from borough to borough. Nevertheless, the top end of the list contains families who have been waiting for many years in miserable housing conditions. What is more, the lists do provide a broad indication of real housing need and every council is under strong political pressure to reduce them.

Table 14   Changes in the housing waiting list (1 April 1975 – 31 March 1976)

	1973/74	1974/75	1975/76
Waiting list cases rehoused by London Borough of Lambeth	71	158	343
Families rehoused by London Borough of Lambeth for other reasons but on waiting list	572	469	425
Families rehoused by London Borough Council		233	241
Families rehoused into new and expanding towns	296	57	95
Families rehoused by Housing Associations		46	24
Cancellations	278	753	480
Total deleted	1217	1716	1608
New registrations on the waiting list	3264	2448	2876
Unknown withdrawals (estimated)[1]	1000	1000	1000
Gain in the period	1047	−268	268

(1) The lists are periodically reviewed to eliminate candidates who have died, moved away or no longer require housing. These reviews normally detect an average of 1000 such 'unknown withdrawals' per year. This may have been greater recently.

Source: London Borough of Lambeth, *Community Plan 1976, Vol. 3: Housing Programme Area.*

In the three years covered by the table Lambeth managed to rehouse in its own accommodation only 572 households from the top of the waiting list. This was despite a massive programme for new housing: the council completed 1626 new dwellings and 502 conversions in the same period.

What were the reasons for this striking anomaly? First, the housing programme was not in fact producing much of an increase in the amount of housing available in Lambeth. With hardly any open land left in the borough, new dwellings could be built only by knocking down old ones. The kinds of area available for such redevelopment were usually populated at densities similar to those of new estates, so there could rarely be much of a 'housing gain' in terms of people rehoused. Furthermore, while it lasted, the programme caused a substantial loss of dwellings from the total stock – those out of use for the seven years or so needed to remove the existing population, demolish the older housing and construct and let replacement dwellings. All this means that the redevelopment programme, though it created new self-contained homes, could not house many more people than before. Decants – that is, people moved out of property to be demolished or rehabilitated – were prominent on the council's letting records, and were comparable in number to the new dwellings being provided (Table 15).

In the year covered by the table nearly 3000 dwellings were let by Lambeth. Less than a third of these were newly built or converted; the remainder were vacancies in the existing stock, created as their tenants moved away or died. Like most councils, Lambeth relies upon such re-lets for the bulk of the accommodation it can offer at any particular time. But it is only new dwellings – whether purpose built, converted or specially purchased on the private market – which can make possible an increase

Table 15   New tenancies by rehousing category (18 May 1973 – 23 May 1974)

	Number	Percentage
Decants from redevelopment areas	617 ⎱ 929	21% ⎱ 32%
Decants from properties for conversion	312 ⎰	11% ⎰
Transfers from other council properties and mutual exchange	869	29%
Homeless families	707	24%
Waiting list	90	3%
Others	376	13%
Total	2971	100%

Source: Special study of tenancy records.

in the overall number of households housed by the council. As we can see, the number of new dwellings completed in the year (966) was about the same as the number of households being moved (929) to make way for new dwellings in the future.

A further reason for the council's inability to rehouse people from the waiting lists has been the increase in 'homelessness'. Lambeth started to rehouse homeless people within its 'normal' stock – as opposed to 'halfway houses' – on a significant scale early in the 1970s. By 1974 the number of households being provided with accommodation in this way had risen to 700 per year, and by 1976 the figure was over 1200. In other words, becoming 'homeless' had largely replaced priority on the waiting list as a principal channel for getting a council dwelling. Many prospective council tenants had undoubtedly realised this and acted accordingly, making themselves 'homeless' in order to get a tenancy.

A liberal homelessness policy poses a fundamental dilemma. On the one hand, to rehouse homeless families in council dwellings is not only humane but also makes sound economic sense, since the cost of doing so is usually far less than the alternatives, such as taking children into care. On the other hand, there is the danger that families will deliberately make themselves homeless to jump the waiting list queue, and it is a political embarrassment for a local authority to be housing large numbers of homeless families at the expense of people who have spent many years on the waiting list. The embarrassment is increased when accommodation is offered to families who have come from other parts of London, and even from foreign countries, allegedly attracted by liberal policies.[1]

It should be explained that a family does not need to be literally 'on the streets' to be categorised as 'homeless'. Families in private accommodation given notice to quit and families living with parents who ask them to leave can normally expect the council to give them accommodation before they are forced to go. We found from the tenancy records of Lambeth that these two kinds of family, and particularly the second, accounted for far more people than those without anywhere at all to live. It has been known for families to move out of a house of their own to live with

---

(1) In Lambeth, such families form only a small proportion of the homeless families rehoused. A survey by the council covering the period from April to September 1975 showed that 83 per cent of homeless families rehoused by the council had lived in Lambeth for at least one year and a further 8 per cent in the rest of London for the same period.

Council housing and its setting.

The GLC's inter-war Kennington Park Estate (above) and the post-war Mursell Estate (below).

parents, on the understanding that they could later, with the parents' help, demand to be rehoused on the grounds that the parents would no longer have them.[1]

Not all homeless households can claim to be rehoused by their councils. The relevant government circular earmarks as priorities: 'Families with dependent children living with them, or in care; and adult families or people living alone who either become homeless in an emergency such as a fire or flood or are vulnerable because of old age, disability, pregnancy or other special reasons'. In spite of such government guidance, the rules are vague and people tend to be rehoused in an ad hoc manner. We heard about families being shunted for many months between their landlords, the rent tribunal and the Housing Advice Centre. One couple moved into a furnished room and subsequently produced two children. Their landlord was then accused of overcrowding by public health officials and gave the family notice to quit. On applying for rehousing at the Housing Advice Centre they were told to ask the rent tribunal for security of tenure. Thus, one arm of the council acted against another, and a third agency – the government-appointed rent tribunal – had to find an uneasy compromise, giving the tenant a period of security to try and sort things out.

One way to deter manipulation of the system is to reserve the poorer parts of the housing stock for homeless families. Now that the 'halfway houses' have been phased out, this involves the use of old tenement blocks like Coronation Buildings. But in any given period of time the number of casual vacancies appearing on such estates can be far exceeded by the number of homeless families, and then there is often no choice but to offer brand new accommodation. In any case, the discrepancy in value for money between the public sector and the private furnished sector is so great that it is doubtful whether even the offer of a dwelling in Coronation Buildings would be an adequate deterrent to most homeless families. To the extent to which homeless families are 'problem families', which is far less likely now than it was in the past, this policy is open to the objection that it concentrates difficult families, creating so-called 'sink' estates.

Homelessness shades into squatting. The recent growth of the two phenomena has arisen from a common cause. The amount of privately rented accommodation available to lower income families has been declining rapidly, principally because of demolition by the councils and to a lesser extent because of 'gentrification'. Since the 1974 Rent Act it has been alleged that landlords are preferring to keep their accommodation vacant, rather than create protected tenancies by re-letting. We have no evidence on this although it seems clear that there has been a tendency to restrict re-lets to short term visitors, which acts against local households.

Alongside this decline in the private sector, there has been a failure to provide adequate housing through other channels, inside or outside Lambeth. As often happens in the housing market, the burden of this failure has fallen mainly on

(1) Lambeth set up a Working Party on Homelessness (composed of elected representatives and officers) which, reporting in March 1976, recommended that the rules should be tightened. But it is difficult to see how the problems could be competely overcome.

newcomers. Established tenants with security of tenure have been able to retain their existing housing or move into council housing. It is new households – whether migrants from outside the area or local people forming separate households for the first time – who suffer the immediate effects of scarcity. For such people, to become 'homeless' or to squat is often the only way of getting reasonable housing.

In Lambeth, as in other parts of Inner London,[1] squatting takes two forms: 'official' squatting by organisations who occupy property by arrangement with the council and 'illegal' squatting by unrecognised groups. At the end of March 1974 the 'official' squatters, principally the Lambeth Self Help Housing Association, occupied 188 properties, all of them short life. At the same time 'illegal' squatters occupied over 100 properties and by 1976 their numbers had risen to over 500.

Council staff spend a considerable time investigating and litigating against illegal squatters. Many squatters undoubtedly antagonise local residents or damage the property they occupy. But many others display a surprising ability to patch up derelict buildings and put a good deal of energy into this task.

So far, we may have given the impression that all is rosy in the council sector. As was suggested by what we reported in Chapter 2 about people's complaints, this is far from true. In recent decades new problems have emerged, rather different from those in the declining private sector. Chief among these are vandalism, other forms of anti-social behaviour, conflicts between neighbours and a general sense of dissatisfaction with many estates. The malaise is deepest on some of the older five-storey walk-up estates.

People's complaints focussed on the bad behaviour of other tenants, especially children, and there was a widespread belief among older residents that some of the estates had deteriorated rapidly. 'A different class of people', the withdrawal of caretakers by the GLC and the subsequent poor maintenance were held responsible.

> 'People moving from slums are creating slums in the flats. We can't ask friends or relations here. The place is filthy, the stairs are in a disgusting state, and the language, you should hear the children. It wouldn't be too bad if it was cleaned up a bit. 25 years ago you could eat off the stairs. Now it's fights and bottle battles. Even the kids take things; you can't leave anything outside.'

Complaints about noise were often connected with problems of neighbours and children and privacy:

> 'Any loud noise carries right through the block – it's really bad. There are too many people on top of each other – we have to pull our curtains because the next block can see in. It's too congested.'

> 'Our problem is having small children in a flat and people below complaining about noise overhead.'

---

(1) Mike Kinghan, 'Squatting in London'.

We argued in Chapter 2 that the underlying causes of many such complaints in council estates and elsewhere, were high child densities and the breakdown of community. Some of the problems could be alleviated by changes in design or management, discussed in Chapter 8.

☐ Housing stress in Stockwell takes a variety of forms and these differ from one housing type to another. Most of the problems – in particular, high rents and prices, multi-occupation, long waiting lists, high child densities, homelessness and squatting – can be explained by the pressures of too many families on a limited amount of land and housing. This raises the question of why so many people are concentrated in Stockwell, which we deal with in the next chapter ☐

6 The housing trap

In recent decades there has been an inconclusive debate about people's attitudes to living in the inner city. One view emphasises the advantages: the proximity to shops, pubs, entertainments and other facilities; the ties with friends and neighbours: community spirit, solidarity and mutual support. On this interpretation, the inner city is a potentially ideal location, its residents are reluctant to leave it, and those who do move to less urbanised areas find them a poor substitute.

The opposite view emphasises the negative aspects: bad housing, squalid surroundings, vandalism, crime and social decay. The inner city is seen as a 'sink', generally undesired, which collects the poor, the socially deviant, the newcomers and others who cannot live elsewhere. The good life is to be found in the suburbs and beyond, and people will get out there as fast as they can.

Clearly, different policy implications would follow from these polarised standpoints. The first would concentrate resources on improving conditions in the inner city. The second would make it easier for people to get out. There is perhaps an element of caricature in this, but it does not seem unfair to place most of the Community Development Projects in the first school, and sociologists such as Rex[1] in the second.

The preceding chapters have documented the bad side of life in Stockwell. We have also shown that the sense of 'community', often thought to be one of the great strengths of the inner city, appears to have declined since the days of the earlier community studies and that many people now find their neighbours a source of threat rather than of comfort. Much of the basis for stable working-class communities has been eroded by the massive population transfers of urban renewal and the collapse of manufacturing industry. Finally, there does not even appear to be much in the idea that areas like Stockwell offer the advantage of cheap housing.

On the other hand, there is strong evidence of the benefits of living in Stockwell. Ready access to urban facilities, in the West End and locally, is widely appreciated. At the upper end of the social scale, many have chosen to put a sizeable investment into living in Stockwell. And while most people appeared to have little sense of community, others, particularly the ethnic minorities, had friends and relatives near them and identified strongly with their area.

So from the outset of the study we were suspicious of the simplifications of these two standpoints. We sought to explore the attitudes of local residents to life in Stockwell.

(1) J. Rex and R. Moore, *Race, Community and Conflict.*

Gans[1] suggests that different types of people experience the advantages and disadvantages of the inner city in different ways. For the 'ethnic villager', a member of a close-knit minority group, the support of his own community and the access to amenities that serve it outweigh the disadvantages. Those he calls 'cosmopolites' – students, artists, writers, musicians and entertainers, as well as other intellectuals and professionals – place a high premium on living near the cultural facilities of the central area. Many such people have the money to insulate themselves from the surrounding shabbiness in their own enclaves, areas like those we have called 'oases'. The unmarried or childless are less affected anyway by this shabbiness, being free from the 'routine family responsibilities which entail some relationship to the local area'. They can enjoy the good things of the inner city without worrying too much about the disadvantages. Lower-income families with children, on the other hand, are less interested in city centre facilities but more worried about local problems such as poor schools, limited play space, vandalism and crime. Thus, depending on social class, ethnic background and stage in the life cycle, different types of people weigh up the positive and negative features of the inner city in different ways.

Potential movers from Stockwell

We tested this by two specific questions in the household survey. First, we asked people whether they wanted to go on living in the district or would prefer to leave it. As we reported in Chapter 2, about half said they wanted to move, compared with only a third in a survey in the London Region as a whole.[2] To clarify people's attitudes to the inner city, it was important to know if they wanted to move within Inner London or to leave it. We asked therefore whether they wanted to move:

'Further in to the centre of London?'

'About the same distance out as this?'

'Further out but still in Greater London?'

'Outside Greater London altogether?'

The overwhelming majority wanted to move further out. These amounted to about a third of all those interviewed.

We asked everyone another question, explicitly about staying in Inner London:

'In fact, is there anything at all that is keeping you from moving out of Inner London? I mean, why don't you move out to the edge of London or out of London altogether?'

As Table 16 shows, this time about a quarter of all the sample said they were planning to move out of Inner London or gave other answers suggesting they wanted to leave it. The main reasons given for staying were connected with work. Attachment to the area or the people were much less important, and only 1 per cent mentioned the proximity of Stockwell to Central London.

(1) H. J. Gans, *People and Plans*.

(2) Michael Young and Peter Willmott, *The Symmetrical Family*, pp. 41–42.

Table 16 People's main reason for staying in Inner London

Can't afford to move; 'Couldn't find anywhere'	18%	
Would like to go (vague answer)	3%	
Already planning to move	3%	
Other reasons	2%	
All who wanted to move		26%
Proximity of work, needs of job	38%	
Attached to district or 'London'	11%	
Because of family or friends	9%	
Don't want to go (vague answer)	8%	
Would disturb children, problems of schools	2%	
Attached to house or flat	2%	
Proximity of centre	1%	
Other reasons	3%	
All who wanted to stay		74%
Total		100%
Number (weighted)		1879

Source: Stockwell Household Survey 1973.

Thus, while the majority wanted to stay, a substantial minority of households seemed to want to leave Inner London. To find out more about this minority, we made a detailed analysis of their characteristics and also carried out further interviews to see why they wanted to move, identify the places they wanted to go to and find out what steps they had already taken to move out.

Characteristics of intending movers

Tables 23 to 31 in Appendix 3 give a profile of the households whose heads wanted to move out. They show that some types of household were more likely to want to move than others.

Chief amongst the potential movers were couples with children. Black people less often wanted to move, even though their households more often contained children. This confirms Gans' analysis: families with children are more likely to feel the disadvantages of the inner city, while blacks are more likely to appreciate the support of a local ethnic community. As we show later in this chapter, black people have as yet made only limited inroads into the suburbs and areas further out. As long as this applies, the inner city will have powerful advantages for them and other similar minorities.

Among white people, those with relatives living nearby were as ready to leave as others. Long-standing residents were, if anything, more likely to want to move; nearly half of those who wanted to move had lived in the area longer than 20 years. As Deakin and Ungerson[1] suggest, it may well be the long-standing 'traditional' resident who feels most severely affected by the changes taking place in the inner city, including the influx of different kinds of people such as black immigrants.

(1) Nicholas Deakin and Clare Ungerson, *Leaving London.*

117

Stockwell Park Estate (above) and the new inter-war Springfield Estate (below)

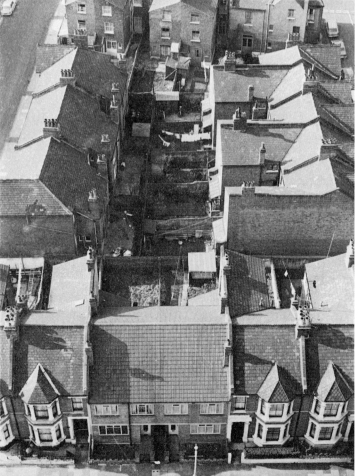

Homes and their environment:

Above: looking from Slade Gardens towards Central London.

Below: terraced houses and their backs in the area north of Landor Road.

119

Owner occupiers and professionals were rather more likely to want to stay. This was probably because many of them had freely chosen to live in the area in the first place, and had been able to buy their way in to the more attractive enclaves. With manual workers, the picture was rather complex. Amongst heads of households, those in the skilled manual class were much more likely to want to move, and lower skilled workers rather less so. On the other hand, taking all working men, there was little difference for skilled manual workers, and unskilled workers were more likely to want to move. Either way, lower skill workers account for a sizeable proportion of potential movers, though as we show later, it is difficult for them to do so under present conditions. Finally, retired people were somewhat less likely to move than people of working age.

The remainder of our information on intending movers comes from the follow up survey which we conducted two years after the original household survey. This second survey probed further into the reasons why people wanted to move and the districts they wanted to move to. It also enabled us to see how serious they were about moving.

It turned out that about a third of the households had moved house in the period between the two surveys. We discuss later where they had moved to. Since most of them were families with children, such households were under-represented among those we interviewed. Nevertheless, as we show, the findings from the interviews were broadly in line with other evidence.

Desired districts

We had realised that it would be difficult to find out where people wanted to move to. Some would have a single district or town firmly in mind, say Carshalton or Haywards Heath; others would be prepared to move anywhere within a large area, such as the whole of Surrey. Others would not have formed their opinions when we came to interview them, and would think things through only after discussion.

We tackled this problem by asking a series of questions, and by helping our respondents to indicate on maps the places they would like to move to. The overwhelming majority – more than four-fifths – said they wanted to move further out but still within Greater London. In discussion, it became clear that nearly half of these would have been prepared to move rather further out. Hardly anybody would have moved beyond the South East Region. Previous studies [1] have shown that out-migration tends to occur within the same sector of a city region. To test this we divided the desired areas into northern and southern sectors using the Thames as the boundary. Most people wanted to stay within the southern sector.

Thus, most people wanted to move only a limited distance, preferably on the same side of London. The reasons were not difficult to discover. They normally expected to be travelling back to Stockwell or nearby places once they had moved, either on a

(1) See, for example, Michael Young and Peter Willmott, *op.cit.*

daily basis to their existing jobs or less regularly to visit friends or relatives. This desire to retain some of their old links made them reluctant to move far. At the same time, most of them realised that the transport links were mainly radial, which argued against a move to another sector.

Why did they want to move? As expected, most mentioned better housing. Over a third were looking for a garden of their own, and a fifth modern amenities. But dissatisfaction with the local environment and local people was far more important than problems with housing.

> 'We used to live near Ashbourne but we moved back here when Dad took up his old job at the pub. I wish I hadn't come back now I've got the kids. There's nowhere for them to play round here; we've only got the yard at the back and they're all over me in the flat. I dread the day they go to school; the big one will be starting next year. You don't send kids to the schools round here if you want them to get on. They're always playing truant or getting into some other kind of trouble.'

> 'There are open spaces in Merton. The houses are more spaced out – it's a nice environment, more village like.'

> 'We want to move to Burgh Heath, Reigate for our health. There's more fresh air and it's much cleaner. And not so much noise – from the traffic or the people. It looks like the country but it's not too far out.'

Altogether, over a third said they wanted an area which was quieter, more peaceful or with less traffic. One in eight were looking for somewhere 'healthier' or more 'countrified' and two-fifths simply wanted a 'nicer looking' area than Stockwell.

Complaints about the district were social, as well as physical. Over a quarter said they wanted to move to live near 'friendlier' or 'nicer' neighbours or 'people more of our class', while a similar proportion wanted a better social life generally. One in eight mentioned 'fewer blacks'. All those with children laid emphasis on moving to an area with better play facilities. The most frequent reason, mentioned by four people out of every ten, was to find an area with less vandalism, violence or crime.

Few people, in considering a possible move, thought they would change their job along with their house. Nearly a third were retired anyway and over half of the rest thought they would keep their present job. In general, people did not seem aware of the job opportunities further out. Such people would be helped by a job counselling service of the kind we have proposed earlier.

Table 17 sums up people's motives for wanting to move, this time giving the 'main' reason. It is clear that most of these potential migrants wanted a 'suburban' environment, in both physical and social senses of the term. This even includes some of those who gave 'housing' reasons, which often reflected a preference for a house with a garden, rather than an inner city flat.

Table 17 Main reason for wanting to move[1]

Better surroundings	40%
Better housing	24%
Better friends or neighbours	15%
Better place to bring up children	10%
Better job	1%
Other reason	12%
Total number of people	67

(1)The percentages add up to more than 100 because two households could not be confined to a single main reason.

Source: Follow-up survey of potential migrants 1975–76

A similar emphasis on the social and physical environment emerged in two other studies of migration from Inner London.[1] However, it goes against impressions we have received from the Shelter Housing Action Centre and other agencies involved in helping people to move outwards, who felt that housing reasons were nearly always paramount with their clients. The reason, presumably, is that the great majority of these clients are in conditions of severe housing stress, and are not therefore a cross-section of all those wishing to move out of Inner London. This has important implications for policy. Housing in the inner city can be improved, thus meeting the needs of those who simply want better homes. But the inner city can never provide a suburban environment: people seeking that will need to move out.

Had people themselves taken any steps to move? Of council tenants, over half had applied for transfers or mutual exchanges and a further few had also applied to the New and Expanding Towns Scheme (NETS). But most of them were well aware of the limitations of the various channels of movement. Some must have not bothered to apply because they knew their chances were slim. And those who were not council tenants had rarely taken any steps to move, usually for the same reason.

> 'What's the point? The Willcox's next door have been on the waiting lists for 12 years. And every time they go to the Town Hall it's the same story – "We'll let you know when we've got something". I don't see how we can ever get out of this place.'

> 'We asked for a transfer to Croydon in 1970. They said we might have a chance now that Gordon (their son) has moved away. So far we've had one offer – and that was a flat in Camden Town.'

So this small follow-up survey showed that most of those who wanted to move were seeking a suburban environment, but were trapped inside the inner city. It is true that a third of the selected households turned out to have moved in the two years between our main household survey and our second visit. But, as far as we were able to gather, most of these had moved only to another home inside Inner London. Thus our conclusions still stand. A sizeable minority of Stockwell residents want to move out and cannot do so.

(1) Nicholas Deakin and Clare Ungerson, *op.cit* and Evelyn Fernando and Barry Hedges, *Moving out of Southwark.*

Successful movers from Inner London

These conclusions were sceptically received by most officers and councillors in Lambeth, who seemed to find it difficult to accept that large numbers of people wished to leave their borough. They felt this ran counter to their personal experience. It is understandable for those who have devoted so much of the efforts to improving conditions inside Lambeth to respond in this way.

Surveys apart, the evidence is that people have been leaving the inner city in their thousands since the beginning of the century. The 1971 census provides the most up-to-date data. For the first time, it gave detailed information about migration from an 'inner ring' consisting of the Inner London boroughs less the four central boroughs of Westminster, Camden, Kensington/Chelsea and the City. Between 1966 and 1971 about half a million people moved out of this inner ring. Some moved to the four central boroughs but the main movement was outwards (Table 18).

Table 18 Destinations of five-year migrants from London's inner ring[1]

Central boroughs	4%
Outer London	47%
Outer Metropolitan Area	22%
Rest of the South East	12%
Rest of Great Britain	15%

(1) Excluding movement to places outside Great Britain. GLC research indicates that such movement was on a similar scale to migration from the inner ring to the rest of Great Britain (E. K. Gilje, *Migration Patterns In and Around London*). This still means that almost 75% of the migration was within the South East.

Source: Census 1971, Migration Regional Report, South East Region, Part 1.

As our surveys suggested, nearly half made relatively short moves to the outer London boroughs and most of the rest stayed in the South East Region. There was, of course, some migration into the inner ring, though on a much smaller scale. Roughly speaking, two people moved in for every five who moved out, so that the *net* loss of population was somewhat smaller than the figure of half a million quoted earlier. Taking account of this, and also allowing for foreign migration and differences in the districts covered by this data, we estimate that the area we defined as Inner London in Chapter 1 has been experiencing a net migration loss of around 75,000 people per year.

The detailed characteristics of the people who moved out and moved in are shown in Tables 32 and 33 in Appendix 3. Most of those who moved out – nearly three-quarters – were families, while most of those who moved in were single people or members of non-family households. This confirms that families with children are attracted to the suburbs and single people to Inner London.

Relatively large proportions of non-manual workers and of skilled workers had moved out, but relatively few semi-skilled and unskilled. The census did not record income levels, but we can get some indication of this from a recent survey of a sample of emigrants from the borough of Southwark,[1] two-thirds of whom moved

(1) Evelyn Fernando and Barry Hedges, *op.cit.*

to Outer London or beyond. 40 per cent of these had gross household incomes over £3,500 a year compared with 25 per cent of households in Southwark as a whole.

Thus better off and higher skilled people are more likely to move out. This is not surprising, since the main channel of movement – accounting for well over half of all emigrants – is buying a house. A further quarter became council tenants and only 19 per cent moved into privately rented accommodation. This pattern was reversed for people who had moved into the inner ring. Over half of them became private tenants, with only 23 per cent buying their own dwelling.[1]

In view of this it is not surprising that most emigrants were well housed after their move. Nine out of ten had exclusive use of the basic amenities compared with under two-thirds of the households in Inner London.

A final piece of evidence from the census concerns migration by black people. During the same five-year period about 19,000 first or second generation New Commonwealth immigrants moved from the inner ring to Outer London. This is 9 per cent of the total migration in this direction – somewhat below the proportion of the inner ring's population who were of New Commonwealth origin (12 per cent). But only a minute proportion had moved outside Greater London.

Migration from Inner London is, then, a high selective process. The movers are most often families with children, skilled workers, well paid and white. They are less often single people, unskilled, low paid or black. Some of these differences can be explained by people's choices. Our surveys show that families with children more often want to leave Inner London and black people more often want to stay. There is no evidence, however, that low skill and low income people do not want to move: indeed many are keen to do so.

Some of them may be tied by their jobs. Many, though, would be able to get better jobs elsewhere, since the demand for low-skill labour is higher in many of the areas they want to move to. Thus they are trapped by the workings of the housing market rather than the labour market.

The housing trap

Under present conditions, owner-occupation is the form of tenure which offers people the greatest choice about where they live. House purchase has been by far the most important channel for people moving out of Inner London. But one needs a lot of money to move this way, either capital (in the form of savings or an existing house) or income to support a mortgage, or some combination of the two. To buy a house in the cheapest areas on the fringes of the South East with a 100 per cent mortgage required a household income of at least £60 per week at the time of the

(1) The data refer to the tenure of households in 1971, which for some households was five years after their move. Changes in tenure could have occurred in the intervening period. However, a separate analysis of people who moved between 1970 and 1971 gave broadly similar results.

124

Stockwell survey in 1973. More would have been needed to buy into the more expensive areas like Outer London. Only 26 per cent of our intending migrants had earnings over this figure, and few of the remainder were likely to have had sufficient capital to make up the difference.

If the rest of the housing market were similarly closed on the grounds of expense, we would be left with the old argument: that people live in Inner London because of its cheap housing. The matter would rest there. But other forms of tenure are to be found outside Inner London, and, as we have shown in Chapter 5, these tend to be less expensive. The 48 per cent of our intending movers who were council tenants in Stockwell, for example, would probably find themselves paying lower rents if they were council tenants in the areas they wanted to move to. But the authorities who control access to dwellings in these areas are primarily responsible to their own residents. Virtually all of them require people to live in their area for several years before they become eligible for council housing and, with a few exceptions, these authorities have no obligations to rehouse people directly from Inner London, however pressing their housing need. Principal among these exceptions are, of course, the new and expanding towns, whose main purpose was to provide housing for Londoners in housing need, particularly those from Inner London. In the event, for reasons we discuss in the next chapter, relatively small numbers of people have been moving from Inner London through this channel.

To some extent, the GLC operates as a regional housing authority apart from its involvement with new and expanding towns. As well as its property in Inner and Outer London, it has a number of estates in the Outer Metropolitan Area, and 'seaside homes' in several coastal towns. But the number of vacancies arising in this stock is limited; most of them are taken up by urgent transfer cases or decants and virtually none are available for people who have a general desire to move out of Inner London.

In theory, it is possible for council tenants from Inner London boroughs such as Lambeth to exchange tenancies with council tenants in outer areas. In practice only a few dozen exchanges take place each year from the whole of Lambeth. This is mainly because council tenants with flats in Inner London have a relatively 'unsaleable' commodity compared with tenants of houses in outer areas and this restricts the scope for direct or indirect exchanges.

These barriers to movement are largely the product of the existing political and administrative priorities governing publicly owned housing. Such priorities can be changed without the need for major additional resources. Whilst accepting that housing should remain in the hands of local authorities primarily responsible to their own residents, a larger proportion of it should be used to assist longer distance moves of the kind discussed in this chapter. The fact that central government provides large subsidies to housing authorities is a good reason for arguing that their housing should not be used exclusively for local purposes. This discussion is developed in the next chapter; meanwhile, we must turn to the final channel of movement available to intending migrants – the private rented sector.

125

We have seen that this is of major importance for immigrants to Inner London. Well over half of all people moving into the inner ring between 1966 and 1971 moved into privately rented housing. However, less than a fifth of those moving out went through this channel.

The private sector is large in Inner London, but private tenancies are relatively sparse elsewhere. In 1971, almost half of Inner London's households were private tenants. The comparable proportion was less than a quarter in Outer London and still lower in the typical settlement beyond the Green Belt. With the general drying up of private lettings which has taken place since the 1974 Rent Act this particular option seems likely to be even less important in the future.

☐ Though most people are attached to Stockwell and wish to stay there, a sizeable minority wish to move out. This minority includes large numbers of families with children, households of the kind for whom the housing and environment of Inner London are particularly inadequate. It also includes many low-skill and low-income workers, the very people who are finding increasing difficulty in Inner London's job market ☐

7 Balanced dispersal

We have seen that the present structure of the housing market is preventing many people from moving out of Inner London. We believe that if this 'housing trap' could be sprung, things would not only be better for such people but also conditions could be more easily improved for those left behind. As we have shown in Chapter 4, many of the problems of the Inner London labour market could be eased by greater mobility of labour, bringing the supply of skills more in line with the supply of jobs. Many aspects of the inner city housing problem result from the pressures of population, and could be reduced by policies to help people move out. Without the need to use every acre of spare land for housing gain, it will be easier to provide social facilities and, perhaps, new jobs. Finally, it seems that some of the more intractable problems of Inner London – such as vandalism, crime and environmental decay – are partly caused by the sheer concentration of population and of certain kinds of family in particular: it is likely that these problems would be eased if such people were helped to disperse as part of a general reduction of inner city densities.

This two-pronged approach to the role of population dispersal in improving the lot of inner city people was, of course, that of Ebenezer Howard[1] and other new town pioneers. Since the late 19th century there has been a powerful movement in Britain arguing for dispersal as a means of solving the problems of London and other cities. But there has also been a powerful opposition, which seems to have been growing in recent years.

Few local authorities like the idea of losing population. If nothing else, it seems to hurt their notions of civic pride: size is often felt to be prestigious and a declining city seen as an unsuccessful one. For this, and other reasons there has been great concern about recent losses in the population of London. At the public enquiry into the Greater London Development Plan, the GLC and a number of London Boroughs developed a series of arguments for stemming the decline. They were not accepted by the Layfield Panel[2] or, more recently, by the South East Joint Planning Team.[3]

The first issue is whether the shifts in population are leaving a growing concentration of low-skilled and low-income families in Inner London. Chapter 2 shows that this is happening. This does not, however, argue for reducing out-migration, but instead for measures to make migration more balanced, in particular by increasing the proportion of low-skill workers moving out. A balanced policy on

(1) Ebenezer Howard, *Garden Cities for Today and Tomorrow.*

(2) Department of the Environment, *Greater London Development Plan, Report of the Panel of Enquiry.*

(3) South East Joint Planning Team, *Strategy for the South East: 1976 Review.*

migration, as well as meeting the wishes of those who are trapped, could strengthen London's employment base by making it easier for those whose skills are least in demand to move out and for some of those whose skills are in great demand to move in.

A second argument is that population decline, by removing ratepayers from the city, is making it harder for local government to provide services. The reasoning here is that certain fixed costs – such as the maintenance of buildings and infrastructure – have to be shared by a smaller number of ratepayers, so that the average costs per head increase as the population drops. This argument seems to be widely accepted but is unproven.[1] In the long run, fixed assets can be renewed on a smaller scale and average costs per head might end up lower. Even in the short run, many services are very expensive to provide in the conditions of congestion which result from high population levels. For example, in 1975, it cost at least £25,000 to provide a three bedroom council flat in most parts of Inner London, and in several particularly difficult areas individual units were costing over £60,000 apiece. At the same time, three bedroom houses in the home counties were costing less than £10,000 on average. These figures include land costs but the differences in construction costs are equally great. The reasons for these higher costs are varied but they all derive from the difficulties of rebuilding in London, including congestion.

The GLC has also argued that high levels of migration from London are producing excessive pressures on the rest of South East England. Whether such pressures are regarded as excessive depends on a comparison with the much greater pressures in places like Stockwell. Certainly the planners most closely concerned do not believe that there is insufficient capacity to absorb further migration from London. The South East Joint Planning Team has specifically recommended planned population increase in a series of growth areas around London,[2] where there is 'slack' in the infrastructure and other facilities.

Finally, the GLC has recently suggested that expenditure on new and expanding towns might be cut back to release public resources for urban renewal in Docklands and other parts of London. We would argue that dispersal and urban renewal are complementary policies and that London needs greater resources for both, but if resources cannot be increased then the main emphasis should be upon new housing outside Inner London. The cost of rehousing an Inner Londoner in Inner London is much higher than rehousing him elsewhere and there is no shortage of prospective emigrants.

These various arguments advanced by the GLC refer to movement out of London generally. The issues are more complicated. The main pressures are in Inner London, the bulk of London's losses have been from there and it is from there that

---

(1) See Department of the Environment, *op.cit.*, p. 63, and South East Joint Planning Team, *Strategy for the South East: 1976 Review. Report of the Resources Group*, pp. 32–34.

(2) South East Joint Planning Team, *Strategic Plan for the South East* and *Strategy for the South East: 1976 Review.*

further migration is needed. Some of this migration, as we argue later, should be to Outer London. Special attention should be given to the needs of the low-paid and the low-skilled.

Migration can be increased by a combination of measures to provide new housing specifically for Inner Londoners and by new allocation policies to give them a greater share of the existing stock. New allocation policies offer the prospect of quicker results and a more efficient and equitable use of scarce housing resources. However, the political resistance to radical changes in allocation policy will sometimes be greater than the opposition to new housing, and there is after all only a limited amount of housing to be allocated. So both these approaches will be needed.

What scale of movement is likely to be necessary? Migration patterns are, of course, notoriously difficult to predict; especially when – as in this case – the basic factors which govern them may be subjected to fundamental change. One possible method is to start with the present level of net migration from Inner London, which we earlier estimated at about 75,000 persons per year. As we have pointed out, this figure includes relatively few low-skill manual workers. If we assume that the rate of migration by other workers is to remain unchanged, then an increase in net migration to around 90,000 persons per year should be adequate to enable low-skill workers to achieve parity.

This is a *net* flow, the difference between the numbers of people moving out and moving in. In the past, for every five people who moved out, roughly two moved in. In the future too, any increase in the numbers moving out will be partly offset by some people moving in. This means that it is difficult to estimate accurately how much out-migration will be needed. It will therefore be necessary to keep programmes under continuous review as new initiatives for dispersal are tried out.

Inner Londoners moving out could go to a variety of places: to Outer London, to other places mainly in South East England and to new or expanding towns in particular. Before we discuss these, there are two general points. First, as we showed in the last chapter, most people who want to move do not want to go very far – the preference is for Outer London or just beyond. Secondly, since the main concern is with the needs of low-income and low-skilled people, and since most of them cannot afford to buy, the bulk of the housing for them has to be public housing for rent.

Outer London

At present, the main way in which a lower-income family can move from Inner to Outer London is through the auspices of the GLC. About 60,000 dwellings are owned by the GLC in Outer London and are available for letting to families from any part of London who satisfy certain priorities. In addition, the GLC has the right to nominate such families for tenancies in a small proportion of the stock owned by the Outer London boroughs.

People who are already council tenants in Inner London can ask to be transferred to this pool. People who are not council tenants, but who are expecting to get a council house, can ask to be nominated for a tenancy in the pool instead of being rehoused in their own borough by its council. Thus, in theory, there are clear channels for existing or potential council tenants to move out. But these channels are difficult to negotiate, as our follow-up survey showed:

Mrs. Stirling, a widow, lived with her son on a Lambeth Council Estate. She worked in Tonbridge. She wanted to move to 'Bromley or nearby' to be nearer her work and her two married daughters, and further away from Stockwell which she found 'filthy and too built up'. She started trying to move soon after her husband died in 1958 but failed and decided not to try again while her children were settled at school. In 1973, she enlisted the support of her vicar and a local councillor to press for a transfer, but only received two offers, in other parts of Brixton and Stockwell. When she pressed again for a transfer, in 1976, her two daughters had left home. She was told at the Housing Advice Centre that the GLC was not accepting any nominations for the time being, but even when they did, her chances for a transfer would be very low. Now that her two daughters had left home she was no longer 'overcrowded'. She was told 'you should have tried earlier'.

Mr. and Mrs. Peters lived in a small flat on an estate owned by the Church Commissioners. They wanted to move to somewhere 'on the borders of London' giving a number of possible places including Edgware, Southgate, Thornton Heath and Croydon. They found Stockwell 'run-down' and 'noisy' and felt little in common with the people who now lived there. Their landlords had discouraged them from applying for a transfer and, when pressed, had only been able to offer flats at Vauxhall or the Elephant and Castle, which the Peters felt were no better. The Church Commissioners were said to be unwilling to accept transfers or exchanges with GLC properties. There was little point in going onto the waiting lists and applying for a GLC nomination, since, with a purpose-built flat, they were already 'adequately housed' and would obtain very few points. People like Mr. and Mrs. Peters, who are well housed in conventional terms, have virtually no chance of transferring to Outer London. Yet, if they were able to go, this would release accommodation for those who want to stay.

Mrs. Palmer, a widow in her mid-50s, wanted to move 'further out to the South of London'. She lived on an older GLC estate and had been on the transfer list for 13 years. Despite being told they had medical priority – Mrs. Palmer was crippled and Mr. Palmer had eventually died of heart trouble – they had only received one offer, in Merton, up to 1976. They lost this through being on holiday at the time the offer was made: it was valid only for seven days. After being advised by us to get in touch again with the GLC and Merton, Mrs. Palmer finally received an offer in June 1976 of a three bedroom house in Morden with a large garden, evidently because the authorities thought that her family was still with her. But, as had been explained, her children had left home by then. She felt that the house would be too big for her, and that, when it came to it, the council would think so too.

Why should such difficulties arise? First, the scale of the operation is extremely limited; only about 2300 households are able to move through this channel every year.[1] This is small in relation to the number of existing and potential council tenants wanting to make such moves. The benefits are anyway confined to those with strong claims upon the attentions of their councils. They will include urgent 'decants' for reasons given in Chapter 5. They will also include people who can provide good arguments for getting a transfer, perhaps for medical reasons or because they are an elderly couple occupying a large dwelling which could be used to rehouse a family. But they will rarely include people who simply want to leave Inner London, however strongly they may feel about it.

There are two ways of increasing movement from Inner to Outer London. One is to give the GLC or the Inner boroughs control over a large proportion of the existing stock. The other is to build new dwellings in the suburbs for Inner Londoners. These should be seen as complementary policies, rather than alternatives.

The objective of extending control over the housing in Outer London can best be achieved by a 'co-ordinated allocation system' for London council housing, along the lines developed by the GLC and the London Boroughs Association. Under these proposals, a new London-wide housing agency would be given letting powers over a proportion of the council dwellings available in each of the London boroughs. This proportion, expected to be around 40 per cent, would be a proportion of current vacancies rather than the total stock. In other words if borough X had, at a given point in time, 100 dwellings available for letting, then 40 of them would go to tenants nominated by the new agency. And as further dwellings became available – whether vacated properties in the older stock or newly built homes, then four out of every ten would be similarly let. There would be no need for any change in ownership or management, which would remain with the boroughs. An incidental and, we think, beneficial aspect of the scheme is that the 180,000 dwellings now owned by the GLC would be handed over to the boroughs.

Such a scheme, if properly implemented, could go a long way towards giving Inner Londoners equal access to Council housing. People who wanted a council tenancy would be dealt with under a London-wide points system, replacing the present order of things where a person who happens to live in an Outer London borough stands a far better chance than someone from Inner London. At the same time, the barriers which prevent existing tenants getting transfers across borough boundaries would be largely removed.

The data processing problems of this scheme could be handled by an extension of the GLC's existing computerised housing system. New legislation will be required, however, to give the new agency powers to require all boroughs to play their part.

The scope for a co-ordinated allocation system will obviously be greater if there are more dwellings to allocate. How can the amount of publicly-owned housing in Outer London be increased?

(1) Nicholas Deakin and Clare Ungerson, op.cit.

For a start, local authorities should buy up existing housing on the private market. This is already being done to some extent, the authorities sometimes buying individual houses and sometimes complete estates. Such purchases, at an average of around £15,000 per house, offer a far cheaper way of getting extra council housing than by new construction. Also, because such houses are normally in good condition, such a policy would not suffer from a major problem of 'municipalisation' in the inner city, where, in the early 1970s the rate at which councils could buy up new houses outran their ability to carry out necessary repairs.

Buying up existing houses in the suburbs will not meet the needs of all those Inner Londoners who want to move, so some new construction will be necessary. Every possible site for housing in Outer London should be identified, and as many as possible used for public housing for rent. But the scope for doing this is limited, unless densities and environmental standards are brought close to those of the inner city, which we would not advocate.

The Green Belt and beyond

There are, however, many possible sites on the edge of London which at present cannot be used because they are within the Green Belt. A reappraisal of the Green Belt is long overdue; it has become one of the sacred cows of British social policy. The reasons for keeping it in its present form are unclear, as conditions have changed since it was first created. One purpose is to preserve the views, amenities and property values of those who are fortunate to live near it. It is also said to provide overcrowded city dwellers with opportunities for open air recreation, although the bulk of it is privately owned and closed to the public, apart from the occasional footpath. Those few parts of it – like the Lea Valley – which have been specifically developed as recreational centres, cater only for a tiny minority of Londoners.

A third objective – probably the soundest – is the need to provide all those who ever travel around the London region with areas of attractive open land to form the occasional visual relief in what would otherwise be a continuous urban sprawl over the 30 miles from Charing Cross to places like Hemel Hempstead, Harlow or Dorking.

More could be done to meet these objectives, in particular by improving access to the countryside and by landscaping those parts which are seen from the major roads. Eventually, some more resources might be devoted to recreational centres for those who are able to get to them and afford the entrance fees. Most of the rest of the Green Belt should, as now, be given over to agriculture, but there is no reason why a small proportion of it should not be developed for housing on carefully chosen sites. Such sites could be far less attractive as open land than alternatives further out, but they would be far more attractive to potential migrants from London.

132

Some people will be willing to move further out, and the obvious places to build for them are the 'growth areas' set out in the Strategic Plan for the South East, near to towns like Reading, Portsmouth, Southend and Crawley.[1] Again, much of this will need to be public housing. Access to it for Inner Londoners will depend upon special institutional arrangements such as the National Allocations Pool for council housing which we describe later.

New and expanding towns

The new and expanding towns are unique in that they already provide, in theory, a major channel for people to move out of London into publicly owned housing.

Each year, about 25,000 people appear to have been moving from Greater London to new and expanding towns. This is only a small proportion of the total out-migration currently running at around 100,000, though it was always intended that they should play a key role in regional planning strategy. In particular, they were originally supposed to take people in housing need from those parts of London where housing conditions were poorest, which meant predominantly Inner London. In his 1944 Greater London Plan, Abercrombie proposed that 60 per cent of London's overspill should come from the LCC area, which was rather smaller than Inner London as conceived in this book.

While the majority of migrants to the overspill towns appear to have been in housing need, relatively few of them have moved from Inner London. In 1973, for example, only 759 households from Inner London moved into development corporation dwellings in the nine main new towns. This was less than 18 per cent of the total immigration to these towns.[2] It is often claimed that Inner Londoners are much more likely to move to expanding towns, since the GLC has more control over migrants to these places. But in the three expanding towns for which we have data, Inner Londoners were still in a minority. In 1973 they formed 44 per cent of migrants to Bletchley, 27 per cent to Haverhill and 16 per cent to Swindon. More recent figures for the first half of 1975, suggest that Inner London has been getting a larger share of houses in new and expanding towns, though still in a minority. Of Londoners moving in this six-month period, only 37 per cent of those who went to new towns and 40 per cent of those moving to expanding towns came from Inner London. Some migrants to the new and expanding towns do not move from London at all.

This bias against Inner London results from the system for selecting tenants. Prospective tenants must normally obtain jobs in a new or expanding town before they can be offered housing there. At the same time, anyone who obtains a job is more or less guaranteed an offer of a subsidised house, although in many cases this can involve a waiting period during which the worker must either live in digs or commute from London.

(1) South East Joint Planning Team, *Strategic Plan for the South-East*.

(2) These figures are from special statistics compiled by the New Towns Division of the DOE.

Most of the firms who move from London to new or expanding towns take a large proportion of their labour force with them. Since the towns attract modern firms and since most such firms are in Outer London, Inner Londoners are unlikely to move out in this way. There is also an arrangement enabling firms to recruit workers after setting up in a new or expanding town or, to put it the other way, enabling workers to move other than with their existing firm. The New and Expanding Towns Scheme (originally the Industrial Selection Scheme) was set up to fill the job vacancies from a register of Londoners willing to move. This register contained 20,000 names in 1976. Because most Inner Londoners who would like to move lack the skills required, however, this scheme helps relatively few of them.[1]

All this means that under the present arrangement, it is employers, rather than housing managers, who decide which people should move to new or expanding towns. Thus the typical new towner is skilled and socially respectable – precisely the kind of person needed to man modern growth industries. Employers in new towns therefore have a unique advantage: they can virtually hand-pick their labour force, while employers in other places have to make do with an existing labour force which may be unsuited to their needs. The present authors, when they worked on proposals for expanding Northampton and Ipswich in the mid-1960s, saw that in both these towns the growing industries, principally in mechanical and electrical engineering, were starved of all kinds of labour, especially skilled. Without the advantage of a large flow of selected migrants they could only meet their needs by 'poaching' from less buoyant industries (such as footwear in Northampton), by laying on private transport to bring in workers from surrounding villages and by carrying out investment projects to substitute capital for labour, which meant, as often as not, providing capital instead of *skilled* labour. Since then, Northampton has become a 'new town' and its industry will be better off than that of Ipswich when the next period of labour shortage comes along.

We recognise the need to provide modern industry with the necessary conditions for growth and below make a proposal to help with this. But we see no reason why employers in new and expanding towns should be given such critical advantages over their counterparts in other places. The inequality has come about only because, in the 1950s when the new towns were started, it was feared that they would have difficulty in attracting industry. Since it was a prime objective that new towns should be self-contained settlements – unlike the peripheral housing estates of the inter-war period – measures to attract industry were gradually given special priority against other objectives. Things have changed since then. Not only have the new towns, contrary to these early fears, succeeded in becoming broadly self-contained, but other industrial growth centres in the South East, such as Reading, Luton and Colchester, have also managed the same thing, without the advantage of industrial selection schemes. And such places have taken a far larger share of the region's population increase than the overspill towns.

(1) See for example, Deakin and Ungerson, *op.cit.*; Francis A. Gee, *Homes and Jobs for Londoners in New and Expanding Towns*; Charles W. Thomson, *The Industrial Selection Scheme – A Study of Conflicting Objectives in Urban and Regional Planning*; and J. B. Heraud, 'The new towns and London's housing needs'.

Thus there are strong arguments for relaxing the employment qualifications of new and expanding towns so as to allow some tenants to move without first getting a job. Instead, they should be selected from the groups which need special help – low-skill people and other disadvantaged people from Inner London. In times of economic recession, such measures may result in an increase of unemployment in the new areas and a measure of extra commuting back to London. But there are strong arguments for spreading unemployment more evenly, as opposed to allowing the present concentrations to persist in the inner city. In particular, the costs to the nation of maintaining a typical unemployed family are likely to be higher in Inner London than elsewhere. In the long run, as the economy regains impetus, such unemployed people will be in a better position to obtain work if they have moved to those areas where manufacturing industry is relatively stronger.

One move to widen access has recently been taken by the Government, which has added a new category – Londoners in housing need who are looking for jobs – to those eligible for rehousing in the new towns. This change is welcome, though it is not yet clear how much difference it will make to Inner Londoners in particular.

It can, of course, be argued that those who move from Outer London create space which can be taken up by people from Inner London. Such 'filtering', as it is called, has undoubtedly taken place in the private sector: it is clear that large numbers of Inner Londoners have bought houses in Outer London, many of which were probably vacated by people moving further out. But, as shown, there is little filtering in the rest of the housing market. The movement of council tenants (existing or potential) from Outer London seems to have resulted in a general improvement for the outer suburbs with few gains for the inner city.

Given that a large proportion of those who move to new and expanding towns are likely to continue to come from Outer London, there are good reasons for ensuring that some of the benefit can be 'clawed back' for the inner city. This might be done by requiring the Outer boroughs to make a proportion of the resultant 'housing gain' available to Inner London. Thus, for example, if 100 families moved from Kingston to new and expanding towns over a given period, then the London Borough of Kingston could be required to make, perhaps, 50 dwellings from its own stock available to Lambeth and other Inner London boroughs. Since both new and expanding towns keep reasonable records of the previous addresses of their tenants it would be technically possible to do this on a year to year basis. It would, of course, be necessary to ignore those households whose movement did not reduce the housing obligations of the Outer borough concerned. Such a measure would not be necessary, of course, if there were a co-ordinated allocation system of the kind described earlier.

A National Allocations Pool

So far in this chapter we have put forward a series of proposals to make it easier for people to move out of Inner London. These have included the construction of new housing but they have also covered new allocation policies to give Inner Londoners a better chance of moving into existing housing in areas further out.

One proposal we have described is the co-ordinated allocation system for council housing in London. As we write, it is not clear how easy it will be to start such a scheme. It would be understandable for Outer London boroughs – and even some in Inner London – to be unwilling to give up their sovereignty over their stock of council housing. Local authorities are responsible to their electorates, and these electorates are unlikely to approve of measures which use local housing for the benefit of others. But local authorities do not provide all the money to build, maintain and manage their council housing. A large and ever-increasing part of the cost is met by central government. Since part of any council's housing funds are provided from central sources, it is reasonable to argue that some of their housing should be used for purposes other than purely local needs.

Helping Inner Londoners is only one of many such purposes: there are other reasons why council housing should be made available to long-distance migrants. Most obvious of these is the fact that the national economy will be able to adjust fully to changing circumstances only if there is greater mobility of labour. But at present, with the private rented sector in decline and an ever-growing proportion of the national housing stock in the hands of local authorities, it is not easy for people to move from one town or city to another.

It might be argued that there is enough scope for increasing long-distance migration by modifying the existing facilities for mutual exchanges between the tenants of different authorities. But the system of mutual exchanges is inevitably limited since it relies on tenants being able to find counterparts in the areas they want to move to with needs exactly complementary to their own.

The only effective way to promote long-distance mobility is by extending the principles of the proposed London co-ordinated allocation system to regional and national levels. Under such a scheme a series of regional housing agencies would control a National Allocations Pool to be made available to long-distance migrants, some on the grounds of housing need and some because they had the skills required by local industry. This need not involve the creation of large new bureaucracies. Co-ordinated allocation systems should be essentially data-processing exercises, with most of the office work carried out by existing housing offices. The main function of the new housing agencies – whether London-wide, region-wide or nation-wide – would be to ensure that individual authorities carried out their obligations under the scheme.

A national scheme would, by extending the principles of the proposed London Scheme, meet the objections of those Outer London boroughs who question why they should be required to make sacrifices for Inner London when their own housing problems are greater than those in many other parts of the country. It would also provide a framework within which houses outside London, for example those built in the growth areas of the South East, could be made available to Inner

136

Londoners and other long-distance migrants without the complicated and time-consuming procedures used for new and expanding towns. Under such a system, a proportion of all council houses in any part of the country could be available to long-distance migrants. And this proportion could be readily increased if any particular local authority wished to allocate extra housing to its regional authority, either by handing over a higher proportion of its existing vacancies (which might be appropriate for councils in declining areas) or by building extra houses (which might, with suitable financial incentives, be attractive to authorities in expanding areas).

☐ To summarise, we are proposing a series of policies to improve residential mobility. While these policies have general advantages, such as increasing mobility of labour, they are particularly aimed at helping Inner Londoners – especially the low-paid and the low-skilled – move further outwards:

1. There should be a co-ordinated allocation system to give Londoners in all boroughs equal access to public housing and facilitate migration from Inner and Outer London.

2. There should be selective intervention to acquire housing in the Outer London market for inner city residents.

3. More public housing should be built in Outer London, in selected parts of the Green Belt and in the 'growth areas' identified in the Strategic Plan for the South East.

4. A National Housing Allocations Pool should be created to help long-distance migrants. The pool would be made up of a proportion of council house vacancies from all local authorities ☐

'Oasis and desert':

Lansdowne Gardens (going up) and Willington Road (going down). The top photograph shows an area being improved by private owners.

On the right is a house boarded up by the council before demolition.

8 Planning and housing policies

We believe that the measures outlined in the previous chapter will increase freedom of choice and the quality of life of those who move out of Inner London. By relieving the pressures on the inner city, they will also make it easier to improve things for those who stay behind. But this will not happen automatically.

What planning and housing policies are needed to take the best advantage of the opportunity? In trying to devise these policies, we have drawn on a number of our studies, reported separately.[1] To examine the causes of problems on council estates, we carried out an additional survey of 18 estates in Stockwell at the beginning of 1976. We brought together data from the 1971 census, the Stockwell Household Survey, GLC and Lambeth housing files and supplemented this with an environmental survey of each estate. As an index of dissatisfaction we took the percentage of tenants who had requested transfers from each estate, which conformed closely with the views people expressed in the household survey. We then looked closely at various features which, since they correlated with this index, seemed to be the main causes of dissatisfaction.

Density

The movement out of families with children will lower the overall level of densities. The objective should be to use this relief to reduce density, and child densities in particular in those areas where they are at present highest. The reverse has often happened in the past, with lower density areas getting most of the benefit from out-migration and the higher density areas staying more or less as they were.[2] The reasons are probably connected with the workings of the tenure system. For example, there was a wide scope for reductions in occupancy and density in areas attractive to owner-occupiers. On the other hand, in areas of private rented housing the pressures were, if anything, in the reverse direction.

To reduce child densities selectively, housing directorates will need to monitor child density levels estate by estate and give priority to transfers from those estates where child density is highest.[3] Given careful controls of this kind, quite large reductions in child density could be achieved for surprisingly small outflows. We have shown that it would be possible to reduce child densities to below 30 children per acre

---

(1) Inner Area Study Lambeth, *People, Housing and District* (IAS/LA/5); Inner Area Study Lambeth, *Policies and Structure* (IAS/LA/7); Inner Area Study Lambeth, *Implications of Social Ownership* (IAS/LA/12) and Inner Area Study Lambeth, *Housing Management and Design* (IAS/LA/18).

(2) See, for example, *Report of the Committee on Housing in Greater London.*

(3) This is already being started on some estates by both Lambeth and the GLC.

everywhere in the study area by moving only 470 households, or 1½ per cent of the total. It would be necessary to transfer only 2700 households to bring child densities down to 'suburban' levels of 15 children per acre.[1] Calculations for the whole of Inner London produced similar findings.

While it should be made easier for families with children to move out of unsuitable accommodation, it is at the same time necessary to ensure that as many as possible move into the kinds of housing most suitable for them. As we have seen, Stockwell has a large number of houses with gardens in single family occupation; they should be retained for families with children wherever possible. Existing pressures are causing many of these houses to be converted into separate flats, not only by private developers, but also by the council. Thus, in Lambeth's first Housing Action Area, which contained several hundred two-storey terraced houses – of the kind well fitted for medium-to-large families – it seemed to be the council's intention to maximise 'housing gain' by converting most of them into flats.

We came across a further pressure towards converting such houses into flats in the Knights Hill area of southern Lambeth.[2] This area contained 220 terraced houses. Though Lambeth had obtained compulsory purchase orders over them, its 'design brief' deliberately allowed for the possibility of a proportion of the houses being retained and improved. Once again the pressures for 'housing gain' were evident: the brief proposed that the area be developed at 100 persons per acre, much more than the zoned density of 70 persons per acre. A further specification was that 45 per cent of the dwellings were to be for small (one or two person) households. These two requirements – on density and dwelling sizes – made it difficult to retain the existing houses, especially as dwellings for single family occupation. They pointed either to complete redevelopment or alternatively to the conversion of the existing houses into separate units for the small households. We, however, used a combination of rehabilitation and redevelopment, improving the best of the old houses for families and infilling with new development, mainly in the form of small flats. The same approach could be used elsewhere: if enough care is taken it will usually be possible to find a means of keeping houses for families with children.

The requirement that around half of all new dwellings should be designed for small households is a common feature of local authority design briefs in Inner London. It has come about as local authorities belatedly realised the prominence of such households in the population structure. Future migration will tend to increase this prominence even further, so that local authorities will need to pay more and more attention to rehousing such people who, despite the change in building policy, have so far taken only a small proportion of their allocations. It is politically difficult for councils to house small households – many of which consist of young people with few local ties – at a time when there is great pressure to house families with children. Once again, if the pressures could be reduced, smaller households would stand a better chance.

(1) Inner Area Study Lambeth, *Housing and Population Projections* (IAS/LA/8).

(2) The Shankland Cox Partnership was commissioned by Lambeth to prepare designs for this area in 1974.

This suggests that existing local authority housing will need to be deployed flexibly. As families with children move out of existing flats – first in the tower blocks and later in lower rise development – more flats will be available for smaller households. But most such flats are two bedroom dwellings. In such a situation it will be sensible to allow two or more small households to share a single flat. There is no reason why this should be resisted. It is, after all, a common and satisfactory arrangement amongst young people in the private sector, many of whom would jump at the chance of moving to the kind of council tower block so unpopular with other kinds of household. Given sensitive management, such a change in letting policy could be the salvation of many local authority flats which could otherwise become redundant over the next 20 years or so.

The first evidence of such redundancies is already at hand; as we show later, many Inner London council estates are now so unpopular that it is virtually impossible to let their dwellings through conventional channels. Most of these estates date from the inter-war period but they include certain post-war tower blocks.

Immigration to London

Many young small households are relative newcomers to Inner London. As we saw in Chapter 6, less than half of those who move in are families, compared with three-quarters of those who move out. Another important difference is that most immigrants move into accommodation owned by private landlords. Historically, the private rented sector has played a key role in enabling Inner London's population to adapt to changing circumstances, such as shifts in the demand for labour.

The decline of the privately rented sector, and the need to maintain the adaptability of London's housing, mean that fundamental changes will be needed in local authority letting policies. They must put more emphasis on new migrants, particularly small households at an early stage in the life cycle. Traditionally, such people have been excluded from council housing although the case for relaxing residential qualifications has been argued for some time.[1] There have been several recent changes. A number of Inner London boroughs, including Lambeth and Southwark, have started to allocate dwellings on 'difficult to let' estates to young single households. The GLC has recently set up a 'ready access' scheme, under which several hundred dwellings on such estates have been allocated, outside the normal channels, on a 'first-come-first-served' basis. This seems to have worked well with no shortage of people willing to accept tenancies, despite their unpopularity with the more 'regular' council clients. People have sometimes queued all night outside GLC offices to be sure of a flat. Remarkable though this scheme is, it is regarded by the GLC only as a stop-gap,[2] is confined to a tiny proportion of the

(1) Central Housing Advisory Committee, *Council Housing: Purposes, Procedures and Priorities.*

(2) In the long run the GLC expects to solve the letting problems on these estates by making tenancies available to married children of existing residents, who could not otherwise expect council accommodation. While such a solution is clearly sensible, it will shift the emphasis away from helping small mobile households.

council's stock and still depends on a residential qualification – one year in London. Local pressures inevitably limit what local authorities will do along these lines. Their efforts need supplementing by other initiatives. A National Allocations Pool, along the lines set out in Chapter 7, can make a major contribution.

The private rented sector

The history of privately rented accommodation seems to be one of the main failures of the 'mixed economy'. Successive governments have tried to control the activities of landlords by restricting the rents they are able to charge and curtailing their ability to evict tenants. These measures have undoubtedly helped the majority of tenants, though a proportion have always fallen outside their scope or have failed to take advantage of them. Attempts to extend the benefits have usually made things even worse for the minority of tenants in the remaining 'free' sector, as a slowly declining group of mobile households has been forced to compete for a rapidly declining number of dwellings. The latest attempt of this kind – the 1974 Rent Act – provided extra security and reduced rents for several hundred thousand 'furnished' tenants. At the same time, it has clearly pushed up rents in the remaining properties and – by reducing the number of re-lets – made it more difficult for people to find fresh accommodation.

These measures have also made landlords increasingly unwilling to spend money on their property. If an improvement project, such as a new bathroom, costing £1000, produces only a £50 increase in the annual registered rent, then the landlord will understandably prefer to invest his capital elsewhere, since other forms of investment offer a greater return for less effort. And if a flat which yields an income of only £300 per year can be sold to an owner-occupier for £10,000 then its landlord will try to obtain vacant possession so that he can sell it off. This kind of arithmetic – fairly typical in present circumstances – has helped to create poor standards in the private rented sector and has caused large scale transfers of formerly rented properties to owner-occupation. Other dwellings have been lost as they fell into dereliction and became candidates for clearance by local authorities.

There have been exceptions, of course. Many landlords have evidently continued to re-let regulated properties after they became vacant. This is demonstrated by Table 33 in Appendix 3 which shows that nearly a third of migrants to London's inner ring moved into unfurnished private tenancies in the late 1960s, contrary to the popular belief that nearly all landlords were at that time converting such properties to furnished lettings or selling them off to owner-occupiers. Similarly, our household survey showed that unfurnished lettings were still being granted on a fair scale in Stockwell up to 1973. But such exceptions are fast disappearing. Many of the large corporate landlords which were able to make profits in the late 1960s have either bankrupted themselves or broken up their holdings in the past three years, and many of the smaller landlords seem to have fallen victim to the panic resulting from the 1974 Rent Act. These recent developments have produced the first examples of tenants' co-operatives such as Fairhazel Gardens in Camden, where a group of private tenants have purchased their flats from a corporate landlord. More often, they have resulted in 'block-busting' operations – where rented flats are sold off to sitting tenants and other customers – or just an increase in the number of vacant properties.

Increasingly, then, the private landlord has proved an unsatisfactory agency for the implementation of housing policies. It seems likely that his decline will continue and that over the next few decades we can expect to see most of the remaining privately rented dwellings pass to local authorities, housing associations, owner-occupiers and other forms of tenure. By the end of the century, the 'purely commercial' landlord will be virtually extinct and the private sector will consist mainly of people letting off spare rooms in their own homes. In general, this is a favourable trend, since it will usually mean that more resources are devoted to improving and maintaining these dwellings. The main problem, as we have noted, will be to find new systems of allocation which benefit those people who at present rely on the private sector. A further problem is that the decline will take some time to be completed. In the early 1970s the complete 'socialisation' of the private sector seemed just around the corner. Since then, the rate of acquisition by local authorities has fallen sharply, partly because of central government 'cut-backs' and partly because local authorities did not have the management resources to support such a high level of acquisition and improvement. At the present rate, it will take several decades for 'complete social ownership' to become a reality. What should be done about privately rented dwellings until then, and what should be done about the rump of the private sector that will still remain at the end of the day?

One solution, often mooted, is to return to the free market by abolishing all controls over rent and security of tenure. In theory, this would attract investment into existing dwellings, prevent their sale to owner-occupiers and even bring about some new building by private landlords. The problem is that, after 60 years of government control, few private landlords are likely to behave in accordance with classical economic theory. Most would believe that controls were likely to be re-introduced in the future and would take advantage of such a respite to sell off their holdings at the first opportunity or extract as much income from them as possible, with little compensating investment. (It is generally accepted that the 1957 Rent Act, which had similar intentions, produced results such as these, in particular a massive increase in the decline of privately rented dwellings.)

A middle course would be to provide better incentives within the present framework of controls. There are strong arguments for a substantial increase in regulated rents. When first introduced in the mid 1960s, these were high enough to attract a fair level of investment into the private sector, but they have failed to keep up with the massive inflation which has subsequently occurred. A new structure for 'fair rents' should make up the existing gap and ensure that future rents would rise along with inflation. But it would be sensible to require landlords to bring their property up to a specified standard, and maintain it at this level, before allowing them to charge the increased rents. In other words, there would be two separate rent scales – 'new' and 'old' fair rents – analogous to the existing dual system of 'controlled' and 'regulated' rents – with transition from one to another dependent on some form of 'qualification certificate'.

Similar arguments apply to public sector rents. The current policy of keeping rents at artificially low levels is, in the last analysis, hurting the tenants themselves, by reducing the potential level of investment in their housing. Many tenants – private and public – would be willing to pay higher rents if this produced a better standard of housing. A logical policy would be to raise rents to make this possible, while at the same time increasing the level of direct subsidies to those who cannot afford such increases. Ideally, this should involve a national income maintenance scheme, as suggested in Chapter 3. In the meantime, something could be done by increasing the maximum levels of the existing rent allowance and rent rebate schemes and taking steps to increase their take-up. In other words, there needs to be a change of emphasis towards 'subsidising people rather than dwellings'.

Another problem of the private sector is security of tenure. The present Rent Acts have prevented arbitrary evictions by private landlords, but only at the cost of making existing tenants virtually immobile. In addition, many landlords now prefer to keep property vacant rather than create tenancies which could last indefinitely. A common suggestion is for all private tenancies to be converted into short leases – three years is the period usually proposed – at the end of which the landlord would have automatic rights of possession. In support of such proposals it is usually argued that most private tenants do not really want absolute security of tenure and would be perfectly satisfied with a few years' peace of mind.

Nevertheless, a simple proposal of this kind would be unacceptable, since at the end of the first three year period there would be large scale evictions of long standing tenants, principally elderly controlled tenants who are least able to fend for themselves. Some kind of compromise is necessary – perhaps a hybrid measure under which the length of the new leases would depend upon the time tenants had already spent in residence. Under such a system elderly tenants who had planned for their retirement on the basis of complete security of tenure would receive, perhaps, 30 year leases, while relative newcomers would obtain a standard three year period. Such a measure would recreate some of the former flexibility of the private rented sector without causing excessive hardship. In addition it would bring extra tenancies onto the market – such as premises over shops, or in investment property – where the owner will not wish to commit himself to letting under present circumstances. The main difficulty is that security of tenure seems to be the principal factor restricting the sale of private rented properties to owner occupiers, and we cannot be certain that revised rent policies will remove this desire to sell. We would regard this as a problem in the absence of any further measures such as the creation of an 'allocations pool' in the public sector and, in the meantime, it might be necessary to take steps to restrict sales of this kind. This could be done by an extension of the existing powers of the 1974 Housing Act which require landlords in selected areas to give local authorities or housing associations the first refusal on any property they wish to sell.

Alternative forms of tenure

The increasing polarisation of the housing market into owner-occupiers and local authority tenants is often seen as a threat to variety of choice and flexibility of allocation. This had led many observers to suggest that alternative forms of tenure be developed.

The best established of these alternatives is rented property supplied by housing associations. The housing association movement is growing rapidly and, though it still only accounts for a tiny proportion of the housing stock in any part of the country, it is now playing a major role in the acquisition and improvement of older properties in Inner London. In recent years about half the public sector conversion work in Lambeth has been done by housing associations. The movement is not able to offer a completely independent system of allocation since a proportion of any association's lettings – sometimes as much as 100 per cent – must be offered to people nominated by the local authority. In Inner London the remaining lettings mostly go to the kind of emergencies – referrals by Social Services departments and other agencies – which often fall outside the local authority net.

It is often claimed that housing associations are more efficient than local authorities at the job of acquiring, renovating and managing scattered properties. This is difficult to prove or disprove, for the differences in performance between individual associations seem to be as wide as those between different local authorities. In any particular borough, however, a good housing association may provide a useful yardstick against which the local authority's own achievements can be measured. In this sense, the advantages of variety are clear cut.

Numerically, the next most important form of alternative tenure is squatting. As we have said earlier, squatting has emerged as a 'grass roots' reaction to the decline of the private rented sector and the growth in vacant properties. Its adherents range from 'respectable' organisations which operate rather like cut-price housing associations, to the political and a-political vandals who form the subject of most press reports. The social costs of squatting – in terms of physical damage, litigation, administrative delays and conflicts with established residents – are large, but it does provide some kind of home for large numbers of people. (A rough estimate is around 30,000 in Greater London). Until the pressure on housing in London is reduced and the stock made available to a wider range of people, squatting will clearly persist, as a strange combination of voluntary welfare and popular bogey. In the meantime, we think that more could be done by local authorities and other bodies to regularise agreements with 'official' squatters.

We discuss housing co-operatives later in this chapter. The remaining possibilities – equity sharing and co-ownership schemes – are best regarded as forms of owner-occupation. They are open only to the higher income groups, in Inner London at any rate. Both of them work by separating the 'owner-occupier' from a portion of the equity in his dwelling. Thus, when he sells, part of the profit goes to the co-ownership society or to the local authority in an equity sharing scheme. In return,

147

his monthly repayments can be kept lower than they would be under a conventional house purchase. In essence, such schemes are devices to lower the 'threshold' to owner-occupation, and offer some of those who would otherwise be priced out of the market a chance to get their 'feet on the ladder'. Co-ownership schemes have existed since the early 1960s and do not appear to be very attractive in London. It could well be that more people will want to take advantage of equity sharing schemes: certainly there appears to be scope, as the level of owner-occupation in Inner London is less than half that of the rest of the country.

As we have pointed out in the previous chapter, proposals of this kind could assist some of those who want to move out of Inner London. Whether they should be available within Inner London is another matter, since they can be realised only by taking rented dwellings from the public or private sectors, and at present such dwellings are urgently needed for lower income households. This issue seems to shade into two other long-standing debates – on the sale of council houses and the merits and problems of gentrification.

In general terms, we can see strong arguments for encouraging the spread of owner-occupation. Most people seem to desire this form of tenure for a variety of economic and psychological reasons. In some circumstances it provides better security and value for money than renting; in others less so. Certainly, it offers greater independence and social prestige. Owner-occupied houses are often high spots in an inner city environment which is generally monotonous and shabby. At the same time, the potential clients for owner-occupation are mostly those whose skills are in great demand by the economy of London. But despite these advantages it would be difficult to support such changes if they made things worse for lower income groups, which will happen in the absence of policies such as those we have outlined for balanced dispersal and the allocation of rented housing.

Rehabilitation and redevelopment

The shift from redevelopment to rehabilitation was evident by the time this report was written. Since 1974, most Inner London authorities had been forced to abandon their new building programmes and had been advised by central government to concentrate on the renovation of existing buildings. In Lambeth, for example, hardly any new areas were being put forward for redevelopment, so that new construction was bound to tail off to a hundred or so houses per year when the existing programmes were completed in the late 1970s.

There is a danger that this shift of emphasis could go too far. In any urban area, a small proportion of the stock will not be worth retaining and a certain level of renewal is necessary, preferably on a highly localised scale. Thus, in the typical housing area, judgements about redevelopment or renovation should be made on a house to house basis, which will often result in a mixture of the two, although the emphasis will be mainly upon rehabilitation. Apart from particular sites like those in Docklands, large-scale redevelopment in Inner London on the scale of the 1960s and early 1970s is unjustified. Such programmes were unduly expensive and socially disruptive. They often involved the destruction of adequate houses and their replacement by dwellings which were poorer value for money. Their main justification was to produce 'housing gain' which, as we argue, is better achieved outside Inner London altogether.

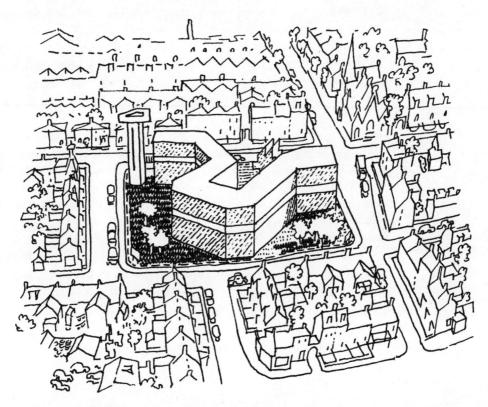

The Inner London authorities will have plenty to occupy them in improving their existing dwellings and those which they are likely to acquire from private landlords. Here, the existing resources are less than adequate, for the rundown in new building has not been matched by an increase in funds for rehabilitation. At present, the tendency is to concentrate local authority efforts into Housing Action Areas or General Improvement Areas. In our experience, this seems to be an inefficient approach. Considerable management resources are needed to get such areas underway – to identify them, carry out necessary surveys, and prepare material for councillors, the DOE and public consultation. Furthermore, such areas are always 'blunt tools' for tackling housing priorities, for they normally contain a proportion of reasonably good properties, while many of the worst are scattered and thus not susceptible to area treatment. In addition, they inhibit the mixing of redevelopment with renovation, since it is difficult to demolish properties once they have been included in a GIA or HAA. While area approaches may be valid, primarily in places which need extensive environmental treatment, resources are normally better employed in tackling individual properties on a priority basis. It would be sensible to extend the special powers and more generous grants at present confined to HAAs, to allow for such an approach over large parts of most Inner London boroughs.

At present, many councils have a somewhat rigid approach to rehabilitation and insist that in any particular scheme all dwellings should be improved to as high a standard as possible. This approach often involves buying out owner-occupiers, and moving residents from their homes so that the contractors can proceed without obstruction. Steamroller procedures of this kind are not all that different from wholesale redevelopment in term of the social disruption they cause. We favour a more flexible approach, which would allow owner-occupiers to keep to modest standards if they wished, and which might involve the phasing of improvement work so that residents did not always have to move out. The GLC, for example, have evolved a 'four day package' under which quite extensive rehabilitation is carried out in four days with the tenants remaining in residence. At present, this technique is mainly used with purpose-built flats but it has also been successfully applied to older houses.

We favour a more flexible approach to improvements by owner-occupiers, giving them greater freedom about the way they modernise their homes. To this end, more use should be made by local authorities of their powers to make loans to cover the owner's share of improvement costs, and there needs to be a review of the arrangements and conditions covering these and improvement grants.

To sum up, there are three main approaches that local authorities should take to redevelopment and rehabilitation, depending on the particular circumstances:

1. Large-scale redevelopment is appropriate where land is derelict or sites already cleared. Such places are relatively rare. As we argue later, even where this is done, the scale of the redevelopment should be broken down, sometimes involving a variety of agencies, to promote a diverse visual character.

Redevelopment and rehabilitation: an integrated mixture.

2. A combination of rehabilitation and redevelopment is needed in areas where the quality of the housing is mixed and where decisions should be taken on a house to house basis.

3. Over most of the inner city, rehabilitation needs to be encouraged in such a way as to maximise investment by owner-occupiers, in a framework in which the future of their property is secure and they have wider freedom of choice.

Both of the last two approaches concentrate on improvement to dwellings and their sites. Such measures will need to be matched by environmental improvements by the local authority.

Existing council estates

A more flexible approach to rehabilitation offers one way of reducing the high level of forced movement which has helped cause the erosion of community spirit in parts of Stockwell. Another way is to strengthen the possibilities for continuity of residence from generation to generation. The present GLC scheme offering vacant flats on older estates to the married children of local tenants is a step in this direction and will be possible on a bigger scale as population pressures reduce. In the long run we can expect to see the presence of friends and relatives playing a sizeable part in the allocation of tenants to individual estates.

Another factor making for dissatisfaction is the concentration of black people on certain estates. In some council estates in Stockwell almost half of all residents are black. As we have seen, these tend to be the older, pre-war estates, which are generally less attractive to most people. It is often argued that such high concentrations are a result of free choice by black people – either because they want to live together, or because they prefer the lower rents. To some extent this may be true, but there is now no doubt that the main cause is a form of unintended discrimination built into the official allocation process.[1] It so happens that black people are not heavily represented amongst 'decants' – those who are displaced from their homes by redevelopment or rehabilitation schemes and who, because they have the power to delay expensive building schemes, are in a strong bargaining position when offered alternative council accommodation. 'Decants' tend to be offered the newer, more attractive properties, while it is those who enter the council sector through other channels who are offered dwellings on the inter-war estates. In Lambeth most black people have obtained council accommodation after becoming homeless, the channel of entry which offers the least bargaining power.

If allocation procedures could be changed, the distribution of black people would become more even. Even so, some estates would have higher than average concentrations simply because members of minority groups often prefer to live

(1) See for example, David Smith and Anne Whalley, *Racial Minorities and Public Housing*. Some local authorities, including Lambeth and the GLC are now keeping records of the ethnic origins of them so as to direct attention to those estates where special efforts are needed to reduce concentrations.

Some of the more successful council estates: South Island Place (above), Spurgeon (below).

Stockwell Gardens (above and below).

together. This should be respected: the main point is to ensure that allocation processes do not cause further concentrations, especially on the least desirable estates.

A separate and even trickier problem is allocation of dwellings to anti-social families. Again, the question is: should they be dispersed or concentrated on a few estates? Official policies are usually claimed to favour dispersal on the grounds that this not only 'evens out the load' but also provides anti-social families with pressure from 'normal' tenants to force them to mend their ways.

In practice, it does not always work out like this. Both Lambeth and the GLC grade families according to their housekeeping standards and other behavioural patterns and this grading largely determines the type of property deemed 'suitable' for them. Those in the highest grade will be offered newly built flats or dwellings attractive for other reasons. Those in the lowest grade will be offered flats in places like the inter-war estates. The most 'anti-social' families will be earmarked for the worst of the stock, such as turn-of-the-century tenement building. This procedure is based on an unassailable fact: that the only available sanction against anti-social families is to transfer them to undesirable accommodation. Eviction, or the threat of it, cannot be an effective sanction, since if these families were evicted they would usually be eligible for re-admission as homeless.

In other words, the effective policy is normally to concentrate 'problem' families. We have no evidence on the effectiveness of these threats to move them – 'management transfers' as they are called. But if families are not deterred by such threats, the policy is an admission of failure, since it assumes that the only solution is to place these families in circumstances where their behaviour will get even worse. The policy is equally unfortunate for those decent families who still live on the estates which are the subject of management transfers.

While appreciating the reasons for what has happened, we must emphasise the dangers of concentration. When compounded with the other factors which make things worse on these estates it can make life almost intolerable for the rest of the people who live there. The end result is the point, already reached on several estates in Stockwell, where it becomes impossible to let vacant dwellings through 'normal' channels and emergency measures have to be taken to lift the estate out of its degradation.

Tenants' participation in management

At present, the main way for tenants to influence the management of their estates is through somewhat remote processes such as voting in local elections (where housing management is only one of many issues), canvassing their ward councillor, or approaching their representative on the local management committee.

Many councils have proposals going further than this. They range from stronger versions of the existing joint tenant-member committees to fully blown transfers of ownership and control to tenants' co-operatives. Several schemes have already been set underway including those at St. Katharine Estate (GLC) and Wellington Mills (GLC and Lambeth). Such experimental schemes will provide guidance for future policy. In the meantime we would make the following points.

One of the main reasons why some councils are interested in tenants' participation is their desire to transfer certain maintenance chores. It seems sensible to us that individual tenants should carry out basic work such as decorating. Minor jobs such as repairing broken windows can often be carried out by individual tenants. More sophisticated work, like the repair of heating systems, could sometimes be carried out by groups of tenants with the necessary skills more efficiently than by a council workforce. Similarly, tenants should have a say in designing major or minor improvements to their estates.

Thus there is a whole range of maintenance tasks which could be transferred to tenants. But it will not be easy to fix rates of payment for this transfer. Neither will it be easy – judging from our observations of Lambeth's Working Party on Tenants' Participation in Management – to come to a satisfactory arrangement with the unions, who are worried about the loss of jobs and about having as masters tenants as well as councillors.

Any transfer of responsibility to tenants will not be primarily to individual tenants but to a tenants' association or some similar form of organisation. As we have said, most council tenants in Stockwell do not play an active part in such organisations. It may be that this will change if they come to have real influence on tenants' life chances. However, there does not seem to have been much response to councils, such as Lambeth and Camden, who have formally requested tenants' ideas about ways they could be involved in management. It seems that what most tenants at present desire is not a greater stake in management but a more efficient and humane version of the present system, including more effective management with a local 'presence' and clearer rules more strictly enforced.

The success of participation in general will not depend upon formal structures such as committee meetings and general discussion but upon ways of giving tenants more say in the decisions which have a direct influence on their immediate environment.

Local management

The estate caretaker is a key representative of local housing management. The best caretakers manage to fill other roles as well as their routine responsibilities. Some of them may act as welfare workers keeping an eye on elderly and infirm tenants and sorting out minor disputes. They are vital mediators between the tenants and the providers of services such as refuse disposal, landscaping and building maintenance.

It seems wrong, therefore, that the status of a caretaker should be so low. Because of this, many are leaving under the harsh pressures of the job and new recruits are hard to come by. In the Stockwell area the GLC has ceased to employ resident caretakers on its estates, providing instead a substitute service of mobile personnel. These travel around their areas in small vans and are on the estate for only a small part of the time. At other periods they must be specially summoned by tenants, by telephone (if the tenant has one) or through special 'assistaphones' provided at key spots on the estate. Many tenants are critical of this system.

> 'We used to have a caretaker living in. Now you have to phone with a dictaphone and the caretaker comes round in a van with "GLC caretaker" written on it. The kids see it and clear off.'

> 'Things have declined on the estate since the LCC became the GLC and the GLC portering system changed. There used to be a link between the tenants and the GLC; now they are just cleaners and maintenance men.'

In our view, estates need to have resident caretakers. We recognise the difficulties, which are partly to do with their low status at present. They need to be given firmer backing by housing managers and, perhaps, perquisites such as specially improved dwellings. Caretakers in other services such as education can normally expect a small house with a garden, and it seems reasonable for estate caretakers to receive similar consideration.

Design of local authority housing

Our survey of housing estates suggested a number of lessons for the design of dwellings and the areas surrounding them. Most of these are relevant not only to new developments, but could also be built into existing estates. In general, the survey confirmed and elaborated many of the ideas embodied in the concept of 'defensible space'.[1] Vandalism and neglect seemed to be concentrated in those areas which were unfitted for informal supervision by residents, or which were so anonymous that residents felt no special responsibility for them. The diagrams illustrate our more detailed suggestions, which can be summarised as follows.

People's sense of anonymity seems to increase with the scale of council estates. Scale is not the same thing as size (Figure 17). A large estate can, if broken up into visually separate units, have a quite intimate scale. On the other hand, a small estate which is designed as a single entity can give an impression of great scale. One way of measuring the scale of an estate as it appears to residents is to count the number of dwellings visible from typical vantage points. We did this on the estates we studied and the results correlated closely with the measures of dissatisfaction mentioned at the beginning of this chapter.

At a more detailed level, the possibilities for natural supervision can be maximised by reducing the amount of 'public' space – which nobody feels responsible for – and increasing the extent of private and semi-private spaces. Most estates contain large

(1) Oscar Newman, *Defensible Space*.

156

Figure 17
**Satisfaction and
the scale and size of
estates**
Dissatisfaction
correlated with the
size of the estate. It
was also related to
'scale', that is, the
number of dwellings
visible from a typical
vantage point on the
estate.

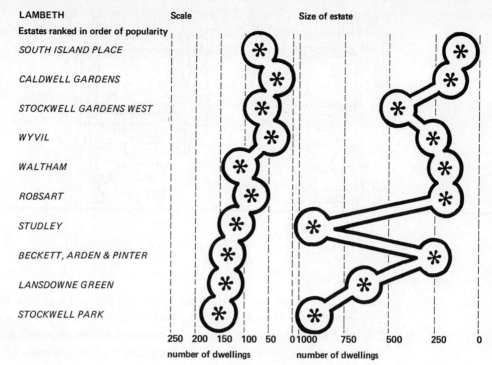

LAMBETH
Estates ranked in order of popularity

Scale

Size of estate

SOUTH ISLAND PLACE

CALDWELL GARDENS

STOCKWELL GARDENS WEST

WYVIL

WALTHAM

ROBSART

STUDLEY

BECKETT, ARDEN & PINTER

LANSDOWNE GREEN

STOCKWELL PARK

250 200 150 100 50   0 1000   750   500   250   0
number of dwellings   number of dwellings

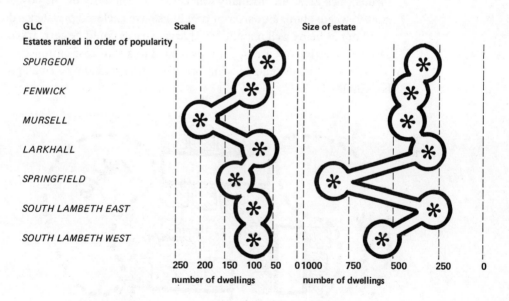

GLC
Estates ranked in order of popularity

Scale

Size of estate

SPURGEON

FENWICK

MURSELL

LARKHALL

SPRINGFIELD

SOUTH LAMBETH EAST

SOUTH LAMBETH WEST

250 200 150 100 50   0 1000   750   500   250   0
number of dwellings   number of dwellings

areas of 'landscaping' not used for any particular purpose and often dirty and neglected. Parts of them could be divided into small gardens for the ground floor flats. This has happened spontaneously in some areas where people have staked out their own plots by their front doors and planted them with flowers or even small shrubs; such areas are normally well cared for. Similarly on the post-war GLC estates, where about a quarter of dwellings have enclosed private gardens, these stand out as being well maintained. Larger spaces could be earmarked as small gardens or sitting out areas, perhaps related to a stair case entrance or other access point. These areas would be 'semi-private', being shared by a small group of households.

Private, semi-private, and public space.

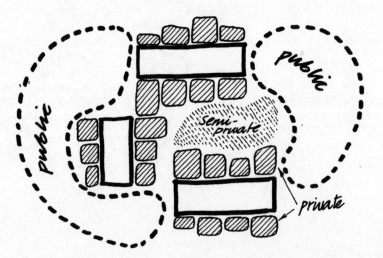

The most depressing characteristic of council estates is their deadening monotony. In general, new designs should take account of people's appreciation of variety and small scale. Existing estates should be enlivened, for example by putting in shops and nurseries, by giving private gardens to ground-floor tenants, or even by pulling down some old blocks to let in light and air.

*An old estate:
before and after.*

*Rehabilitation of old
estates could provide
gardens for ground
floor dwellings and
introduce new uses
such as playgroups.*

Access points are often a focus for vandalism and neglect. This happens most frequently when they lead into large numbers of dwellings so that they become over-used and anonymous. The number of dwellings accessible from each entry correlated with the extent of vandalism and dissatisfaction. Deck access schemes suffer especially in this way, since each entry point to the deck can theoretically give access to all dwellings opening onto the deck. They are also difficult to police, since they offer burglars and vandals a wide variety of potential escape routes. The local police were especially worried about this feature of the Stockwell Park deck access estate.

*Location of vandalism
in access areas.*

*The figures denote the
number of dwellings
accessible from a
single point of entry in
the blocks affected by
vandalism.*

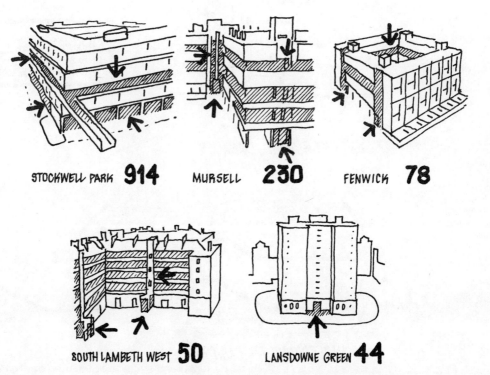

STOCKWELL PARK **914**   MURSELL **230**   FENWICK **78**

SOUTH LAMBETH WEST **50**   LANSDOWNE GREEN **44**

Many high-density estates have groups of garages in underground or lower level galleries. These are usually vulnerable to vandals, being almost invisible from the dwellings or from pedestrian routes. Often, the only protection to vehicles is a wire mesh gate which is easily penetrated by paint aerosols, blazing sticks or other missiles. Few motorists are willing to leave their vehicles in such places. On the Stockwell Park estate cars were normally left out on the roads or even on landscaped areas. On several other estates the grouped garages were completely unused and sealed off. The few estates where such garages were successful provide pointers to what should be done. At one such estate – South Island Place – the parking decks had a single entry point provided with a padlocked gate. Car owners

Garaging and parking.
The garaging and parking arrangements shown on the right hand side of the illustration are vulnerable to vandalism, whereas those on the left have been found workable.

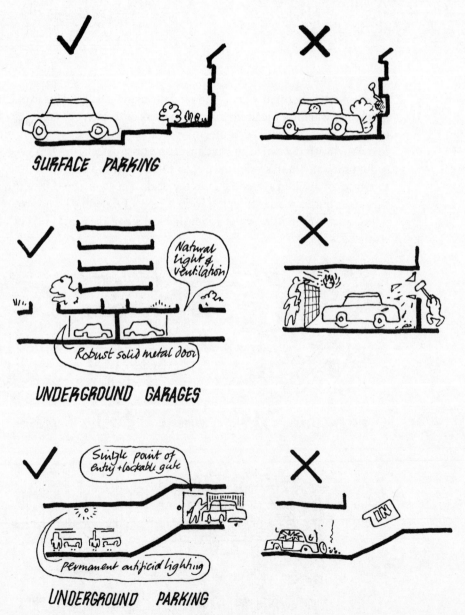

SURFACE PARKING

UNDERGROUND GARAGES

UNDERGROUND PARKING

had their own keys. Some of the garages at Stockwell Park were to be converted to this arrangement. On another estate the underground garages worked satisfactorily because they were fitted with individually-locked robust doors. All such areas should be well lit day and night and supervised by resident caretakers.

The measures outlined in the last few pages could go some way towards easing the problems found on inner city housing estates. We would not, however, wish to overestimate the results. There are limits to what can be achieved by sensitive management and design. Strategic measures are needed to relieve the overall pressure on inner city housing and enable it to respond to changing circumstances.

A role for town planning

The picture we have painted so far in this book must cast doubts on many of the traditional functions of the town planner. What scope is there for local planning in areas like Stockwell where the basic structure of land uses is unlikely to change over the foreseeable future? We can see the need for local plans in expansion areas on the edges of towns or cities, or in urban districts likely to experience major redevelopment. But there is little point in devoting scarce staff resources to such activities in places where there is no likelihood of new houses, parks, roads, shops or other major developments. In our experience, they result in nothing more than a charting of miscellaneous piecemeal decisions already made, with relatively few new proposals. Most of the local planning exercises in Lambeth fit this model.

There is a clear need, in a typical inner city borough, for some form of structure plan to crystallise the council's thinking on strategic issues such as population change, industrial development, or transport policy. Such a plan will be mainly concerned with management issues. It should provide a series of principles for the control of development and will need to be supplemented by fine-scale proposals and detailed plans for those few major developments likely to occur.

There does not seem to be room for any other kind of planning until one descends to the level of individual development sites, which will normally be small – perhaps a small group of houses, a disused church building, or a one acre clearance site. It was sites such as these which formed the subject of our multi-space action project, to be reported separately.

In this project, we identified a number of derelict sites for improvement, after learning from the household survey that many residents were concerned about such dereliction. We evolved proposals for improving these sites, in consultation with local residents. Some involved temporary uses, such as an adventure playground built upon a cleared area which was eventually intended to be laid out as part of a public open space. Others involved relatively minor works, such as the provision of a gate in the wall of a garden belonging to a government office, so that the garden could be used by patrons of an adjoining library. The total cost of the project was modest, some £20,000 for a total of six schemes.

Our experience showed why sites of this land are often left unused. The problems of implementation were out of all proportion to the task. Virtually every directorate of the council was involved at one stage or another, and a meeting to deal with minor landscaping works and a wall painting on one of the sites included no less than 12 people. The institutional barriers to innovation were formidable.

This suggested the need for a new kind of planning at the very local scale. If properly used, small sites and buildings could be a valuable community resource. But identifying them, devising appropriate uses and implementing these proposals can be a very tricky business. Carrying out this task would seem to be a more effective use of existing planning staff than much of their present work.

First, some kind of intelligence unit will be needed to detect such sites as they become available. At present, they emerge through the workings of individual council departments – or other agencies – with no single body being responsible for building up a comprehensive picture or deciding how they can be used. Finding new uses for them will involve an insight into the needs of different parts of the borough and close liaison with local community groups who really come into their own when developments of this kind are discussed. Finally, the implementation stage will usually require detailed negotiations with a plethora of bodies, since small-scale proposals involve proportionally more administrative processing than major development schemes.

We are thus proposing a new role for planning in districts like Stockwell. The planner needs to change his role from that of a 'policeman' or a promotor of large-scale projects to become an initiator and manager of small-scale urban change.

☐ To sum up, we have made the following proposals in this chapter:

1. Housing allocation and management should reduce high child densities where these are causing problems.
2. In inner areas the objective of seeking 'housing gain' should be dropped as an overriding principle for new housing schemes and rehabilitation.
3. To replace the private rented sector, a programme of social ownership should use different forms of agency and sponsorship, encouraging a more flexible provision and allocation of housing.
4. To improve the housing remaining in private tenancy 'fair rents' will need to rise. Controls will be required to ensure that improvements are carried out.
5. For similar reasons, public sector rents should also rise. To avoid hardship among poorer tenants, public and private, assistance with rents needs to be maintained at adequate levels and more effectively distributed.
6. New forms of tenure such as equity sharing should be developed by initiatives at both national and local level. There should be a switch from conventional fixed repayment to index-linked mortgages to help lower income groups become owner-occupiers and move out of the area.

162

7. Decisions on redevelopment or rehabilitation should be taken on a house-to-house basis. The resulting schemes will often combine rehabilitation with some redevelopment.

8. While the general aim of allocation policy should be to encourage dispersal of ethnic groups, individual choices should be respected even if they lead to concentration.

9. The scope of tenants' participation in housing management should be established by a series of experiments involving various degrees of delegation and responsibility.

10. The quality of housing management on estates needs to be improved. To this end caretakers, who need to be resident, should receive better housing and increased status.

11. The design of buildings and layouts should take account of the 'defensible space' concept, particularly in terms of access ways, grouped garages and open public areas.

12. Housing design and layout should avoid high density. For any level of density there is a strong link between the level of investment and the cost of management. Since investment in housing is likely to continue to be low in future, new schemes should be designed more simply so as to reduce the demands on maintenance.

13. New designs should recognise people's preference for variety and small scale. Cost yardstick arrangements and regulations inhibiting variety should be amended. Existing estates should be enlivened, for example by putting in shops and nurseries, by giving private gardens to ground floor tenants, or even by pulling down some old blocks to let in light and air.

14. Town planning in inner areas needs to shift its emphasis towards encouraging and managing small-scale urban change by public and private initiative and develop more sensitive ways of managing urban renewal, conservation and minor improvements. Planning and other staff should be redeployed to undertake this work ◻

9 The delivery of welfare

If implemented, the policies just suggested on housing and planning, together with those on jobs and deprivation put forward in earlier chapters, will go a long way to easing the problems of people in inner areas like Stockwell. It is however clear that, quite apart from such measures as these, local services need to be organised in ways that will help residents more effectively. There are two reasons why this is particularly important at present. The first is the financial constraints on public spending; since services cannot be increased and may even be reduced, it is all the more essential to see that they are used effectively. The second reason is that, as shown in Chapter 3, a large minority of inner city residents need help and support.

There is ample evidence, from our own research as from elsewhere, that many do not receive the help for which they are eligible.[1] It seems likely that most of those shown in Chapter 3 as being below the 'poverty line' would have been eligible for the various relevant forms of financial support. Yet, among these households, 37 per cent of those where the head was not working were not receiving supplementary benefit. Among those of the same poor households who were council tenants, 40 per cent were not receiving rent rebates. Of those who were in privately-rented unfurnished housing, 83 per cent were not receiving rent allowances. Among all poor households, only 18 per cent were receiving rate rebates. These examples are all of financial help but, as we illustrate later, local people eligible for other kinds of support, for example with home helps, services for the disabled, advice on housing or on family planning, found difficulty in getting it.

How, then, can local services be more effectively delivered?[2] This was our central question. We should make clear that, in trying to answer it, we did not feel able to examine the much wider issue of the adequacy of existing services in terms of resources, manpower, quality of staff and so on.

We extended our perspective beyond local authority services and considered also those provided by other bodies. But we narrowed our focus by studying only the delivery of services to local residents as individual consumers or 'clients'. We therefore covered only those services whose effectiveness depended upon local people being able to make direct and personal contact.

This meant that we excluded, for example, environmental services such as refuse collection and street cleaning. It is true, as we showed in Chapter 2, that these

---

(1) Other studies include Molly Meacher, *Rate Rebates: a Study of the Effectiveness of Means Tests* and T. Lewis, *The Haringey Rent Allowances Project: Second Report*, Department of the Environment, 1975.

(2) Our work on this subject is reported in detail in Inner Area Study Lambeth, *Interim Report on Local Services* (IAS/LA/3), *Local Services: Consumers Sample (IAS/LA/9)*, and *Multi-Service Project: Report of the Working Party* (IAS/LA/14).

particular services are a source of dissatisfaction among local people. But a refuse collection or street cleaning service is either adequate and efficient or it is not; as long as it is, the detailed form of organisation is of no great interest to the residents. They rarely need to be in personal contact with the workers in such a service, as for example they sometimes might with a health visitor, a social worker or someone dealing with their social security payments.

Thus we concentrated on what might be termed 'personal', 'family' or 'community' services. Within this framework, we still had to narrow our focus. We could not, for instance, examine the delivery of the services provided by every general practitioner in the study area. Nor could we study the delivery of hospital services or education (though we tried, unsuccessfully, to mount a separate study of the role of education and, in looking at local services, we included some study of the education welfare service provided by the Inner London Education Authority).

Methods of study

We examined the services at two levels. We collected information about the location and boundaries of a fairly wide range; and we looked more closely at the organisation of some that seemed particularly crucial – income maintenance, community health and welfare.

In addition, we collected survey information from two other sources. First, we sought the views of people working in the services. We saw over 80 officers employed in local services and we had formal and informal meetings with fieldworkers and with representatives of local community groups such as Neighbourhood Councils.

We supplemented these personal contacts with postal questionnaires circulated to certain workers operating in the study area. These included social workers, community workers and home help organisers (Lambeth Directorate of Social Services), health visitors (at that time in Lambeth's Directorate of Health Services but, after the reorganisation of the National Health Service in April 1974, employed by the new St. Thomas' Health District) and education welfare workers (Inner London Education Authority). They were asked about their experience of – and their views about – other workers and services they had contacted on behalf of clients, and their suggestions for improving the co-ordination of services.

Our second main source of opinions was the potential users of services themselves. We selected, from the sample interviewed in the main household survey in Stockwell, two categories of people particularly likely to need services – those in households containing old people or children under five. We deliberately biased the selection towards households identified as poor or deprived, and re-interviewed 23 old-person households and 30 with children under five. People were asked about three things: their knowledge of the services relevant to their needs; their satisfaction with the accessibility of services they had sought or used; and their experiences of any failure or success of services.

Services and their areas

We plotted the location of the local bases of a number of services and mapped their boundaries, which usually defined where residents had to go for help. Changes in the location of offices and in boundaries are common; we describe things as they were on 1 April 1974.

For national insurance contributory benefits three offices of the Department of Health and Social Security (DHSS) served Stockwell. Each office covered one or more postal district. One of the three was inside the study area. A second was about two miles away in Balham, and the third also about two miles away on the far side of Battersea Park.

For supplementary benefits most of the study area was served by yet another DHSS office at the Oval to the north-east of – and just outside – the study area.[1] The remaining south-west corner of the study area was served, again for supplementary benefit only, by the DHSS office in Clapham High Road, south of the study area.

The Department of Employment was also involved with the payment of money – unemployment benefit, and supplementary benefit when paid as an addition. Young people similarly used the ILEA youth employment 'careers offices' to get their benefits. The local Department of Employment office covering most of the study area was just south of it. The south-west corner of the study area was covered by an office in Battersea. The two Inner London Education Authority (ILEA) youth employment 'careers offices' serving Stockwell were the 'Brixton office' (on Brixton Hill) for those living in the south of the study area, and the 'Elephant and Vauxhall office', on the west side of the Wandsworth Road and just outside the area, for those in the north.

Lambeth's Directorate of Housing, together with its Housing Advice Centre and Lettings Office, was in the Town Hall complex, just to the south-east of the study area and easily accessible to at least half of it. Like the rent officer service and the Rent Tribunal (which were both just south of the study area), these were centralised services covering all of Lambeth but the management of public housing was locally run. The GLC's district housing office was outside and north of the study area, and there were two area offices within it each serving a large estate. There were five Lambeth area housing management offices serving the whole borough, of which four served parts of the study area; only one of the four was within it. Each office covered a specified area, but the areas were subject to change as tenant numbers rose

(1) This was one of the few remaining offices dealing only with supplementary benefit. Since 1966 government policy has been to combine national insurance and the Supplementary Benefits Commission (SBC) in one building. As part of implementing this policy, the office near the Oval was to be closed, its work being transferred to combined offices organised on the basis of postal districts.

or fell through new building or clearance. The Directorate's housing welfare service (also responsible for homeless families) was based at the Town Hall but, as far as staff shortages allowed, individual housing welfare officers worked to the area management districts.

The National Health Service is organised into health districts within Area Health Authorities. The St. Thomas' Health District covers part of Wandsworth and the half of Lambeth which includes the study area. Three child health centres served the study area, two inside it and one outside.

Lambeth's Directorate of Social Services had its headquarters in the study area, and a number of its services, such as residential care and housing liaison, were administered centrally. Social work services, and others such as home helps and community work, were organised on an area basis. Two of the eight area offices covering Lambeth were located in the study area. One, based at the Directorate's central offices, covered all but the south-west corner. The other office was in the south-western part of Stockwell.

The Divisional Office of the ILEA, covering the whole of Lambeth, was located just south of the study area. This was also the base from which some of the Division's education welfare officers worked, and there was an educational welfare section at the Divisional Office responsible for part of the study area. There was also a branch education welfare office north of the Oval and the workers from this covered the remainder of the study area and beyond.

There was one probation office in Stockwell. Though just outside the boundary of the area it served, it covered most of the study area. Probation areas were based on ward boundaries and two other offices outside the study area served the rest of it. A fourth office outside the study area was responsible for the after care of offenders and the welfare of prisoners' relatives for the whole of the borough.

Some needs are met by voluntary organisations. The large organisations such as Lambeth Old People's Welfare Association (LOPWA), All Lambeth Voluntary Action Services (ALVAS), the Lambeth Association for the Disabled (LAD) and the Women's Royal Voluntary Service (WRVS) are borough-wide. The smaller bodies usually worked to a local 'catchment area'. The WRVS office was near the study area, LOPWA's just south of it, and LAD's and ALVAS's inside it. These last three were all in premises of the Directorate of Social Services.

The Borough Information Bureau and Housing Advisory Service were both based in the Town Hall complex. There was also an information service at the office of the Social Services area team in the south-west part of the study area, and an enquiry office in the central premises of the Directorate of Social Services. One neighbourhood council had opened a Saturday morning information service in a local library, and another had experimented with an information stall in a busy street. Other information centres serving Stockwell but outside it were the Citizen's Advice Bureau (CAB) in Kennington Road (about half a mile north of the study area boundary); the Brixton Advice Centre (voluntary), the Consumers' Advice Centre and the Planning Advice Centre (both Lambeth Council). A Law Centre (funded by Lambeth Council) opened after April 1974.

Finally, the police. There was one police station in the study area, but this covered only part of Stockwell, as did two other stations. All were in the Metropolitan Police 'L' Division, covering the whole of Lambeth. In the course of the study, two local 'home beat' policemen had been reintroduced in part of the study area, but the police would not, for reasons of 'security', tell us the boundaries of their 'beats'. The police Community Liaison Officer, responsible for relationships with all young people in the Division, was based at Brixton Police Station.

Figure 18
Local boundaries
The local boundaries adopted by various agencies bore no relationship to each other.

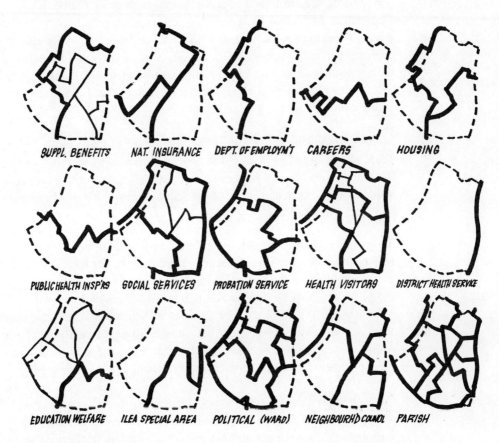

SUPPL. BENEFITS   NAT. INSURANCE   DEPT. OF EMPLOYM'T   CAREERS   HOUSING

PUBLIC HEALTH INSP'RS   SOCIAL SERVICES   PROBATION SERVICE   HEALTH VISITORS   DISTRICT HEALTH SERVICE

EDUCATION WELFARE   ILEA SPECIAL AREA   POLITICAL (WARD)   NEIGHBOURH'D COUNCIL   PARISH

Boundary confusion

The boundaries of areas and sub-areas of most of these services are shown in Figure 18. Some further boundaries relevant to services have been added to those already mentioned. These are the ward boundaries, the traditional ecclesiastical parishes, the neighbourhood councils and the ILEA 'special area'.

The maps show that, though some services shared common boundaries at some points – major roads, the railway line in the south and the boundary of the borough itself in the west– the general pattern was confused. No two services shared identical boundaries for areas or sub-areas.

Does this lack of correspondence matter? We think it does, both to consumers, for whom the services are presumably ultimately intended, and for workers in the services trying to help their clients. The difficulties for the consumer are mainly because the area in which a person lives also, for most services, determines the office to which he needs to go. There are exceptions. Sometimes, as with libraries, there is no defined area limiting the use of a particular centre to local residents. With one or two services, the prescribed boundaries may in practice not be rigidly enforced. The Department of Employment, for instance, does not require people to use the office serving the area they live in if they find it more convenient to go elsewhere. Likewise, a mother can take her child to the child health centre most convenient for her, though because the centre-based health visitors themselves make regular home visits within fixed geographical areas, mothers are encouraged to use the same centre to ensure continuity of care.

More commonly there are firm rules about which office or centre one has to go to. There were in April 1974, about 30 centres serving the Stockwell study area where the caller, if he were to avoid an unnecessary journey, would have needed to know in advance the particular office of the relevant service within whose prescribed boundaries he lived.

To give an extreme example, there were no fewer than nine offices with responsibility for some social security payments. In our interviews with consumers we were told of the difficulties people had met in finding their way to the right one out of the nine. Most people wanting benefits sensibly began by trying the DHSS office nearest to their home. For those in the south-east of the study area this was in Brixton; but visitors discovered that, though it was the right office for people wanting or enquiring about sickness benefit, it was the wrong one for unemployment benefit or supplementary benefit.

One young family seeking supplementary benefit went to the Brixton DHSS office, which was within easy walking distance of their home, but found after the inevitable waiting that 'for some reason they wouldn't entertain us there'. They were referred to the office near the Oval, a bus ride away. All those re-interviewed who had not been in touch with social security offices were asked which one they would go to if they needed benefits. They gave answers which were varied and usually incorrect, as in the examples quoted here:

'I'd go to the Town Hall' (for supplementary benefit).

'I'd go to the social security at Brixton' (for unemployment).

'There's an office in Battersea and one in Tooting. I'm used to the one in Balham so I'd probably try that one first' (for unemployment benefit).

'I'd go to the same place as the Labour Exchange' (for sickness benefit).

170

As we have said, social security provides but one example, if perhaps the most extreme. It is clear that the confusion over boundaries makes things difficult for people who might use them. There is also confusion among the workers. It is sometimes difficult for workers, particularly new ones, to know where to refer their clients for services they need. The confusion can also act as a barrier to communication between workers in different services. Even for the most experienced and knowledgeable workers, it is time-consuming to maintain contacts with several offices and workers covering different geographical areas overlapping their own. This uses time which could be more profitably spent in other work for their clients, and thus has a further detrimental effect on consumers themselves.

In some ways it is more difficult for the worker than for the consumer. This is because the worker acting on behalf of his client may need to know of boundaries that the consumer does not. For example, to get help from the Supplementary Benefits Commission the client needs to know the correct office. He then either goes to it or is visited at home by a worker from it. The social worker, if she is to be effective in helping a client, may need to have direct contact with the officer who knows the particular client. This will be easier if she knows not just the boundaries but also the sub-area in which the client lives and which relevant SBC officer is responsible. Where her own working area does not match that of the SBC officer (which it usually does not) she will, of course, need to know more than one.

To sum up so far, the complexity of boundaries affects the delivery of services in two crucial ways. First, it makes it difficult for the consumer to get the service he needs. Secondly, it impedes contact between workers in different services trying to act on behalf of their clients.

Difficulties of co-ordination

Boundary confusion is not the only cause of difficulty. Residents are often confused about what the different services do, and as a result they often do not know where to begin. When we re-interviewed people, they sometimes thought, despite our careful explanations, that the interviewer was herself 'from the welfare'. One elderly woman reeled off the names of a range of 'nice ladies' – and one 'nice man' – who had been to see her. She had no idea where they were all from, though they were, she thought, something to do with 'the welfare' or the Town Hall.

Such confusion is understandable. On the face of it, for example, one might imagine that a person called a 'rent officer' would be the right person to go to if one wanted to enquire about rent allowances or if one was in arrears with one's rent. In practice, of course, the rent officer is concerned only with fixing the levels of 'fair rents'. Though his staff would no doubt politely refer an enquirer to Lambeth's Housing Advice Centre or to the appropriate local housing office, the caller's visit would have been a wasted one.

We were given more complex examples. One disabled old woman wanted a wheel-chair:

> 'I didn't know how to get a chair. The people at the club said the Town Hall. My home help went there. They sent her to Ferndale Road (LOPWA) which sent her to somewhere else. My husband 'phoned Social Services, who put him on to the Red Cross. They charged a rental of 25p per week but this was too expensive so my husband refused. Then we got this social worker round the corner who got this "therapist" to come from Social Services.'

A younger woman, with interrelated difficulties of the kind discussed in Chapter 3, had gone to the Social Services office about what she thought was her main problem – housing. Her basic problems were mainly financial and marital. But the problem, as she presented it to Social Services, was judged by them not within their responsibilities. The interviewer reported:

> During her efforts to get some attention to her plight over the past four years, she has visited Blue Star House (Social Services) three times to see if a social worker would help. No one ever called on her. Friends advised her to go the Probation Office who in turn sent her to the WRVS clothing depot, where – after a long walk – she was most upset at being made to sign a chit for a pair of boy's trousers.

This illustrates the problem of what might be called 'diagnosis', which is obviously linked to the present complexity and poor co-ordination of services. The woman who took what she saw as a housing problem to Social Services may just have had the bad luck to see the wrong worker each time. But in general it is clear that even those reaching one of the services may still not get through to the particular service they need. When workers, in all services, decide that the need or problem – as diagnosed and presented by the client – is not their responsibility, they often seem to fail to pick up other needs and problems for which their or other services are required. As things are at present, even where they do see the need for help beyond the limits of their own responsibility, this may involve – for the worker, the client or both – the difficult task of getting at the other service or services.

Some workers in the services may have been relatively unaware of this problem of 'diagnosis', but most certainly recognised the general difficulties of co-ordinating their work with that of colleagues in other sections or departments. It was clear from the postal survey among workers that they needed to contact others fairly often, and also that this was not always easy.

The fieldworkers were asked about the 'accessibility of other offices and workers' and how 'satisfactory' they found the arrangements for contacting them. One worker pointed out the biggest difficulties:

> 'Unless you know your way around it's very difficult to get in contact with the exact person you want. This is especially so with large establishments like the DHSS, electricity board and housing departments.'

The difficulties were intensified by the high turnover of staff in most agencies.[1] We ourselves found in the course of the study that often workers we had got to know – the Social Services' community worker, a senior social worker, a DHSS manager, a housing official – had moved on. Among Social Services' workers who replied to our questionnaire, as many as two-thirds had been in their present job for a year or less. The workers themselves explained that this constant coming and going made it all the more difficult for them to 'know their way around'. It takes time to build up a knowledge of the boundaries of other services and of the roles of workers within them. It takes time to build up personal contacts. When a worker moves, his or her own 'investment' of knowledge and contacts is lost to the area – the replacement person has largely to start from scratch – and life is made more difficult for all those other workers who in their turn are without one of their 'contacts'.

The workers' ideas for improvement gave further evidence of what was wrong with the existing system. The commonest suggestion was to improve contacts with other workers by discussions with, and visits to, other agencies. The notion of bringing workers together under one roof was also put forward. People realised, of course, that all agencies could not be together locally in the same building, but they were asked to suggest those they thought most crucial. Those in Social Services gave priority to social security (SBC/DHSS) and to housing. Health visitors and education welfare workers laid less stress on income support; their priorities were social workers and, secondly, other health workers. This suggests that, along with easy access to those dealing with debts in the electricity and gas boards, the biggest need was for improved day-to-day contacts between Social Services, community health, supplementary benefits, housing and education welfare.

The workers made other suggestions indicating their current problems. The difficulty of knowing about and making effective contact with other departments and services was constantly emphasised, confirming our strong impression from our initial interviews with administrators and organisers. The gaps were evidently as wide between departments, even between sections of one department, within Lambeth's own services as between those and others. The workers' suggestions included: organisation charts of agencies and departments, job descriptions of the workers in them, improved telephone and reception services, better circulation of information, up-to-date lists of names and telephone numbers (with extensions) and more liaison officers.

Thus the evidence from workers and clients alike confirmed that, if services could in some way be co-ordinated more effectively, this would make better use of the workers and, most important of all, would ensure a better service to the public. To conclude this chapter, we discuss various ideas about how this might be done. The discussion includes several proposals that we have already tried to implement within the framework of the Stockwell study.

(1) One likely reason for the high turnover was that this was in a period of rapid growth, particularly in local authority Social Service departments. It was our impression that an additional reason, in all services, was the stress of working in the inner city together with the problem of finding suitable housing there.

Can boundaries be rationalised?

Our first proposal is that more should be done to co-ordinate the boundaries of different services. The need is particularly urgent in inner areas like Stockwell with special problems and an unusually complex pattern of services.

The present location of service centres and the boundaries within which they work arise from decisions made at different points in time. When decisions are made about service centres and boundaries, those responsible do not always give primary consideration to convenience for the consumer, seeing it as only one of a number of factors to be taken into account. Other criteria include the premises available, the size of the population it is thought reasonable to serve, the type of service provided and the type of need to be met. Over time, as the needs or the service change, the location and boundaries of a particular service may likewise have to be changed. Because services change at different times, and have to meet specific needs at different times, it is not easy, and in practice not common, for those organising services to take into account how their own boundaries will relate to those of others.

Since boundaries have been created by separate departments and agencies at different times to meet what were then seen as their own specific needs, they are inevitably unrelated. There is no external pressure to ensure that the boundaries of any one department or agency are compatible with those of others. We think this external pressure is essential; it could be provided by a Location and Boundaries Committee.

This would be a Standing Committee of the local authority (for example, Lambeth) but arrangements would be made for other public services, such as the health district, the DHSS, the police and, in London, the GLC and ILEA, to be represented. The purpose would be to move towards common boundaries and towards an orderly pattern of location for offices, clinics and other local bases. An obligation would probably need to be placed on all public authorities to notify the Committee of any proposed changes affecting the local authority's area. In its turn, the Committee would have an obligation to seek the views of voluntary organisations, community groups and the public at large on any proposed changes. We hope that some local authorities will be willing to set up such committees on an experimental basis. They would need the full backing of the council and of central Government, which would have to put pressure on its own services to collaborate. If all went well, the committees would be recommended to all local authorities.

We have no illusions about the difficulty. Through the working party of representatives of various services convened in the so-called 'multi-service project' (discussed more fully later), we tried to move towards more co-ordinated boundaries at the local scale. In exploring the reasons for existing variations and the possibilities of realignment, the working party faced the familiar difficulties already mentioned and had to conclude that there was no immediate hope of advance. In particular there was no chance of persuading the DHSS to change its boundaries either for social security (which, in line with its national policy, were in process of being related to postal districts) or for health (the new health districts, and their sub-areas, having been only recently created). It seemed that any co-ordination in the foreseeable future would probably have to be confined to Lambeth's own directorates and ILEA's education welfare service. The working party acknowledged that progress would be difficult and slow without some outside pressure, such as the proposed Location and Boundaries Committee.

Bringing workers together

More needs to be done to improve liaison between workers so as to ensure that they do not ignore, duplicate or, even worse, undermine each other's work. The objective, clearly, is for them to work co-operatively in the interests of clients, each making their own special contribution.

We have just mentioned the Stockwell 'multi-service project'; though one of its purposes was to consider boundary realignment, starting from the 'bottom' end instead of the 'top', the main objectives were to examine the possibilities of co-ordination and in particular to see whether there might be a case for a local 'multi-service centre'. The project concentrated on only a part of the physical area of the Stockwell study: the south-eastern sector, covering about half a square mile and with a population of about 15,000. This area was convenient for the Inner Area Study office, where meetings were held, and it did not cut across any major boundaries, for example between one Social Services area team and another. The population size was something like that suggested by a 'desk study' that we had undertaken to explore a possible basis for a future reorganisation of services within common boundaries.[1]

The multi-service project operated mainly through a working party of senior officers representing the basic personal or community services whose collaboration seemed most urgent.[2] The project also involved a series of meetings of fieldworkers from the same services. At the first meeting, convened to explain the purpose of the project and seek workers' views, came the suggestion that regular meetings would be useful. Although this meant workers regularly giving up their lunch hours, they enthusiastically supported the meetings. They were of direct value to the project in that various ideas were put forward by the fieldworkers, for example on joint training, which were incorporated into the report and put to the relevant agencies for action.

(1) This desk study suggested a borough-wide network of 'basic centres' (incorporating a health clinic, a Social Services area team and representatives of most other services), each serving a population of about 18,000.

(2) The members were senior officers from Lambeth's Social Services, Lambeth's Housing, St. Thomas' Health District, the Supplementary Benefits Commission and ILEA Education Welfare – together with representatives from Lambeth's Management Services and its Chief Executive's Office, and of the Inner Area Study team, acting as convenors. For fuller details, see Inner Area Study Lambeth, *Multi-Service Project: Report of the Working Party* (IAS/LA/14).

The meetings were also of value to the fieldworkers themselves. Some initial hostility was expressed, with people showing that they felt that those in other services were at fault. But the workers said at the end that they had learnt a good deal about the operation of services other than their own and were able to work more effectively as a result. Meeting other workers face to face, instead of 'just a voice on the telephone' as one put it, had facilitated liaison. In ways like these, the meetings illustrated yet again the initial difficulties and the need for some measures to promote better co-ordination.

Out of this multi-service project, and incorporated in its report, came a number of minor but nevertheless useful proposals. One was that 'multi-service manuals' should be produced for local areas. These would be local guides giving information about the functions and responsibilities of other agencies; such guides would enable workers to know what other services could and could not do, and how they operated. There was also a need for the kind of detailed multi-service directory referred to earlier, giving the names, telephone numbers and extensions of workers; because of staff turnover, this would need to be revised more often than the manual. Such manuals and directories would be produced by one service on behalf of all, with the others contributing their own material to a standard format.

Another suggestion was for forms of training, both at the induction stage and in-service, which included some multi-service element at the local level, again so that workers would know more about other services. It was specifically suggested that, as part of this training, workers should spend some time working in the local offices of other agencies than their own; this would both introduce them to local colleagues and enable them to learn about the resources and constraints of those with whom they needed to co-operate.

Helpful though these proposals are, they are not enough. Hence our own suggestions, supported by the working party, to bring workers closer together at the local level in their day-to-day work. This would mean creating a multi-service team of workers from different services. At a minimum the services represented would include community health, Social Services, housing, supplementary benefits and education welfare, though in the longer term it would be extended to include others. Workers from the various services would meet regularly so as to keep in touch with other services and promote liaison.

An even better arrangement would be for such a multi-service team to be based in a community service centre, where workers from the different services would be in frequent contact with each other and where the most important services would be made available, though not necessarily all on a full-time basis, to people living locally. Liaison between workers would be improved through informal contacts in the common room, over coffee and the like, and through more formal discussions.

This is obviously a difficult period in which to propose building new centres. But it seemed, from our investigations as part of the project, that it would be perfectly possible for services to make immediate progress by co-operating in the joint use of existing premises. This would indeed have advantages because it would be more flexible.

In the autumn of 1976 discussions were taking place about continuing with the multi-service project and creating a multi-service centre. Lambeth Council had taken over responsibility for the project from the Study Team, and was seeking funds to continue with it, including the capital resources which would allow the adaptation of a suitably-placed existing building to serve as an experimental centre.

Access from below

Our final proposal concerns information services. It is virtually impossible for the consumer to find his way about in the present maze except on the basis of trial and error. There are, as already mentioned, a number of information centres in or near the study area. Yet, on the evidence of our household survey, these have not done much to help the considerable numbers of residents who are ignorant about all kinds of services – rate and rent rebates, housing advice, social services, personal and environmental health services. Lambeth's Housing Advice Centre provides an example. It was one of the first, and most widely publicised, remains one of the best and is obviously extremely busy. Yet when in the household survey we asked people who were 'seriously thinking of moving' whether they had used the Centre, although 40 per cent had been to it, 26 per cent said they had not even heard of it.

What lessons can be learned from the experience of such advice centres? We made a brief study of the records of the Housing Advice Centre itself, examining the records of about 1000 personal calls and nearly 200 telephone enquiries to the Housing Advice Centre during a two-week period in November 1973.[1]

The analysis showed that, excluding referrals by other Lambeth Departments and other official bodies, the most common reason given for going to the Housing Advice Centre was that the enquirer had noticed it as he or she had passed: 'I saw it was there when I was round that way'; 'I noticed it once when I was going by on a bus'. The next most common reason was the personal recommendation of friends or relatives.

When we plotted the addresses of enquirers we found that they were concentrated among people living within about a half a mile radius or living on a main bus route that passed the door. There were in consequence few enquiries from people living in the extreme north of Lambeth. We had also noted from our household survey that more people living in the eastern half of Stockwell – that is, nearer the Town Hall complex – had heard about the Centre than those living in the western, and further-off, half.

(1) We made a similar study, in February and March 1974, of the records of the recently-opened Citizens' Advice Centre in Kennington Road. The findings were broadly consistent.

The conclusion we draw is that, although a conspicuous and well-placed centre of this kind has advantages in attracting members of the public, it cannot ensure that those most in need will use it. A well-located centre will not necessarily be easily accessible to those most in need nor necessarily in a position where they will notice its existence.

Thus in our view information needs to be made accessible to people at the most local level. Our own suggestion for meeting this need is through a series of localised referral points that we have called 'local information posts' (LIPs). The basic idea is that a local resident, working at home on a part-time basis, would provide an accessible service, usually giving neighbours elementary information about where to go and how to get the help they need, but sometimes even sorting out the problem on the spot. This worker could be a housewife or a retired person, who would be provided with a telephone and given some modest payment. He or she would have an initial training on the structure of services, sources of information and methods for dealing with inquirers, and would be backed up by appropriate directories and professional support.

We have in fact implemented this proposal in another action project within the Lambeth Inner Area Study. Our suggestion, after initial discussion, was that the training should be provided by the Citizens' Advice Bureau, who would employ the LIP worker and provide a back-up worker to assist with inquiries and help in the evaluation of the project.

Our original proposal was for ten LIP workers to be appointed to work in the study area, backed by one CAB worker. Because of doubts about the proposal on the part of Lambeth, the number of LIP workers was reduced to two and the start of the project delayed; by the autumn of 1976, the two workers had been in post for less than a year. Since one would expect such a service to take much longer to become firmly established, and since the salary of the CAB 'back-up worker', along with CAB overheads, were supporting only two workers instead of the proposed ten, the cost per inquiry was high – over £20. In the view of the Department of the Environment, the scheme was too expensive to justify its continuance or wider application. Lambeth continued to support the project for a limited period, but when this book went to press it looked as if the experiment would be discontinued.

If this happens, the decision will in our view have been wrong. Had there been ten workers, as proposed, instead of two, the CAB costs per LIP worker, and per inquiry, would obviously have been much lower. Had the experiment been allowed to continue for longer, more local people would have learned about it and the flow of inquiries probably increased. Of course, our proposal may have been wrong in detail. For instance, the LIP workers were employed for set hours totalling ten a week, at £1 an hour. Perhaps we over-estimated the likely level of demand for their services and a smaller fee, together with the free telephone, would have been adequate pay for them to be 'on call' to neighbours at reasonable times. If the LIP workers' input were reduced in this way, then one back-up worker might well be able to support 20 or 30, and the costs per inquiry would be lower still.

Certainly the project showed that there were valuable untapped resources within the community; the LIP workers proved extremely good at their job. Thus we showed both that there was a need to be met – well over a hundred inquiries were dealt with over a six-month period – and that local people could be found to meet it. We still believe that the proposal deserves a reasonable trial, and we hope it, and other alternative forms of localised and community-based advice, will be tested out in future.

This chapter has made it clear that a better 'delivery' at the most local level of all – on people's own doorsteps, as it were – is needed if services are to do their job effectively. People often need the help of someone they know and trust to put them in touch. This link is almost wholly lacking at present: in general authority has so far proved reluctant to encourage or support such access from below.

We hope, therefore, that a variety of schemes for localising information and referral will be tested experimentally. Many of the other proposals in this chapter depend, ultimately, on an effective form of two-way diffusion, which will facilitate the flow of information in the reverse direction, feeding back consumers' views about what is needed and what is going wrong.

☐ In considering how to improve the delivery of welfare, we have not come down in favour of mini-town halls, as usually conceived. In authorities of Lambeth's size, there seems to us to be no advantage in devolving administration, policy-making or political power to a very local level. To try to do this would, in the London context, be returning to something like the scale of local government before its reorganisation in 1965. As we explain in the next chapter, we put the emphasis instead on the functional approach, proposing 'task force' teams to help with the problems that arise in localities affected by immediate programmes such as Housing Action Areas.

We have in this chapter made the following proposals to help bring about improved accessibility and delivery of services, and thus make better use of all available resources:

1. Location and Boundaries Committees (initially on an experimental basis) should be set up to rationalise the local areas of local and central government services.
2. Multi-service teams should be created to improve links between workers in different services, and between those workers and their clients.
3. Multi-service centres should be established; these would be the bases for multi-service teams, offering some services and providing advice about others.
4. Localised information channels are needed to improve access from the potential consumers of services to those who seek to offer them ☐

10 From study to action

We have reached the point in the book where we start drawing together the various threads of the study. Before we summarise our conclusions and try to show their relationship to each other, we need to do two things. The first is to discuss the role of studies of the kind we undertook in Stockwell. The second is to discuss some of the problems to be overcome in carrying out policy proposals. These are the subject of this penultimate chapter.

How useful has our study been in explaining the problems and identifying policy options? What in future could be the value of local studies of this kind? How can they help shape policy? Our answers, of course, must be both personal and provisional.

Our reaction to the terms of reference and the consequent evolution of our work programme has been described in Chapter 1. We were first commissioned to define a study area and produce a work programme.[1] The Department of the Environment, rightly in our view, did not impose any common work pattern on the three inner area studies, which have developed very differently in terms of method, subject matter and work style. At the time we write this, no systematic comparison of findings had been undertaken. It is, however, already clear that there is a significant correspondence between many of the policy recommendations. At the same time, each of the three studies has been able to make its distinctive contribution and in this way achieve a broader coverage.

The Department's approach for these studies was to set out brief and somewhat general terms of reference, and request a statement from the consultants describing their approach to the work and making detailed proposals for its first phase. Perhaps it would have been better if a sharper distinction had been made between two kinds of task. The first would involve analysis in depth of key problems. Why, for instance, does unemployment co-exist with labour shortage in the inner city? The answers to this sort of question would lead to a better understanding of the problem and hence indications of possible policy options. The second kind of task would be to suggest answers to clear policy alternatives already apparent. This applies, above all, to priorities and to decisions already in the pipeline.

It is vital for researchers to maintain a dialogue with those who will take decisions in the light of their findings. In this study the intention was that this need would be met by the Steering Committee, representative of the relevant institutions, and meeting regularly.[2] We reported progress to it and, as each of our studies and action

(1) Inner Area Study Lambeth, *Project Report* (IAS/LA/1).

(2) The Steering Committee met about three times a year.

projects was completed, submitted our recommendations with the aim of influencing current policies.

As well as reporting to the Steering Committee we also sought to provide a wider discussion of our work by holding three seminars. The last of these in January 1976 considered in draft form the findings and recommendations set down in the next chapter.[1] The main purpose of this seminar was to explore with those in key political and administrative positions, the likely relevance of the conclusions for Inner London as a whole.

Stockwell had been selected as a test bed, and most of our work was confined to this area of some 50,000 people. Only a limited amount of work could be undertaken, because of the resources and time given to us, to establish the relevance of our conclusions to Inner London containing nearly three million people. So we attached great importance to this seminar. In the event, both members and officers of virtually all Inner London boroughs considered that the main problems had been correctly identified. There were some exceptions, but most participants also broadly supported our recommendations. We discovered, to our astonishment, that this was the first time that the representatives of Inner London, as apart from Greater London, had met alone specifically to discuss its problems.

Gaps in the work

Our work on most studies and action projects finished in April 1976. Inevitably some gaps were left in the overall pattern and some work must be regarded as incomplete. Readers will, no doubt, spot other gaps, but in our view there were two kinds of omission. The first kind relates to work we sought to do but failed to convince the Steering Committee to authorise. The second is in the nature of 'unfinished business' which we have not had the opportunity to undertake. Under both headings we give some examples of jobs which still need to be undertaken by someone.

In the first category, various possible tasks were put to the Steering Committee but not authorised. One of these was our proposal that both the DOE and Lambeth should list some of the more obvious policy decisions they would have to make in the coming year as part of their normal procedure, coming within the orbit of the inner area study, on which we might be able to comment usefully.

This proposed advance look at an agenda of future decisions never materialised. It is not clear to us why. Some policy reviews require a long gestation period, but action on others could be taken immediately. For better or worse, policies are being confirmed or amended month by month without the benefit of being tested against research conclusions. Surely better arrangements can be devised to secure quicker reaction? This is even more important at a time of financial stringency.

(1) They were published in the spring of 1976 under the title *London's Inner Area: Problems and Possibilities* (IAS/LA/11).

Since we made our proposal the Central Policy Review Staff has put forward a similar suggestion. In this they say:

> 'The Central Policy Review Staff, in consultation with departments, has prepared a pilot version of a forward look at the social policy field. This lists the main items likely to be coming up to Ministers collectively in the next 12 months or so . . . one of its main aims is to help Ministers and officials to look at impending decisions in a wider context, and to identify possible links and possible inconsistencies.'[1]

This was exactly our intention, though more precisely expressed. We consider that central and local government need to devise similar arrangements for urban policy.

Researchers do not expect to usurp political decisions, but to make sufficient impact on the administrative process to see that their latest findings and suggestions are considered in time by those responsible for making key decisions in respect of matters coming before them in the normal course of events. Urban policy is not only a matter of new initiatives, but requires re-examining the direction of existing programmes, most of which ought to be regularly reviewed in any event. Corporate planning procedures in local and central government were devised to make this task easier; but the gearing of research findings with the normal process of decision making appears still spasmodic.

The second example was a proposal for an action project involving equity sharing put forward at the beginning of the study. We proposed:

> 'To investigate the possibility of applying subsidy to houses for sale, sponsored and built by the local authority, in which owners have some degree of partnership with the local authority in the equity. The objective of such a study would be to bring the price of a house within the range of the middle income group and explore the financial and legal implications of this.'[2]

This was taken no further because it was unacceptable to the Steering Committee. On reflection, we can understand why Lambeth should have hesitated: with so much pressure on housing and land in Inner London, it would have been difficult to marshal support for proposals benefiting middle income households.

Since then, the principle of equity sharing has been adopted in Birmingham and is being considered in London for Docklands, Hillingdon and a number of other areas. Such schemes can help the inner city in two ways. Equity-shared houses, old and new, could be made available in suburban areas to migrants from Inner London: this would ease outward movement for those who at present cannot afford to buy outright. Within the inner city there will be scope for increasing home ownership by such means: this will become politically more feasible if the pressure on housing is reduced in the ways we have suggested. Thus while one aim of this policy would help people to move out, another would make it easier to attract and

(1) Central Policy Review Staff, *A Joint Framework for Social Policies.*

(2) Inner Area Study Lambeth, *Project Report* (IAS/LA/1).

retain within the inner city professional workers and others whose skills are particularly needed there.

Perhaps the most important omission was education. This featured in the first draft of the terms of reference from the DOE but for some reason did not appear in the final version, and the Inner London Education Authority (ILEA) were not initially represented on the Steering Committee.

We became increasingly concerned about the quality of education in Stockwell and particularly the problems that school leavers were facing in getting jobs. Although we recognised that other research on education was being carried out in Inner London by the ILEA, we proposed an examination of the subject in the context of the Stockwell study. Our suggestion was that detailed information about education in the area should be related to material gathered on other aspects, for example from our household survey and labour market studies.

The ILEA rejected this proposed study, arguing that it was unnecessary. In response the Steering Committee asked it to supply a summary of relevant research conclusions but it provided only a list of schools in the study area, a brief policy statement and a general bibliography. Our own view is that this was an inadequate response. The ILEA has many problems and we would not wish to add to them, but the inner area study still needs to be matched by a complementary examination of educational issues, particularly at secondary school level.

Unfinished business

The second group of omissions is of new tasks suggested in the course of the work but not started before the study came to an end. Early in 1976 the Department indicated they were not prepared to consider any further studies or action projects in Lambeth, and directed our energies to writing up our conclusions on work so far undertaken.

Our local employers study concentrated on large firms, those with 30 or more workers. It was also deliberately biased towards manufacturing industry, which had particular importance for the local labour market. Though the study provided useful information about the problems of firms, it did not cover a number of issues. Hence our proposals for the following three further studies of aspects of employment.

Traditionally, Inner London, like the inner areas of most older metropolitan cities, has acted as a seed bed for new firms. Now, however, the birth of new firms in the inner city is not keeping pace with the demise of old ones. Why is the inner city now failing in this role? What is the rate at which new firms are being created and where is this happening? What conditions favour their birth? The new towns and development areas have a battery of inducements to new industry; are any of these relevant to Inner London and, more generally, what measures are needed to encourage the birth and growth of new firms? Study of these issues is crucial to the maintenance of Inner London's vitality.

A second set of questions relate to small businesses and, in particular, those in what has become known as the informal sector. Many new firms start out small, often with well below 30 workers. Many, though they remain small, flourish in the older urban areas, making a major contribution to the national economy. In Britain they are said to provide some six million jobs and produce 20 per cent of the gross national product. Many have a reputation for inventiveness and entrepreneurial dash. It is a very varied field, statistically difficult to measure, which is one reason why this is seldom done. It can provide a first foothold on the economic ladder for marginal workers, including new immigrants to the city. These trades do not usually conform to the norms of large-scale bureaucratic management, finance and operation. Yet their function is underestimated, economically and socially, and the sector may be growing rather than declining, offering as it does goods and services cheaper or different from those provided by big organisations dedicated to mass production.

In Lambeth and Inner London these enterprises take many different forms; small full-time manufacturing, women working at home, street traders, independent professionals, family shops, mini-cab drivers, cobblers, tailors and plumbers. The contribution of this sector to the economy of Inner London is important, but little is known about how it operates. It might make a bigger contribution, particularly suited to the skills, buildings and environment of Inner London. It has been widely acknowledged as valuable but so far has received 'all aid short of real help'. It deserves sympathetic and systematic study.

The work needed to modernise, re-equip and refurbish the inner city will extend over several decades. This will depend on efficient performance in the construction industries (building, civil engineering, building supplies and component manufacture). The industries could play an important part in creating immediate job opportunities with career prospects, as long as a continuous programme of housing and environmental improvement were guaranteed. Many local people have relevant skills and experience which are being under-used. Construction could also employ a sizeable number of the local unemployed, both in unskilled jobs and those for which training could be given. The industries, currently in their deepest recession since the war, need a firmer work base now to secure their ability to perform in the 1980s and, unlike most manufacturing industry, will not be inhibited in expanding by lack of space and bad communications. A study is needed to determine how best to devise a programme to meet these ends.

One of the central problems of conventional urban renewal projects is the necessity to move families out before building work can start. As we have shown, established communities are often disrupted as a result. The buildings lie empty for long periods and this waste prompts squatting and vandalism. The whole process is costly to administer.

More could be done in devising rehabilitation schemes which eliminate movement entirely. Work of this kind has been carried out by the GLC on a number of purpose-built old local authority estates. For example, a 'four day package' has been evolved, which provides a full central heating system, hot water and renovated bathroom and kitchen, without the tenants needing to move out of their homes. So far such techniques have been mainly used on purpose-built flats on large estates. They could have wider reference. We therefore propose an action project using a research and development approach, to test the possibilities of phased improvement of older houses. This would take the form of a series of packages, none of which would require tenants or owner-occupiers to move out of their homes. Such a project would be in three phases. In the first, a pilot project would be prepared. In the second, the rehabilitation work would be carried through. In the third, the project would be evaluated covering the implications for finance, legislation, building regulations and administrative procedures.

The role of action projects

We have described in Chapter 1 how we divided the research programme into studies and action projects, and we have just given an example of a possible future project. Here we want to discuss more generally the use of action projects to test new ways of doing things.

A problem which continually arises, even when the general direction of policy is clear, is how to decide on the best means of carrying out a task in practice. The framework of procedures and standards frequently inhibits the personal initiative it is meant to encourage. Yet if public money is to be spent, there must be justification and control. Action projects, being experimental, can show how such dilemmas can be resolved. One of the best ways of testing out new ideas and procedures is by a carefully designed action project, which is independently monitored and from which lessons can be drawn for changes in procedures and, if necessary, new legislation. The advantage of this is that ideas can be tested without the government being committed in advance to endorsing a particular method. For the purpose of such planned experimental projects, existing rules and legislation can be set aside and new ones tested. If successful, the idea can be followed up. If not, what might have proved a costly mistake will have been avoided. The evidence of the projects can in this way provide the case for subsequent major commitments. Traffic management has used the device of the 'experimental scheme' for many years, and it has also proved valuable in testing public acceptability.

An action project programme for the inner city can be as large or as small as available resources permit, and its staffing and financing can be relatively easily adjustable compared with public authority programmes and their fixed establishments. It can be applied selectively without being open to the usual objection of partiality. No programme of inner city renewal, however modest, should be without its planned experimental component, otherwise innovation is likely to be either frustrated or capricious. A continual search for innovation should be built into the system. This requires a firm commitment by the DOE and other departments to identify funds for this work, distinct from their other research activities.

While the costs of such projects can often be shared with local authorities, the main brunt is likely to be borne by central government. Particular projects could be proposed by consultants, local authorities or the departments, and shared out so that different local authorities tried out different initiatives. The success or failure of all such projects could also provide a reservoir of national experience, provided it was properly evaluated, explained and publicised.

Local authorities should not always wait for a nudge from central government before experimenting. Some do not, and they are often the very authorities who complain about the limits central government places on their power to innovate. Lambeth has a consistent record of achievement and innovation. The fact that it volunteered to be the focus for the London inner area study and the fact that the DOE eventually chose it indicates that, when choosing partners in experiment, you choose partners whose record suggests competence and open-mindedness. The problem of the most backward authorities, however, remains.

How can a measure of experimental innovation be made a more normal feature of local authority programmes? There are many ways this can be done, and here we would make one proposal. All departments, either annually or at frequent intervals, could be required to initiate new short-term action projects and to allocate in advance a modest fixed percentage of their planned expenditure to this end. Once a year, presumably in the autumn, the work for that year would be agreed and any spare money added to the sum allocated. These projects would take immediate effect and be strictly limited in time. Some could be highly topical, such as schemes to help young unemployed in Brixton. Others could try out existing staff on new tasks. Our experience on our action projects in Lambeth is that it is difficult to win departmental support for them unless they are already in tune with the department's own approach. Yet experimental projects are designed to change established attitudes and practices. One way of breaking this vicious circle is to build innovation into normal budgetary procedures by providing a slot for such programmes in advance. Nonetheless, if traditional departmental opposition to innovation is to be overcome, strong leadership in the authority's key central policy committee will be needed, as will muscle exercised by the corporate planning team.

A similar device might prove useful in securing local community involvement in identifying priorities for minor local improvements. The council could identify an annual sum well in advance for locally determined minor improvements. Following adequate publicity the local community would be consulted for their views on priorities with a roughly costed shopping list. Projects need not be confined to any one directorate. The local ward member would be associated with this from the outset so he could act as interpreter between the council, its service committees, and local community representatives. Some projects should be deliberately chosen to require inter-directorate and inter-professional staffing and decision making.

Quite apart from these suggestions, we recommend an immediate programme of action projects in Inner London and other inner areas. These projects would suggest further lessons for policy and would give early relief to deprived areas, and should include some which test new forms of local authority initiatives involving several departments.

Obstacles to action

Our aim so far has been to identify what should be done by indicating the general directions policies should take. To stop here might suggest that we thought our proposals existed in a benign political and institutional vacuum and that there were no special problems about getting things done. But proposals on ends must be matched by a discussion on means. So in the rest of this chapter we discuss some of the more formidable obstacles to action.

There are four main kinds of difficulty; strategic, political, resource allocation and institutional. All of these obviously interact. To overcome them will require decisions and actions on strategic aims, major political commitments, changes in the distribution of resources, and new institutional initiatives.

The vital strategic issues include those concerned with the allocation of resources and positive discrimination in favour of Inner London. One example is the decision on whether to allocate the resources requested by the local authorities for major capital expenditure on new infrastructure in Docklands. This is the kind of decision which in any event only the DOE or the Cabinet can take. But it is also clear that where there is an absence of consensus among the authorities concerned, central government initiative may be needed to secure, for example, a co-ordinated housing allocation system for London.

Why has such a consensus not been achieved after a decade of debate and negotiation on the Greater London Development Plan, the strategic housing plan, and London's transport strategy? A quick reading of our recommendations suggests that the reasons include not only the complexity of the problems, but also the difficulty of disentangling causes from effects before finally identifying policy options.

A more fundamental reason for the lack of consensus on strategy is that there are real conflicts of interest. Any programme for the inner city following the social objectives set out in our terms of reference must be re-distributive in character. If the inner city and its residents are to get more resources, other places and programmes must get less. This will not happen automatically, because of the weak political bargaining position of those who need help.

Inner London contains only 40 per cent of Greater London's population and only about a third of the local authorities are Inner London boroughs. It is even more outnumbered in the counsels of the wider region. Inner London is in a minority on all the bodies where crucial issues are debated: the London Boroughs' Association (LBA), the GLC, the Standing Conference for South East Regional Planning, the South East Economic Planning Council and Parliament. In particular, within the GLC the marginal constituencies whose allegiance secures overall political control are those least deprived. They will not directly benefit from the programme put forward here, yet have to be asked to forego money, land and housing allocations to help Inner Londoners.

Thus, despite the apparent all-party support for a programme to help Inner London and despite the efforts of the GLC, there are limits to what Outer Londoners and other suburbanites will acept, and their votes count. This, for example, explains why the GLC has so far made little progress in persuading outer boroughs to yield up more housing allocations and sites.

The GLC and the LBA can take effective action on most of these issues only by securing a consensus among themselves. So any bold political initiatives are likely to have to come from outside. Only central government can grasp these nettles.

The political leverage of Inner London is further weakened by the fact that no one voice speaks on its behalf. Yet its problems and potentialities are distinct and demand debate and action. So a focus is needed for a continuing dialogue to agree the specific issues which characterise Inner London, and to debate a programme of action. Some Inner London forum seems to be needed, articulating collective needs and helping to resolve the mutual suspicions which impede common action; it could study and identify priorities, often seen most sharply at the local level, and thus help to secure a more constructive debate within and between the authorities concerned. So long as these matters are left to the present organisations, the minority position of Inner London will ensure that its voice is muted.

The main political decisions affecting the inner city to be taken during the next few years are likely to be about short and mid-term resource allocation. Problems are not necessarily solved by spending more money, as the experience of the United States shows. Indeed, over-generous local authority budgeting can lead not only to waste but also to misdirected effort and, in particular, to a failure to enlist local community support and initiative. Many of our recommendations propose a reallocation of existing resources and the wiser spending of what is to be spent anyway. Generally, what is involved is a transfer from 'big' schemes to a multiplicity of small ones. This is particularly true at the local authority level where we propose less expenditure on major redevelopment and more on housing and environmental improvement. Nevertheless, in many inner city areas more resources will be needed for certain kinds of programme.

We have stressed the need for more work to be done on housing maintenance and environmental improvement. This is a sensible use of resources in two ways: it protects the fabric of the inner city, securing the extension of the life of the housing stock, and it uses the skills of residents who would otherwise be unemployed. There are also latent resources of voluntary effort and initiative which could be enlisted.

Such a programme would yield some benefits in promoting pride of place and community enterprise.

New proposals which could affect resource distribution to the inner city are put forward in the Layfield Report.[1] The report examines two polarised alternatives for local government finance: 'centralist' and 'autonomist'. Under the first, the finance for local services would increasingly come from central government, with correspondingly tighter government control. Under the second, local sources of finance would be strengthened, producing greater local autonomy and accountability. Layfield seems to favour the second. But the more autonomous local authorities become, the more difficult will be the task of positive discrimination between them. It might also be more difficult to discriminate inside authorities, since central government would have less power to direct resources to specific deprived areas.

The inner city's needs require a differential, not a uniform, allocation of resources. The rate support grant has been the main means to this end and has been one of the ways in which national accountability has taken precedence over local. On this score, the inner areas are likely to do better under a 'centralist' than an 'autonomist' model, at least as long as there is an 'inner city' problem.

If the Layfield proposals were adopted, it would be all the more necessary for the central government to intervene with some corrective redistributive mechanism, and all the more difficult to ensure that it worked effectively. Similar problems will arise with devolution.

There is a further difficulty with the 'autonomist' model. It depends on substantial additional funds being made available and the means suggested for this is a new local income tax. The logic of the autonomist argument suggests that this tax should be collected on the basis of where people live rather than where they work. Any form of local income tax based on the place of residence rather than the place of work acts against the inner city, as in Central London there are many more jobs than people. It is just this difficulty of the separation of the tax base from the spending base which has caused such problems in American cities.

Furthermore, a new local income tax levied in this manner would require a separate system of administration to PAYE, costly to administer. If, on the other hand, local income tax were collected at the place of work it would be necessary only for the Inland Revenue to add a percentage to its normal charges. If the objective is 'autonomy' and cost effectiveness, might it not be simpler to raise the rates?

Layfield is mainly relevant to the distribution of resources between authorities. But there is a separate question about discrimination within them. Only parts of some boroughs need special help; in Lambeth, Stockwell does but not Streatham; so does North Kensington but not Chelsea. So there will be difficult political problems of

(1) *Local Government Finance: Report of the Committee of Enquiry.*

resource allocation even within the same local authority. Our colleagues on the Liverpool inner area study have rightly drawn attention to this and provided evidence of the failure to apply positive discrimination.[1] Ratepayers may be reluctant to forego benefits in favour of other ratepayers. There is no point in the taxpayer providing special resources if they are not to go to those parts of boroughs in greatest need.

Within local authorities, priority for deprived areas depends on political will, matched by strong executive direction and monitoring by the Chief Executive. The day-to-day business of local authorities is carried out mostly by means of subject-orientated committees. The force and impetus of current programmes and the loyalties generated by them makes them, as we found in our own action projects, difficult to penetrate or modify. Normal political horse-trading, too, tends to work towards an even distribution of expenditure within these programmes. Differential resource allocation, interprofessional field work and new initiatives have to battle against this strongly established system. The battle ground is principally the Central Policy and Resources Committee and other committees determining the overall spending and staffing priorities. But the issues will go by default unless these central committees have more than a policeman's function. They should be enabled to debate and decide on the broad context of comprehensive programmes in specific areas and have the power to ensure decisions are carried out.

Institutions

Though many aspects of London government have been criticised we are likely to have to live with its present structure for some years. Responsibilities for policy and action in London on the issues discussed in this book are diffused among six central government departments, the GLC, the ILEA, 32 London Boroughs and the City of London. How can this collection of agencies be brought together to decide priorities and agree programmes for Inner London? We have already indicated where central government will need to intervene. What contribution can the boroughs themselves best make?

The main strength of the boroughs lies in their being most-purpose authorities. Lambeth has been one of the most effective, with a record of vigorous intervention and departmental achievement. This experience, transmitted through the personalities and professional background of senior personnel, has stamped Lambeth actions with its own work style, characterised by the largely independent activities of directorates with strong centralised departmental loyalties and political and professional direction. Its faults stem from such virtues. This pattern is common among London boroughs, despite other differences.

(1) Inner Area Study Liverpool, *Area Resource Analysis: Methodology* (IAS/LI/5) and *Area Resource Analysis: District D Tables 1973–74* (IAS/LI/9). We cannot be sure whether there was any 'positive discrimination' within Lambeth in favour of deprived areas like Stockwell; we had hoped to undertake an 'area resource analysis' of the kind carried out by the inner area study team in Liverpool, but were told by Lambeth that it would be difficult and by the DOE that it would be an unnecessary duplication.

The boroughs enjoy much freedom of action and are eager for more. They do not become much involved in each other's affairs, save when they have to, for instance, in participation in the London Boroughs Association's activities. There appears to be little systematic exchange of experience. This is a great loss; a considerable amount of professional and administrative innovation is going on in London, but the initiatives of individual authorities are not generally known. If all that happened in Inner London was the raising of the general level of performance to that of the best, by pooling experience and by healthy competition, this would bring about a marked improvement in local authority performance generally.

For the most part, the boroughs go their own way, but sharing, unfortunately, a distrust of the GLC. The GLC/borough friction, which transcends political affiliations, is born of overlapping responsibilities and conflicting interests. It frustrates decisions on both strategic and local matters, which often become entangled. When large projects (like the redevelopment of Docklands) have to be undertaken, the proliferation of responsibility coupled with the demand for participation make particularly formidable the problem of translating strategic objectives into local proposals.

It is not surprising that the consistent success of the new town development corporations in doing just this has led to the suggestion that this form of agency should take over the implementation of urban renewal in the inner city, supplementing the existing authorities. We do not consider this idea realistic. The boroughs are there, and in one way or another their abilities have to be harnessed to those of others in the pursuit of wider objectives. Powerful democratic institutions are not easily displaced, and proposals for new overriding executive agencies which seek to do this will not get far. We consider it would be more effective to seek new ways of combining present institutions to work together, supplemented with outside advice. There should be the maximum encouragement to existing bodies, public and private, to carry out without unnecessary interference the tasks they alone can best undertake.

We have approached the question of area management in a similar spirit. Deprived areas need a comprehensive approach to their problems as well as effective and responsive local management in the field. This is hindered by the difficulties of co-ordinating decision making and action between different departments and the reluctance of senior officials to delegate responsibility. The same factors also weaken the ability of local government to respond to complex new problems. Local government has grown up to carry out the routine delivery of specific services and has therefore been organised along strong departmental lines. Its departmental and committee structures still reflect this and, despite attempts to introduce corporate planning and inter-professional co-operation, local authorities have much to learn from other fields where combined operations have proved successful.

Our terms of reference enjoined us to 'examine whether the problems of the area can be dealt with more effectively by bringing together the administration of the local authorities' functions on an area basis', and we have discussed some aspects of this in Chapter 9. Another approach is through area management which is seen as a means of achieving co-ordination and delegation at the local level. Our colleagues working on the Liverpool inner area study have promoted an area management team, separate from the City's Directorates and attached to the office of the Chief Executive. This experiment is initially supported by DOE funds.[1] The DOE's interest in such schemes was further highlighted when it announced that grants would be made available for local authorities under approved experiments in area management.

To be effective, an area management team must contain officers sufficiently senior to bargain with the established Directorates. This suggests that its chief executive would need to be fairly senior, which in turn means that in any permanent structure the areas need to be large, to carry the cost of this fixed establishment. The area chosen in Liverpool had a population of 60,000.

Our study area in Stockwell (population 50,000) is a myriad of smaller pockets, some deprived, others less so. Each has its set of special problems, which may be shared with some similar pockets but rarely with the study area as a whole. In such circumstances a permanent management structure would probably end up with a set of largely irrelevant areas, in which the specific needs of small pockets could be submerged.

Insofar as problems can be regarded as area problems, we think they can only be located in areas of a fairly small size – about that of a housing estate or small group of streets. There is a certain consistency, for example, in the problems experienced by residents of the Stockwell Park Estate, and some of these problems could be met by a clear set of policies for the estate. But the problems and remedies are quite different in the Landor-Hargwyne area, and they would be different again on the Springfield Estate.

We have sought more fluid structures which can concentrate resources where they are needed in a more flexible way. Why should area management structures necessarily be permanent? Small urban areas may have particular crises at various stages in their history. A sensitive management team can be deployed to tackle such a crisis, or at any rate reduce it to an acceptable level. When this has been done the team could be dissolved. In another area a different kind of crisis may arise and require a new local management team, but with an altogether different composition. We see the team set up by Lambeth for the Landor-Hargwyne Housing Action Area as one pointer to what could be done more widely.

We favour a flexible approach to inter-directorate co-ordination. Teams drawn from different directorates should be brought together to tackle new problems as they arise and should be tailor-made to handle a set of specific problems. The focus will sometimes be a particular geographical area. Sometimes it will be an issue or set of issues not geographically concentrated: an obvious example is interdepartmental collaboration on a programme of housing improvement for a whole local authority area. 'Task force' teams of this kind should become a normal instead of an

(1) Inner Area Study Liverpool, *Proposals for Area Management* (IAS/LI/3).

exceptional feature of local authority staff deployment in the inner city. Since the normal functioning and structure of committees, directorates and departments is traditionally protective, there will need to be a strong lead from the office of the Chief Executive. We consider experiments in mobile area task forces of this kind should also receive the support of DOE funds.

Quite apart from proposals of this kind, there is value in inventing new forms of organisation for new tasks; they can offer new opportunities and work perspectives for personal creativity. There is great scope for this at middle management levels, where officers too rarely meet and collaborate,[1] but to have real effect chief officers have to be persuaded to delegate power to this level.

Much of a local authority's activities, however, are routine in character and do not offer such opportunities. Many of these problems are met with in other large organisations. But in manufacturing industry, a product which is badly designed or too expensive will not sell, and the effect of this makes its impact in a matter of months on management and workers. No such sanctions apply in local government. The powers, political influence and spending of local government have grown greatly in the last decade, but not the accountability of the service it offers; the ballot box is a poor monitor of regular performance. In the absence of market forces, new means are needed, backed by political determination, to secure value for money.

This is a topical issue. London boroughs and the GLC are currently spending much more than the national average on many of their services. To an extent these costs are inevitable in a metropolis and can be justified by the unique services a national capital offers. In part they are a product of size and congestion. Living in London has long been recognised as more expensive, thus justifying 'London weighting' in salaries. The rate support grant has been sharply tilted to help London and other big cities. Inevitably, questions are being raised if this level of subsidy is justified and whether it seems to diminish financial discipline. The case for diverting further national resources towards the big cities cannot be taken for granted but will have to be convincingly argued.

We have one suggestion to make which should improve the public accountability of local authorities and their method of work. Every year a council could present, in the form of a report on its own objectives and performance, an audit and commentary on the previous year and a statement of its immediate future priorities and of how it proposed to meet them. The report should be comprehensible to the ratepayers, and quantified in sufficient detail to support the case the council will be making for a rate support grant. It would explain what it sought to achieve and how far it had fallen short. The report would be a critical examination of performance and a recognition of mistakes.

The DOE should ask every local authority to make an annual statement on these lines, and could also suggest the indices of financial accountability which it might

(1) See our proposals in Chapter 9 for multi-service teams.

196

cover.[1] Some of this information is already being given by individual services to different Ministries. But there is no easily understood general account across the board. This could be a step towards more open government, arousing ratepayers' interest and in rebuttal of the charge that there is a community of interest between officers and members to cover up each other's mistakes. Eventually this statement should be mandatory, like its equivalent in the private sector under Company Law.

There is a danger in assuming that changes in organisational structures, innovations in management and new forms of accountability will, by themselves, solve the problems. Important though these all are, we believe that at least as much weight must be given to changes in the thinking and work-style of local government officers.

Policies and people

Everything we have said so far has been in terms of the contribution of various public authorities. But such measures will not succeed unless they evoke a response from the people themselves. Many changes in policy already made by local authorities have followed questioning and protest by local community groups. Cumulatively the actions of such groups have led to changes in local government policy and style, particularly in planning, housing and conservation. Most of these changes have improved the workings of local authorities and led to better results.

The local community cannot, however, normally be expected to make bigger decisions than their limited collective interest in their area, or current topics, require. They may even come into conflict with neighbouring groups and rival interests. Inevitably their influence is local in effect and often conservative in character. They cannot contribute much on the major strategic planning and housing decisions.

At present the role of local community groups is largely confined to protest and consultation. They could in future make a positive contribution to the kind of small-scale urban changes we have recommended. They could play a more active part in devising proposals and helping to implement them, for example by self-build projects in improving the local environment and by the organisation of services for residents and their children.

One possibility would be for local authorities to give community groups more power to make decisions affecting their immediate environment, along the lines suggested earlier in this chapter. Central and local government find such proposals difficult to accept. Authority shelters too easily behind the defence of its monopoly of public accountability. But the risks in delegating decisions of this kind within a fixed budget are not great. A more relaxed posture by authority, with a less monopolistic attitude to knowing what is best for people in their locality, might produce a better relationship between the governors and the governed and also some surprising results on the ground.

(1) Examples of the kind of indices that might be used are given in a pioneering report on five district councils. Epping Forest District Council, *Performance Measurement in Local Government*.

Consulting the local community is never a substitute for positive decision making by a council, which alone possesses final powers. Consultation is nonetheless essential to evaluate the quality of services and effectiveness of delivery, to overcome the information gap on proposals with local impact, to enable members and officials to reappraise their actions and to give local people a chance to influence policy.

Most people are not active members of local community groups or organisations. What part can individual people and families play? One of our central themes has been to increase people's opportunities, above all in jobs and housing. We have made a number of recommendations, for instance the job counselling service and the local information posts, to bring advice and help closer to people so that they can make better informed and more effective choices. We have sought to make it possible for people to contribute, if they wish, to the improvement of their own housing and local environment. We have shown, in our action projects on local information posts and salaried childminding, that local people have skills and resources so far largely untapped.

At present people's choices are very limited. They are discouraged from making a contribution themselves because most of the initiatives are still firmly held by the authorities. The common reaction of a conscientious public body confronted by a new problem is to charge itself with some new act of intervention. But continuous regulatory intervention can be counter-productive. It has led, for instance, to a plethora of rules and procedures which present a labyrinth not easily penetrated by the owner-occupier or the tenant, the potential client of social services or the small businessman. In turn, it buttresses a patriarchal style of government, discouraging to personal and private initiative. Often, therefore, a relaxation or abolition of the policing activity of government may be the most useful way of effecting improvement. When money is tight this could be one of the first places to look for economies, instead of simply axing the next item of capital expenditure.

Successful achievement in Inner London will, of course, depend first of all on the response of the authorities. But policies will, however well-conceived, falter unless the manner of carrying them out also takes account of the part people themselves can, and increasingly seek to, play. A common thread running through our proposals set out in the next and final chapter is the overriding need to encourage, not only greater freedom of choice for people, but also greater opportunities for them to contribute to the shaping of their own lives and environment.

☐ We have in this chapter, as well as discussing some general suggestions, put forward the following specific proposals:
1. There should be an immediate programme of action projects in Inner London and other inner areas. These should be designed to have an immediate effect in deprived areas and should include some which test new forms of local authority initiative involving several departments.

2. A new forum is needed for Inner London, helping to secure a more constructive debate, articulating collective needs and agreeing priorities. This forum should include both elected representatives and senior officers.

3. Local authority teams, drawn from different directorates, should be brought together to tackle particular problems focussing sometimes on a geographical area and sometimes on an issue or issues not geographically concentrated. 'Flying squads' of this kind should become a normal feature of staff deployment.

4. Each local authority should be asked to publish an annual statement setting out past objectives, quantifying the extent to which they have been achieved and defining priorities for future action ☐

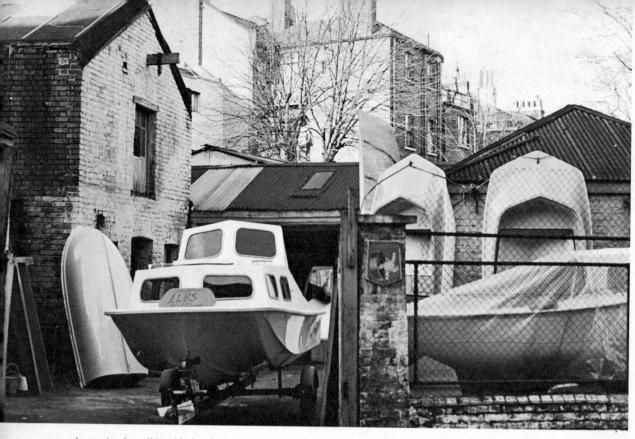

A couple of small local industries.
Fibreglass boats ready for the Thames at Landor Road. The old vinegar factory in South Lambeth Road.

Corner shops to suit all tastes.
New parts for your motor at Larkhall Lane; orange juice, bananas and toy guns at Landor Road.

11 Policies for dispersal and balance

In this concluding chapter we set out our policy proposals in full. We start by indicating how the component parts of the study fit together into a coherent programme. After listing the proposals subject by subject, we show what is needed to carry them out and put forward a shorter list of those measures which, in the autumn of 1976, we thought called for immediate action. We end the chapter with a brief sketch of what, if our proposals were accepted, Stockwell might be like in the year 2000.

Whilst recognising the need for studies of the different elements, we were conscious from the start of the dangers of artificially isolating the various aspects of the study from each other. We became more aware of the connections between these different aspects as the studies deepened and as the policy implications became clearer. We therefore need to trace some of the links between the elements and show how the logic of one set of conclusions leads on to a search for action in another field.

Links between elements

We start with employment, where the most striking conclusion is the mis-match between people's skills and the jobs available. Even before the present recession there was a serious shortage of low-skill jobs of the kind needed by Stockwell men. On the other hand, although good jobs were available nearby, many local people did not have the skills to perform them.

This could be remedied by stimulating more jobs in London but there are limits to what can be achieved by such measures. In the longer term they are unlikely to prove adequate to deal with the fundamental inner city problem of disappearing jobs, low incomes and unemployment.

So we suggest other means. The most urgent is training. At the moment few training facilities are accessible to Stockwell workers, more must be provided locally, along with help in travelling further afield. In the longer term better basic education is needed to fit the next generation of inner city workers for the more skilled jobs required by Central London and the inner city.

Measures such as these will not be enough. There must be far more effective measures to help the less skilled and less affluent to move, if they so wish, to Outer London and further out in the London Region where there are more jobs for them. Not only will some Stockwell workers find it easier to get new jobs if they move out, but our evidence shows that a sizeable minority would like to move in any event. At present there is little or no rented accommodation available to them outside Inner London.

The new towns housing allocations are under direct public control, and subject to central government direction. Their housing has been largely reserved for the workers demanded by industrialists, and more recently for the children of the first new town residents. So far, this national programme conceived in the 1940s to help the inner city has done little to help those who most need it.

Low-skill inner city residents need access to rented accommodation in Outer London and beyond. This would mean changing existing housing allocation procedures already wholly under public control. But a more equitable sharing of the existing housing stock is not enough; more new housing to rent will need to be built in the suburbs and beyond.

Thus we favour new policies to open up to low-skill inner city workers the opportunity to move out that has so far been denied them. Since the turn of the century hundreds of thousands of families have left Inner London. So far, most of them have done so on their own initiative; they have generally been earning enough to buy a house. But this had excluded low income families, who have remained trapped even if they wanted to move. Dispersal has helped the better off and left out the worst off. At the moment there is little effective action to provide rented homes near jobs for those low-skill workers who want to move out of Inner London.

The disappearance of some traditional jobs from Inner London has at least one advantage. It has reduced the need to house so many workers near their jobs. This reduction of population pressure, together with a more balanced dispersal, can offer great opportunities for the inner city. It is the overwhelming pressure of numbers that has in the past been a major obstacle to improvement. If the opportunities are seized, those who stay behind will benefit as well as those who go.

Even allowing for what happens in Docklands, the total amount of housing space in Inner London is unlikely to increase. So any reduction in pressure will largely depend on a further reduction in population. This reduction, reinforced by our proposals for a more balanced outflow, will open the way to more sensitive renewal and rehabilitation schemes in scale with the locality, to the admission of more open space and recreational uses, and to the many minor improvements and developments needed to modernise and adjust the urban fabric to life in the next decades.

Clearly, the improvements will not just be physical. Above all, the management of the environment and of public housing should be eased by the relaxation of the pressure of numbers, leading in turn to a reduction of occupancy and of child density on estates which will make management and good maintenance easier. The benefits of the reduction in pressure will not automatically help those who most need it. Just like balanced dispersal, it will need to be selectively managed to ensure that the benefits are shared.

A balanced programme for dispersal and renewal should not just help to bring homes and work into better relationship in the London region as a whole, but should ensure that out-migration includes a greater proportion of those who would otherwise be left behind, thus leading to a more equitable sharing of the burden of local social services.

Because of the social costs of forced movement within Inner London, we have argued for more population stability inside the inner city. The break-up of settled communities and the erosion of community spirit lie at the root of many of the residents' complaints about other people, and the conflicts between neighbours over such things as children's play. The resulting anonymity, and the consequent lack of informal control by familiar neighbours, partly explain the prevalence of vandalism.

Encouraging greater population stability depends on planning policies as well as on housing allocation and management. It will be greatly helped by the abandonment of wholesale clearance and its substitution by more selective small-scale rehabilitation and development, which can cause less social disruption and allow greater sensitivity to community ties. Where continuity of residence has occurred it has helped community and race relations. The household survey showed that in many respects black residents in Stockwell, particularly those of West Indian origin, were more often attached to the place – and less often disposed to move away from it – than were their white neighbours. They have already created the basis of their own local community. Insofar as white and black residents alike become more settled, race relations are likely to improve.

Our proposals could be summarised by saying that it should be made easier for people to move if they wish to move and stay if they wish to stay. This apparent contradiction is not a real one. In fact, people differ in what they want; they also want and need different things at different times in their lives. Some seek new homes, usually houses with gardens, and are prepared to search outside Inner London to find them. Others prefer inner city life. We favour helping voluntary dispersal; being voluntary it will, unlike clearance, not normally be concentrated in areas, so it would be far less socially disruptive. Essentially our policies add up to an argument for giving people more choice over their lives.

Although our dispersal policies will reduce the load on family and community services, the need for intensive support will remain in the inner city. Our proposals for the improvement in the delivery of welfare services call for boundary co-ordination, bringing together workers from different services, and improving access from below. Such ideas, relevant in any community, are vital in inner city areas because there are relatively more people needing such help and because of the strain this places on welfare services.

Much welfare support is, however, residual in the sense that it would not normally be needed if incomes and housing were adequate. There are of course special cases – the elderly, the disabled, 'problem families' – where special help will be required.

One important conclusion of our study of deprivation was that there was not a strong association between income poverty and bad housing in Stockwell. In other words, the availability of public housing to nearly half the households had proved a key factor in reducing deprivation even though incomes were low. Clearly this is an argument for continuing support to the public housing programme within the inner city and in the areas outside it.

We suggest a comprehensive national income maintenance scheme to raise the incomes of the poor, particularly old people and families with children, while recognising that the resources are not likely to be immediately available for such a measure. This is a redistributory measure, inevitably related to the size of the national income and to a political willingness to share it more widely.

To sum up, the main links in our chain of reasoning are:

1. As well as measures to strengthen Inner London's employment base and improve training programmes, an essential part of policy must be to help low-skill people to move where the jobs are increasingly found.

2. Since many such people want to move out of Inner London anyway, a scheme for balanced dispersal will have no shortage of applicants. It will arrest the social 'bi-polarisation' of Inner London.

3. Balanced dispersal will make it possible to reduce densities among those who stay behind, and generally to improve housing conditions and the local environment.

4. A parallel policy of encouraging population stability among those who remain, helped by the abandonment of wholesale clearance and its substitution by more selective small-scale rehabilitation and development, will contribute to better relationships between residents and more effective informal control of vandalism and petty crime.

5. More sensitive housing management, resident caretakers supported by better maintenance and cleaning services, fuller involvement by tenants, and housing designed to a more human scale will all help to improve the quality of inner city life.

6. A new government programme, giving extra help to inner areas where deprived people are concentrated, will ensure that more resources are available locally. Improved access from below, boundary co-ordination and the creation of multi-service teams will lead to a more effective 'delivery' of services and a more efficient use of resources. In time, the introduction of a comprehensive national income maintenance scheme will relieve poverty inside and outside the inner city.

The policy proposals

Our detailed recommendations, set out in the following pages, are of many different kinds. All are derived from our studies in Stockwell which is only a part of Inner London; nobody has yet undertaken a study of the whole of Inner London. Further work will be needed to define Inner London, to quantify these proposals and devise appropriate mixtures for different areas.

In commissioning this study the Department of the Environment made the assumption that from such a sample it would be possible 'to provide a base for general conclusions on policies and actions . . . appropriate to such inner city residential areas'. We have sought, therefore, to generalise from our experience of Stockwell and to indicate the key problems likely to occur in similar Inner London and inner city situations generally.

Most of our proposals are likely to be relevant to other British inner city areas. This applies particularly to those related to 'The people and their views' (Chapter 2), 'Poverty and deprivation' (Chapter 3), 'Stresses in housing' (Chapter 5) and to those related to housing design (Chapter 8). Every city inner area should have its own priorities and in other cities other proposals may be more important. Our proposals should, however, be considered for inclusion in any comprehensive programme for Britain's inner cities.

Some of our proposals, however, are specific to London. All British metropolitan regions are different in their functions, location, form and history. No package of solutions to their inner city problems is likely to be identical; each set of proposals will have to be purpose designed, from regional to local level. Though some of our policy suggestions match those from the companion studies in Liverpool and Birmingham, for example, others do not. In particular, we argue that there are parts of Inner London, unlike Inner Liverpool and to some extent Inner Birmingham, where the population pressures are still so strong that further dispersal is needed.

Where our proposals are confined to London, the name of the capital is given. This applies particularly to the proposals (Nos. 4–17) on 'The job market' (Chapter 4) and to the proposals (Nos. 18–22) on 'Balanced dispersal' (Chapter 7). Alongside the proposals, set out subject by subject, we have placed the initials of the main responsible agencies.[1] Where the role of central government is to prompt other bodies to action we have not shown their initials.

(1) The following abbreviations have been used:

DE	Department of Employment	ILEA	Inner London Education Authority
DHSS	Department of Health and Social Security	LA	Local Authority
DI	Department of Industry	LHA	Local Housing Authority
DOE	Department of the Environment	LPA	Local Planning Authority
GLC	Greater London Council	MSC	Manpower Services Commission
HC	Housing Corporation	TR	Treasury

Poverty and deprivation (Chapter 3)

1. A new comprehensive national scheme for income maintenance should be designed, to ensure in particular higher pensions for old people and higher children's benefits. Such a scheme should redistribute income to those who are poor, by a method which is automatic (avoiding low take-up) and preserves the incentive to work.

    TR/DHSS

2. Area based initiatives are needed to direct resources for both physical improvement and welfare support into districts where concentrations of poverty have produced physical decline and have generated particularly heavy demands on services. Study will be needed to determine the most appropriate areas for help of this kind, and the criteria for selection.

    DOE/DHSS/ LA

3. Changes in the physical fabric and in the population structure of areas adjacent to the inner city need to be monitored so that resources can be switched to these areas as needed.

    DOE/GLC/ LA

The job market (Chapter 4)

4. A positive statement is needed by central government and the local authorities that they now favour the retention and development of industry in Inner London.

    DOE/DI/GLC/ LA

5. IDC controls should be completely removed from Inner London.

    DOE/DI

6. There should be a complementary relaxation of planning controls in Inner London over industry and commerce.

    LPA

7. Some office development should be allowed in or near Inner London in areas well served with public transport and with a surplus of clerical skills.

    DOE/GLC/ LPA

8. More land in Inner London should be zoned for industrial and commercial uses. Local authorities should set aside land for small industrial estates, providing workshops in advance.

    DOE/GLC/ LPA

9. Local authorities in Inner London should provide a range of other services, including advice to small businesses.

    LA

10. Areas in Inner London containing small businesses should not be subject to wholesale clearance.

    LPA

11. Mixed use zones should be protected and where necessary created in Inner London.

    LPA

12. Immediate measures must be taken to regenerate employment in the construction industry in Inner London, particularly in housing rehabilitation, leading to a secure long-term programme in both public and private sectors.   DOE

13. A major expansion of training schemes should be undertaken, including both existing and new forms. Private training schemes should be underwritten with public funds.   MSC

14. More emphasis should be given in school curricula to basic academic skills and to vocational preparation.   ILEA

15. An experiment should be mounted to provide a new form of home counselling service to people with employment problems in Inner London.   DE

Balanced dispersal (Chapter 7)

16. There should be a co-ordinated allocation system to give Londoners in all boroughs equal access to public housing and facilitate migration from Inner to Outer London.   DOE/GLC/LHA

17. There should be selective intervention to acquire housing in the Outer London market for inner city residents.   DOE/GLC/LHA

18. More public housing should be built in Outer London, in selected parts of the Green Belt and in the 'growth areas' identified in the Strategic Plan for the South East.   DOE/GLC/LHA

19. A National Housing Allocations Pool should be created to help long-distance migrants. The pool would be made up of a proportion of council house vacancies from all local authorities.   DOE/LHA

Planning and housing policies (Chapter 8)

20. Housing allocation and management should reduce high child densities where these are causing problems.   LHA

21. In inner areas the objective of seeking 'housing gain' should be dropped as an overriding principle for new housing schemes and rehabilitation.   DOE/GLC/LPA

22. To replace the private rented sector, a programme of social ownership should use different forms of agency and sponsorship, encouraging a more flexible provision and allocation of housing.   LA/DOE/HC

23. To improve the housing remaining in private tenancy 'fair rents' will need to rise. Controls will be required to ensure that improvements are carried out.   DOE

24. For similar reasons, public sector rents should also rise. To avoid hardship among poorer tenants, public and private, assistance with rents needs to be maintained at adequate levels and more effectively distributed. — DOE/LHA

25. New forms of tenure such as equity sharing should be developed by initiatives at both national and local level. There should be a switch from conventional fixed repayment to index-linked mortgages to help lower income groups become owner-occupiers and move out of the area. — DOE/LHA

26. Decisions on redevelopment or rehabilitation should be taken on a house-to-house basis. The resulting schemes will often combine rehabilitation with some redevelopment. — DOE/LA

27. While the general aim of allocation policy should be to encourage dispersal of ethnic groups, individual choices should be respected even if they lead to concentration. — LHA

28. The scope of tenants' participation in housing management should be established by a series of experiments involving various degrees of delegation and responsibility. — LHA

29. The quality of housing management on estates needs to be improved. To this end caretakers, who need to be resident, should receive better housing and increased status. — LHA

30. The design of buildings and layouts should take account of the 'defensible space' concept, particularly in terms of access ways, grouped garages and open public areas. — LHA

31. Housing design and layout should avoid high density. For any level of density there is a strong link between the level of investment and the cost of management. Since investment in housing is likely to continue to be low in future, new schemes should be designed more simply so as to reduce the demands on maintenance. — LHA

32. New designs should recognise people's preference for variety and small scale. Cost yardstick arrangements and other regulations inhibiting variety should be amended. Existing estates should be enlivened, for example by putting in shops and nurseries, by giving private gardens to ground floor tenants, or even by pulling down some old blocks to let in light and air. — LHA

33. Town planning in inner areas needs to shift its emphasis towards encouraging and managing small-scale urban — DOE/LPA

change by public and private initiative and develop more sensitive ways of managing urban renewal, conservation and minor improvements. Planning and other staff should be redeployed to undertake this work.

The delivery of welfare (Chapter 9)

34. Location and Boundaries Committees (initially on an experimental basis) should be set up to rationalise boundaries of local and central government services. — DOE/DHSS/ LA

35. Multi-service teams should be created to improve links between workers in different family and community services, and between these workers and their clients. — LA/DHSS/DE

36. Multi-service centres should be established; these would be the bases for multi-service teams, offering some family and community services and providing advice about others. — LA/DHSS/DE

37. Localised information channels are needed to improve access from below to services. — LA

From study to action (Chapter 10)

38. There should be an immediate programme of action projects in Inner London and other inner areas. These should be designed to have an immediate effect in deprived areas and should include some which test new forms of local authority initiative involving several departments. — DOE/GLC/LA

39. A new forum is needed for Inner London, helping to secure a more constructive debate, articulating collective needs and agreeing priorities. This forum should include both elected representatives and senior officers. — All agencies

40. Local authority teams, drawn from different directorates, should be brought together to tackle particular problems, focussing sometimes on a geographical area and sometimes on an issue or set of issues not geographically concentrated. 'Flying squads' of this kind should become a normal feature of staff deployment. — LA

41. Each local authority should be asked to published an annual statement setting out past objectives, quantifying the extent to which they have been achieved and defining priorities for future action. — DOE/LA

A balanced programme

This programme needs to be conceived and carried through as a whole. It has to be composed of both national and local initiatives. As the inner city presents a many-sided set of problems, it would respond only partially and unevenly to unilateral solutions. The success or failure of particular initiatives need to be tested against the whole programme if resources are to be sensibly allocated. New policies usually have some unexpected side effects. These need to be monitored and harmful effects countered. Are the original objectives being met? They often need action in different and disparate fields; are efforts being dissipated through simple political expediency or under the daily pressures of managing the programme?

Other balances also have to be struck, for instance, between the short and the long term. Long-term proposals have to be carried on the backs of political credibility, generated and maintained by short term actions. Both area-specific and client-based initiatives will be needed; so will physical proposals as well as management measures.

Perhaps the most important balance of all is the overall make-up of the programme. The issues have been confused by empty debate between false alternatives, particularly as between inner city renewal and dispersal. The most powerful and lasting policies for the inner city are bound to be medium or long term. They will take time to generate and will need consistent following through. If policies are reversed without adequate study, or are allowed to run down through lack of drive and commitment, strategic planning will be further discredited and the urban crisis deepen.

Our proposals can be grouped according to the means by which they can be realised. First, there are those proposals which can only be administered nationally. The national income maintenance scheme is one of these. It would require national initiatives and new legislation, and would apply everywhere, only being selective by being personal and not identified with specific areas, except by the concentration of beneficiaries in them.

Secondly, there are those which would be nationally administered, but which can and should have selective local application. Training and retraining is an example.

Thirdly, there are those which have markedly different regional and local characteristics, but which may require differing allocations of national resources. Dispersal policy is the obvious example. Is further dispersal needed from particular areas? Who should be helped to move? Are incentives needed to encourage or discourage dispersal and, if so, who should offer them?

Fourthly, there are those programmes which it will be the job primarily of local authorities to operate, but which will need the initial encouragement of central government. Help to industry is an example.

212

Fifthly, there are ideas and initiatives which can and should be originated by the local authority on its own.

The main emphasis of our proposals, short and long term, will be on those with local application. While their success will depend on local enterprise, public and private, central government will need to outline the framework and open the dialogue. The package of proposals will differ from city to city, and from borough to borough, as the needs and possibilities are different. While the same set of problems often occur in different parts of the inner city, the detailed measures cannot be standardised.

To decide which parts of Inner London should receive special additional help, appropriate indices of deprivation will need to be devised and the areas defined. The amount of public resources being spent there should be received and resources reallocated from more fortunate areas. New management and monitoring arrangements for these areas must be worked out, additional funding from the State identified and annual reviews conducted.

An immediate programme for Inner London

Some of our specific proposals have already been accepted or are under discussion. This is not surprising: there has been a continuing debate over the last three years or so in which we have participated. Some London boroughs, including Lambeth and Wandsworth, are already taking a more flexible line over planning decisions affecting industry. Some housing authorities are trying to reduce child densities and starting to widen access to their older stock. The Department of the Environment has somewhat relaxed the rules governing access to new towns. However, these constitute only the first steps towards a comprehensive programme for the inner city.

Most of our proposals have, moreover, not yet been accepted. The scarcity of resources will delay some of them. But an early start can and should be made on others. We put forward here a short-term package of measures which are both urgent and immediately feasible.

The first thing is to end unnecessary restrictive interventions by central and local government. Examples are the removal of IDCs in Inner London, the relaxation of ODPs and the complementary relaxation of planning controls in Inner London over industry and commerce. Action on these could have an immediate effect on the attitudes and decisions of employers and investors (proposals 4, 5, 6, 7).

The second set of measures are those particularly urgent because of their effect on jobs. Local authorities should play a positive role in collaboration with private enterprise in promoting employment (proposal 9). There is also an urgent need to expand job-training facilities in or near Inner London and give travelling and other help to improve access to training elsewhere (proposal 13). A guaranteed and continuous programme of inner city renewal and improvement, including building small factories and workshops, is needed not only in its own right, but also because of the opportunity it offers for schemes of 'on the job training' in the construction industry in Inner London (proposals 8 and 12).

There should be an immediate start on the purchase of existing homes outside Inner London, together with more generous assistance with removal expenses, as the first stage in the programme of balanced dispersal (proposal 17). The necessary legislation should be passed and the arrangements made for a London co-ordinated allocation system (proposal 16). This should be the first step towards a National Allocations Pool of council housing, to help not only Inner Londoners but the labour mobility needed for industrial recovery (proposal 19).

Inside the inner city, selected schemes of local environmental improvement should be mounted in areas where physical and social conditions are bad, and where a rapid change can be effected. Local authorities should be asked to identify such areas and propose to the central government suitable schemes for them (proposal 2).

Finally, further lessons for policy would be learned and some relief given to inner city areas, elsewhere as well as in London, by launching further action projects in the field (proposal 38). These projects, funded by central government and carried out by local authorities or other agencies, should be designed to have an immediate effect in deprived areas and should include some which test new forms of local authority initiative involving several departments.

Action along these lines could produce results within months, bringing recognisable improvements in the daily lives of the most disadvantaged residents of Inner London. This would, of course, be only the first stage in carrying through the fuller set of proposals which, over a longer period of time, would offer a means of bringing the society and economy of Inner London into a better balance.

Stockwell 2000

What kind of place could Stockwell become if our longer term proposals were acted on? Fixed blueprints and precise predictions command little credibility, but a set of scenarios for the study area should help to bring the ideas in this book into local focus.

The picture will be composed of three elements: enduring features of the present scene, such as the housing stock, our estimates of likely and future trends and our judgements on what should be done. We rule out dramatic events, not because they may not happen, but because they cannot be predicted. Though 'Stockwell 2000' has a futuristic ring, it is less than a quarter of a century away, well within the lifetime of most of us.

Our first conclusion is that in many ways the part Stockwell plays in Inner London will not change. It will remain a predominantly residential area mainly dependent on jobs in Central London, but with some others scattered around Inner South London. In contrast to the last quarter century, change, though substantial, will be small-scale rather than dramatic. Most of the present housing will still be there and so will the existing mosaic of sites and roads. Some big changes lie just outside the study area; these include the Brixton Centre redevelopment, although we do not expect this to be on the large scale earlier envisaged.

By contrast, other features of Stockwell will change. Outside the new housing estates, we expect to see a sizeable decrease in the residential population and changes in its composition. The proportion of one and two-person households, at present 60 per cent of the total, may rise to 75 per cent by the end of the century. Families with children, who now comprise a third, may only account for a fifth.

London will continue to be economically the most buoyant among Britain's big cities. Manufacturing employment in Inner London will continue to decline. There will be some new jobs created in Docklands and elsewhere, but very few in or near Stockwell. Inner London will continue to be attractive as a place to live for people working in Central London, so that the proportion of Stockwell residents who work there will increase. Non-manual workers, at present about a third of Stockwell's working residents, may rise to a half by 2000. Skilled manual workers may hold their share, while the proportion of low-skill workers could drop from well over a quarter to a fifth. Despite measures to strengthen manufacturing industry short and mid-term, the long-term trend in Inner London and the country as a whole will probably be towards services, as has been the case in virtually all advanced economies.

Given the present age structure and the larger families of West Indians and other blacks, they are likely to increase in Stockwell numerically and, even more, proportionately over the next decades. As we have argued, to the extent that this represents a genuine desire for concentration on their part, it should not be resisted. But we would expect that increasingly members of West Indian and other ethnic minorities will seek to move to the suburbs and beyond, and we see our policy of balanced dispersal as enlarging the opportunities for them to do so along with other inner city residents. If this happens, the general effect will be to bring about greater balance, this time in ethnic terms, throughout the metropolitan region as a whole.

Incomes should increase in real terms, partly in response to these changes in the occupational structure, and partly as a reflection of a general long-term rise in incomes. While a few years ago a doubling of real incomes by 2000 would have been predicted, present forecasts are much more modest. Even so, there should be more taxable and disposable income. Some of the taxable income will, if our proposals are adopted, go to reduce the gap between the poorest and the average in Stockwell, as elsewhere. Some of the disposable income will go into improving the housing and services of the area.

The future pattern of working hours is less predictable. There may be an increasing polarisation with more senior people working at least as long and more of the majority working shorter hours. Hours worked per week in Britain have fallen very little since the 1920s, but our present and short-term economic state is likely to lead to demands for a greater sharing out of such work as is going. The likely response is to have more workers working less time rather than, as at present, a few working long hours with overtime. In the longer term, a shorter working week, rather than a shorter working day, seems likely if the pattern set in the United States is followed. This could have great importance for the home-work relationship as longer journeys to work would be possible and wider job perspectives opened up to Stockwell residents.

As the normal working week contracts, 'leisure' may well take the form of more second jobs, paid or unpaid. The 'do it yourself' enthusiasts and gardeners already do the latter. The impact of this would be felt first in the home and the street, with new resources and skills turned to improving homes and their immediate surroundings.

Stockwell people are already relatively well served with public transport and will continue to use it for most journeys, provided London Transport maintains the quality of its services. We do not expect the resurrection of the motorway box through central Brixton or any other major changes to the highway pattern outside of peak periods. Despite current proposals for traffic restraint, traffic on Stockwell's main roads will become heavier. This will be compounded by some increases in car ownership, locally, from the present figure of about 30 per cent towards 40 per cent or more.[1] We expect more cars, and more households with one or more. They will not, however, be so much used for journeys to work as for week-end and evening leisure. The need to find parking space will limit numbers and even ownership.

We expect local government and other authorities to respond positively to these challenges, despite what we have said in this book about their shortcomings. The services they will be providing, at ascending costs in a labour intensive industry, will be increasingly offered on a buyer's market. As Stockwell's residents' incomes rise, so will their demands for better standards of service, maintenance and environmental improvement. Some demands will be relatively easy to meet. It would be possible for every family with children still in the area to have a home on the ground and for the flats in tall blocks to be allocated to young or sharing households without children and to people coming to London looking for their first job. Other demands, such as those for more owner-occupation and even equity sharing, will be more difficult for some authorities to accept. But, increasingly, they will have to adjust to such aspirations or lose many of the households they seek to keep, or attract. Rising incomes and better job prospects, reinforced by our policy of balanced dispersal, will offer the chance of moving out of London altogether to many more and it will have to be made worth people's while to remain in the more run-down parts of Inner London. These boroughs will have to work hard to make themselves attractive to the population of the 1980s.

(1) In 1971 46 per cent of households in Greater London had cars.

These gains will not automatically help the low-skilled or the poor. The authorities will have to continue to discriminate positively to help such people, through maintenance work on older council estates, through the management and allocation of public housing, and through family and community services. It will take time for the better education for white collar jobs to work its way through the education system and not all inner city children will have the capacity to benefit.

In Stockwell and other parts of Inner London there will be a large continuing programme for the renewal of the urban fabric. This will take a different form from earlier programmes, but represents a challenge to the construction industry, architects and builders. Rebuilding and improvement to a more intimate scale; modernisation and remodelling of old estates inside and out; conservation and conversion to new uses of old buildings; development of a programme of small open spaces for multi-use; street improvement and tree planting. Owners and tenants will be making a bigger contribution than before. All this will lead to a more varied and interesting street scene. In Stockwell these kinds of improvement have so far been largely confined to the 'oases', and in Inner London to the smarter boroughs. Now this can be extended, over time, to every street.

Such an environmental programme itself could become a much more important focus for voluntary community effort, in execution as well as ideas. Many residents, black as well as white, feel some pride in Stockwell, despite its generally shabby appearance. Most home owners and tenants will become involved in home and street improvement, as well as the council, so that this kind of urban change, unlike clearance, can be a force drawing people closer together.

There should be other forces working to the same end. Most Stockwell families will stay there; only a minority will want to move and will do so. The policy of balanced dispersal is designed only to help the minority who want to leave, and will be matched by the discouragement of forced movement. So Stockwell 2000 should contain more people who know their neighbours and feel attached to the place. The young managers and professionals moving in or moving up are likely to be more socially adaptable than anybody else.

This kind of perspective, taken as a whole, leads us to be optimistic about social harmony. The relief of the pressures of numbers, children and strangers, and easing of worry about jobs, should allow people to settle down and live more easily together. The little extra elbow room afforded by dispersal will give them space in which to do it. At the same time they will, as now, be close to the metropolitan centre and all the opportunities it offers. Some may consider that these would be modest achievements. We think they represent what most people want. They are, after all, the very substance of inner city life.

Enduring landmarks of the area.

On this page, the 18th century: modified along Clapham Road (above), rather better preserved in the United Reform Church at Stockwell Green (at right).

On the page opposite, two later churches: St John's, Clapham (top), Beresford Pike's Christ Church on Brixton Road with its external pulpit (bottom).

All of them will probably remain in Stockwell 2000, though it would be hard to guess what they will be used for.

Appendices

Appendix 1

Announcement of Inner Area Studies and Terms of Reference

The Inner Area Studies were announced by the Secretary of State for the Environment in April 1972.

'There is concern about a variety of growing problems in many of our inner city areas, and a general feeling that not enough is being done about them. It may be that slum clearance, redevelopment and economic growth will remove them in the long run. But one cannot be sure. In any case, long-term solutions are not much help to the people living in inner areas now: the blighting effect of longer term plans may make life worse for them in the meantime. There is an urgent need to discover what should be done in relation to the physical environment to help these areas, why it is not being done already, and what measures are needed; and to do this in a way which tries to see problems in the totality and how they relate, and not piecemeal.

The Department of the Environment has decided to invite selected Local Authorities to work in co-operation with consultants appointed by the Department to investigate these matters. The purposes of the work will be to:

discover by study a better definition of inner areas and their problems

investigate by experiments on the ground the actions affecting the physical environment of these areas which could usefully be undertaken for social and environmental purposes

examine whether the concept of 'area management' can usefully be developed, and what the practical implications would be for the local authority

provide the base for general conclusions on statutory powers, finance and resource questions, and techniques.

The work will be derived from an examination of the problems of the area, the experience of the local authority, and the circumstances and views of the residents. It will be primarily concerned with the physical environment, and thus may cover housing and other land uses, open space and cleared sites, pollution, traffic and transport, refuse collection, and street cleaning and so on. Emphasis will need to be given to the social implications of actions affecting the physical environment. The local authority may want to consider relationships with actions outside the sphere of the Department of the Environment, e.g. in the social and educational fields.'

Our terms of reference were as follows:

'The Consultants, under the direction of the Steering Committee, are to propose an area within Lambeth in which a programme of study and experimental action can be undertaken, what that programme should be and how it could be implemented.

The programme, with others in other towns, is to provide a base for general conclusions on policies and actions, within the sphere of DOE, appropriate to such inter-city residential areas as present a combination of poor or declining housing, bad environment and a concentration of social problems.

The programme will be concerned primarily with policies and actions affecting housing, its ancillary buildings, facilities and amenities and its physical environment. It will have regard to the conditions and needs of the inhabitants. It will consider the full range of relevant local authority responsibilities and the central government functions relating to them within the DOE sphere and their relationship to other services. It will examine whether the problems of the area can be dealt with more effectively by bringing together the administration of the local authorities' functions on an area basis.'

Appendix 2

The Household Survey

This appendix briefly explains how the household survey was carried out and how the data from it have been interpreted.

The survey covered the Stockwell study area. We used the rating records to select a sample of rating units within the area. Because we wanted to boost the numbers in private housing. particularly among owner-occupiers and furnished tenants, we deliberately weighted the sample to give twice as many private as council estate addresses. We calculated in advance that, to get a sample of the size we wanted, we would need to draw out one address in 12 (and one in 24 on council estates). Of the 998 addresses selected by this method, 102 proved to be demolished or empty, leaving 886 that were called on.

The survey was designed, like the General Household Survey covering Britain as a whole,[1] to provide both a sample of households and a sample of individual adults. The interviewers tried to interview a representative (usually the head of household or the housewife) of each household living at the sample addresses and every person aged 16 and over in each of those households. If household members could not be interviewed, another member (usually a spouse or parent) could be used as a proxy, and parents similarly acted as proxies for their children. This meant that factual information, if not opinions, was collected for children and for some adults. Even if no proxy interview could be conducted, some limited information was collected about every household member.

At 15 per cent of the 886 occupied addresses in the sample we failed to interview anybody. We cannot be entirely certain how many households there were at the sample addresses. Our estimate is that there was a total of 1140. Of these, we interviewed 931 – a success rate of 82 per cent. Most of the failures were where household representatives refused to participate, but about one in five were because the head of household or the housewife could never be contacted. Further details about the response have been separately reported.[2]

The survey results presented in this book were re-weighted so as to correct the deliberate over-representation of private as against council addresses. Since the sampling fraction in the former was twice as high as in the latter, and since the response was broadly similar in the two kinds of property, we simply doubled the data from households (and individual people) living on council estates.

This re-weighting meant that the figures more accurately reflected the population of the study area as a whole. But it also meant that the total numbers of households or people shown in tables are not the exact numbers. As a reminder, in all household survey tables the absolute numbers are labelled 'weighted'; the same weighting procedure was applied to percentages or proportions cited in the text. Quite apart from weighting, the totals sometimes vary from table to table. This is firstly because the base can vary: some tables refer to households, some to all adults for whom limited data were collected, some include children as well; on matters

(1) Office of Population Censuses and Surveys, *The General Household Survey: Introductory Report.*

(2) Inner Area Study Lambeth, *People, Housing and District* (IAS/LA/5).

of opinion the people are obviously limited to the adults who gave full interviews. Numbers may also vary because the information was not always available for some people or households: either the particular question did not apply or, if it did, the interviewer failed to get an adequate or clear answer.

A familiar question with social surveys is whether the variations in behaviour or attitudes between one group of people and another are sufficiently large, given the numbers on which the percentages are based, for it to be reasonably certain that they reflect real differences in the population and not chance ones, resulting from sampling bias. We have followed the usual rules and in general draw attention to differences only if the probability is less than one in 20 that they could have arisen by chance. If apparent differences are less firmly based but nonetheless seem worthy of comment, we have used a more cautious form of words.

Copies of the questionnaires (household and individual) used in the survey can be obtained from the Institute of Community Studies, 18 Victoria Park Square, London E2 9PF. There will be a small charge to cover the costs of photocopying and postage.

Appendix 3

Additional tables

This appendix contains the additional tables referred to in Chapters 4, 6, 7 and 8.

Table 19   Industrial composition of local employment (males and females in employment by workplace, April 1966 and April 1971)

Industry (1968 S.I.C.)		Percentage of total employment			Percentage change in employment 1966–1971 in Inner South London
		Inner South London		Greater London	
		1966	1971	1971	
I	Agriculture, forestry, fishing	0·05%	0·05%	0·13%	−13·6%
II	Mining, quarrying	0·07%	0·02%	0·12%	−71·4%
III	Food, drink, tobacco	4·24%	3·66%	2·59%	−22·4%
IV–V	Coal, petroleum products, chemical and allied	1·06%	1·77%	2·00%	+50·6%
VI	Metal manufacture	0·36%	0·18%	0·52%	−54·6%
VII	Mechanical engineering		2·41%	3·12%	
VIII	Instrument engineering	5·89%	0·71% (5·32%)	0·93%	−18·8%
IX	Electrical and electronic engineering		2·21%	4·05%	
X	Shipbuilding, marine engineering	0·09%	0·07%	0·14%	−35·0%
XI	Vehicles	0·29%	0·34%	1·61%	− 6·6%
XII	Metal goods, n.e.s.	1·65%	1·41%	1·76%	−23·3%
XIII	Textiles	0·38%	0·39%	0·44%	− 8·1%
XIV	Leather, fur	0·56%	0·48%	0·32%	−23·2%
XV	Clothing, footwear	1·37%	1·02%	2·20%	−32·9%
XVI	Bricks, pottery, cement, glass, etc.	1·04%	0·82%	0·57%	−29·3%
XVII	Timber, furniture	1·25%	1·21%	1·32%	−13·2%
XVIII	Paper, printing, publishing	5·12%	5·03%	3·90%	−11·7%
XIX	Other manufacturing	1·02%	1·02%	1·29%	− 9·5%

Table 19 (continued)

Industry (1968 S.I.C.)		Percentage of total employment			Percentage change in employment 1966–1971 In Inner South London
		Inner South London		Greater London	
		1966	1971	1971	
III–XIX	All manufacturing industries	24·32%	22·72%	26·76%	−15·9%
XX	Construction	8·99%	8·32%	6·11%	−16·8%
XXI	Gas, electricity, water	2·45%	1·86%	1·52%	−31·7%
701	Railways	2·09%	1·72%	1·34%	−26·1%
702	Road passenger transport	1·66%	1·87%	1·47%	− 1·6%
708	Posts, telecommunications	2·75%	3·77%	3·11%	+23·2%
703–707, 709	Other transport and communications	4·18%	3·08%	4·42%	−33·8%
810–812	Wholesale distribution	3·81%	3·55%	3·09%	−16·1%
820–821	Retail distribution	11·59%	9·65%	9·10%	−25·2%
831–832	Other dealing, etc.	1·60%	1·27%	1·22%	−28·2%
XXIV	Insurance, banking, financial and business services	3·88%	4·01%	9·28%	− 7·2%
872	Education	4·94%	6·35%	4·60%	+15·7%
874	Medical and dental services	5·61%	6·26%	4·15%	+ 0·5%
871, 873, 875–879	Legal, accounting and other professional	1·46%	1·79%	3·66%	+ 9·3%
884–888	Hotels, catering	2·78%	2·33%	2·99%	−24·5%
892	Laundries	1·11%	0·30%	0·43%	−35·2%
894	Garages	1·77%	1·70%	1·59%	−13·7%
899.7	'Other' services (includes contract cleaners)	0·43%	0·74%	0·50%	+54·6%
881–883, 889–891, 893, 895–899.6	Other miscellaneous services	4·61%	4·64%	5·39%	− 9·6%
901	National government, defence	3·55%	4·98%	4·22%	+26·0%

Table 19 (continued)

Industry (1968 S.I.C.)		Percentage of total employment			Percentage change in employment 1966–1971 in Inner South London
		Inner South London		Greater London	
		1966	1971	1971	
906	Local government	5·67%	6·32%	3·52%	+ 0·1%
	Industry inadequately described or workplace outside United Kingdom	0·61%	2·17%	1·30%	—
Total %		100%	100%	100%	−10·1%
Number		424,04	381,23	4085,53	

Notes:

1. The figures are derived from the Census 1966 and 1971, 10% economic activity tables. Figures such as 424,04 correspond to the estimates which would be produced by grossing up the sample, in this case 424,040.

2. The figures are not corrected for bias or under-enumeration. The latter was serious in 1966 (several percent in London), so the rates of decline between 1966–1971 are under estimates.

Tables 20 and 21: Selected indicators of the local demand for labour

These tables contain two sets of analysis; at different levels of detail both are concerned with measuring the demand for labour in different occupational groups in the local area as against London or the country as a whole.

The first table uses six socio-economic groups and compares Inner South London (Lambeth, Southwark, Wandsworth) with London or Britain. The second table uses 15 occupational categories and compares Inner South London with a wider area (which also includes the City, Camden, Hammersmith, Kensington, Merton and Westminster) as well as London. The first table includes five measures of demand and three estimates of the unemployment rate, the second five and one respectively. All figures relate to *males*, and are derived from the Census 1966 and 1971 10% economic activity tables or from the Department of Employment EDS 68 sheets for September and December 1973.

The definitions of these measures are as follows:

D1 = the vacancy rate = notified unfilled vacancies (1973) as a percentage of employment by workplace (1971) in the same area and occupation.

D2 = job/worker ratio = employment by workplace as a percentage of economically active residents in the same area and occupation in 1971.

D3 = percentage rate of growth (+) or decline(−) in employment by area of workplace between 1966 and 1971 in the given area and occupation (*not* corrected for bias or under enumeration).

D4 = index of 1971 jobs ÷ 1966 jobs as a percentage of index of 1971 economically active residents ÷ 1966 e.a. residents in the same area and occupation.

$$= \frac{D2\ (1971)}{D2\ (1966)} \times 100$$

D5 = difference between absolute change (1966–1971) in jobs by workplace and absolute change in economically active residents, as a percentage of 1966 economically active residents, in given area and occupation.

U1 = registered unemployed adult males in area in 1973 re-coded into OPCS occupational categories, as a percentage of 1971 resident economically active males in same area and occupation.

U2 = U1 multiplied by a constant to give an overall average male unemployment rate the same as U3.

U3 = estimated males out of employment in April 1971 (census) as a percentage of resident economically active males in same area and occupation.

D1, U1 and U2 rely upon the use of data based on employment exchange areas, which had different boundaries from the boroughs – it is assumed that the two main 'overlaps' (Tooting and Putney) cancel each other out.

The U3 figure for all S.E.G.'s excludes the unclassified, and this is the basis on which U2 is calculated.

Table 20   Selected indicators of the local demand for labour: Inner South London (ISL), Greater London (GL) and Great Britain (GB)

Socio-economic group	D1		D2		D3		D4		D5	U1	U2	U3
	ISL	GB	ISL	GL	ISL	GL	ISL	GL	ISL	ISL	ISL	ISL
1, 2, 3, 4, 5 Professional, managerial, intermediate	0·10	0·61	125	119	+ 9·0	+13·9	99	106	+1·33	1·04	1·78	3·14
6 Junior non-manual	1·07	1·52	86	130	−15·8	−12·1	89	101	−1·23	1·95	3·33	2·82
7 Personal service	1·43	4·31	53	116	+ 1·0	+ 2·4	100	105	−1·22	2·46	4·20	3·84
8, 9 Supervisory, skilled manual	1·47	1·71	96	113	−15·4	−12·0	102	101	+2·84	1·88	3·21	4·76
10 Semi-skilled manual	1·11	1·34	88	120	−22·4	−16·5	97	101	−0·18	2·40	4·10	5·26
11 Unskilled manual	1·04	2·11	63	102	−30·0	−16·5	88	99	−3·65	11·20	19·13	7·08
All groups	0·63		89	101	−11·7	− 5·9				2·77	4·73	4·73

Table 21   Selected indicators of the local demand for labour: Inner South London (ISL), the wider area (WA) and Greater London (GL)

Occupations	D1	D2			D3		
	ISL	ISL	WA	GL	ISL	WA	GL
1 Management	0·00	172	348	143	+ 0·7	+ 8·4	+ 8·9
2 Professional	0·04	133	255	128	+11·0	+ 6·9	+ 7·9
3 Sales	0·43	105	227	118	−14·1	− 5·3	− 5·8
4 Clerical	0·42	78	285	120	−13·6	−12·3	− 9·6
5 Service	0·77	71	153	102	+ 1·3	+ 3·1	+ 3·2
6 Electrical	0·68	93	192	119	− 1·0	− 0·9	− 3·3
7 Engineering	1·37	80	119	103	−21·9	−22·2	−14·3
8 Woodworking	2·37	97	149	101	−11·3	−18·0	−18·1
9 Printing	0·09	112	254	114	−16·6	−10·8	−10·2
10 Other operative	1·18	84	126	100	−28·7	−21·9	−16·6
11 Construction	0·57	95	125	97	−15·7	−16·0	−12·6
12 Painting	0·33	80	109	92	−21·1	−24·4	−24·4
13 Transport	0·66	74	162	105	−21·7	− 9·4	− 2·6
14 Warehouse	1·00	73	130	100	−24·5	−26·1	−16·1
15 Labouring	0·92	71	106	93	−22·3	−19·9	−19·6
All occupations	0·63	89	190	110	−11·7	− 6·2	− 5·9

Occupations	D4			D5		U1
	ISL	WA	GL	ISL	WA	ISL
1 Management	96	195	196	− 3·8	+24·4	0·03
2 Professional	102	103	104	+ 4·9	+13·4	2·08
3 Sales	100	108	103	− 1·3	+ 1·3	1·11
4 Clerical	99	101	102	+ 1·0	−21·9	2·53
5 Service	103	106	101	+ 2·3	+ 7·3	3·02
6 Electrical	116	134	103	+13·6	+24·3	1·81
7 Engineering	95	100	100	− 0·6	− 4·8	2·04
8 Woodworking	111	112	101	+10·1	+ 2·8	1·40
9 Printing	107	109	102	+ 4·3	− 7·3	6·77
10 Other operative	93	91	99	− 2·1	−15·3	4·23
11 Construction	107	105	100	+ 7·0	+ 0·7	0·88
12 Painting	95	95	93	− 0·6	− 7·8	3·88
13 Transport	88	105	101	− 6·9	− 0·5	2·35
14 Warehouse	92	96	99	− 1·1	−12·5	3·58
15 Labouring	100	101	98	+ 5·5	0·0	21·60
All occupations						3·69

Table 22   Industry of workers living in Stockwell 1973

		Full time men	Full time women	Part time women
I, II	Agriculture, mining	0·8%	0·9%	1·0%
III–XIX	All manufacturing	18·9%	13·8%	8·0%
XX	Construction	14·8%	0·7%	0·0%
XXI	Gas, electricity, water	3·3%	0·9%	1·0%
XXII	Transport, communications	16·6%	7·2%	1·0%

Table 22   Industry of workers living in Stockwell 1973 (continued)

	Full time men	Full time women	Part time women
810–812, 831–832 Wholesale distribution			
	10·5%	15·4%	22·0%
820–821 Retail distribution			
XXIV Financial business services	6·1%	12·1%	9·0%
872 Education			
874 Medical, dental services	8·3%	16·6%	19·0%
871, 873, 875–879 Other professional services			
XXVI Miscellaneous services	12·6%	19·4%	26·0%
901 National government			
	8·3%	12·9%	11·0%
906 Local government			
Total %	100%	100%	100%
Total number (weighted)	800	428	208

Source: Stockwell Household Survey 1973.

Tables 23 to 31: *Characteristics of potential migrants*

These tables set out the characteristics of people who, when interviewed in the 1973 household survey, said they wished to move to areas further out than Stockwell. These, the 317 'movers' are contrasted with the rest of our sample, the 829 'stayers'.

Table 23   Household type

	Movers	Stayers
Single person	14%	28%
Couple, husband under 40	6%	6%
Couple, husband 40 or over	22%	15%
Couple with children under 16	35%	27%
Couple with children 16 or over	13%	6%
Other households	11%	18%
Total %	100%	100%

Table 24   Age

	Movers	Stayers
16–19	6%	6%
20–34	35%	32%
35–44	14%	16%
45–64	35%	30%
65+	10%	17%
Total %	100%	100%

Table 25 Social class of head of household

	Movers	Stayers
Professional, managerial	3%	5%
Intermediate	9%	10%
Junior non-manual	15%	13%
Skilled manual	34%	21%
Semi-skilled manual	17%	27%
Unskilled manual	22%	25%
Total %	100%	100%

Table 26 Colour of head of household

	Movers	Stayers
Coloured	7%	20%
White	91%	79%
Not observed	2%	1%
Total %	100%	100%

Table 27 Tenure of household

	Movers	Stayers
Owner-occupier	5%	13%
Council tenant	48%	46%
Private unfurnished	32%	27%
Private furnished	11%	12%
Other	2%	2%
Total %	100%	100%

Table 28 Place of work

	Movers	Stayers
Stockwell	12%	7%
Elsewhere in Lambeth	12%	11%
Central London	39%	49%
Elsewhere in Inner London	18%	14%
Outer London	9%	10%
Other places	9%	9%
Total %	100%	100%

Table 29 Relatives

	Movers	Stayers
No relatives living locally	68%	69%
One or more relatives living locally	32%	31%
Total %	100%	100%

Table 30 Friends

	Movers	Stayers
No friends living locally	52%	46%
One or more friends living locally	48%	54%
Total %	100%	100%

Table 31 Time in district

	Movers	Stayers
Under 2 years	10%	17%
2 years but less than 10	24%	30%
10 years but less than 20	17%	17%
20 years or more/always	48%	35%
Total %	100%	100%

Table 32   Characteristics of migrants to and from the inner ring

Socio-economic group	Emigrants Five year migrants from the inner ring to the rest of Great Britain				Immigrants Five year migrants to the inner ring from the rest of Great Britain			
	In wholly moving families		Not in wholly moving families		In wholly moving families		Not in wholly moving families	
Professional (3, 4)	19,59	5·0%	7,04	4·6%	6,06	6·5%	7,12	6·3%
Managerial (1, 2, 13)	57,55	14·7%	12,16	7·9%	12,82	13·7%	8,48	7·5%
Other non-manual (5, 6)	80,67	20·6%	47,45	30·9%	20,60	22·0%	47,24	41·9%
Skilled manual (8, 9, 12, 14)	143,31	36·6%	20,15	13·7%	26,15	27·9%	11,38	10·9%
Semi-skilled manual (7, 10, 15)	46,57	11·9%	14,27	9·3%	11,63	12·4%	10,16	9·0%
Unskilled manual (11)	20,95	5·3%	5,16	3·4%	5,75	6·1%	3,77	3·3%
Armed forces, inadequately described (16, 17)	9,64	2·5%	13,44	8·7%	3,35	3·6%	5,18	4·6%
Retired (included above)	23,42	6·0%	18,80	12·2%	2,33	2 5	5,38	4·8%
Students	1,39	0·4%	3,37	2·1%	1,16	1·2%	6,46	5·7%
Other economically inactive	12,31	3·1%	29,75	19·4%	6,25	6·7%	13,09	11·6%
Total population	391,98	100·0%	153,67	100·0%	93,77	100·0%	112,88	100·0%

Notes:
1. This information was obtained from a 10 per cent sample. Figures such as 19,59 correspond to the estimates which would be produced by grossing up the sample, in this case 19,590.

2. The figures for migrants in wholly moving families classify all persons by the socio-economic group of the head of their household. Migrants not in wholly moving families are classified by their individual socio-economic group.

Source: Census 1971, Migration Regional Report, South East Region, Parts I and II, HMSO 1976

Table 33 Characteristics of migrants to and from the inner ring

	Emigrants Five year migrants from the inner ring to the rest of Great Britain			Immigrants Five year migrants to the inner ring from the rest of Great Britain		
	In wholly moving families	Not in wholly moving families	Total	In wholly moving families	Not in wholly moving families	Total
Tenure						
Owner-occupier	58·5%	53·3%	57·1%	27·9%	18·0%	22·7%
Rent from a council or new town	27·2%	15·4%	24·1%	25·3%	9·8%	17·2%
Rent unfurnished from a private landlord or housing association	11·8%	18·0%	13·4%	34·6%	27·4%	30·8%
Rent furnished	2·4%	13·3%	5·3%	11·9%	44·6%	29·1%
Not stated	0·1%	0·1%	0·1%	0·2%	0·2%	0·2%
Amenities (included above)						
With exclusive use of bath, hot water and inside w.c.	93·0%	84·4%	90·8%	74·6%	59·0%	66·4%
Density (included above)						
Over 1½ persons per room	2·5%	2·7%	2·6%	9·7%	5·8%	7·7%
Over 1 and up to 1½ persons per room	2·6%	5·6%	8·6%	17·4%	8·4%	12·7%
Less than ½ person per room	11·4%	28·5%	15·9%	7·4%	13·6%	10·7%
Total	100·0%	100·0%	100·0%	100·0%	100·0%	100·0%
Total number of persons in private households	391,98	141,28	533,26	93,77	103,77	197,50

Notes:
1. This information was obtained from a 10 per cent sample. Figures such as 19,59 correspond to the estimates which would be produced by grossing up the sample, in this case 19,590.

2. The figures for migrants in wholly moving families classify all persons by the socio-economic group of the head of their household. Migrants not in wholly moving families are classified by their individual socio-economic group.

Source: Census 1971, Migration Regional Report, South East Region, Parts I and II, HMSO 1976

Appendix 4

References

Allen, S. *New Minorities, Old Conflicts: Asian and West Indian Immigrants in Britain*, Random House, 1971.

Banton, M. *Racial Minorities*, Fontana, 1972.

Cartwright, A. *How Many Children?*, Routledge and Kegan Paul, 1976.

Central Housing Advisory Committee *Council Housing: Purposes, Procedures and Priorities*, HMSO, 1969.

Central Policy Review Staff *A Joint Framework for Social Policies*, HMSO, 1970.

Central Statistical Office 'Social commentary: social class', in *Social Trends No. 6*, HMSO, 1975.

Centre for Environmental Studies *Ninth Annual Report*, CES, 1976.

Community Relations Commission *Unemployment and Homelessness: A Report*, HMSO, 1974.

Deakin, N. *Colour, Citizenship and British Society*, Panther, 1970.

Deakin, N. and Ungerson, C. *Leaving London: Planned Mobility and the Inner City*, Heinemann, 1977.

Department of Employment/Manpower Services Commission *Training for Vital Skills*, HMSO, 1976.

Department of Industry *The Decline of Manufacturing Industry in London*, paper submitted to the Development of the Strategic Plan for the South East and given at CES Inner City Employment Conference, September 1976.

Department of Health and Social Security *Two-Parent Families*, HMSO, 1971.

Department of the Environment *Greater London Development Plan, Report of the Panel of Enquiry*, Vol. 1, HMSO, 1973.

Docklands Joint Committee *London Docklands: A Strategic Plan: A Draft for Public Consultation*, Docklands Development Team, 1976.

Douglas, J.W.B. *The Home and the School*, MacGibbon and Kee, 1964.

Dugmore, K. (editor) *The Migration and Distribution of Socio-Economic Groups in Greater London: Evidence from the 1961, 1966 and 1971 Censuses*, Research Memorandum 443, Greater London Council, 1975.

Epping Forest District Council *Performance Measurement in Local Government*, 1976.

Eversley, D. 'Old cities, declining population and rising costs', *Greater London Council Intelligence Unit Quarterly Bulletin*, No. 18, March 1972.

Fernando, E. and Hedges, B. *Moving out of Southwark*, Social and Community Planning Research, 1976.

Field, F. *Unequal Britain: a Report on the Cycle of Inequality*, Arrow Books, 1973.

Fried, M. *The World of the Urban Working Class*, Harvard University Press, 1973.

Gans, H.J. *People and Plans*, Basic Books, 1969.

Gee, F.A. *Homes and Jobs for Londoners in New and Expanding Towns*, HMSO, 1972.

Glass, D.V. and Hall, J.R. 'Social mobility in Britain: a study of inter-generation changes in status', in Glass, D.V. (editor) *Social Mobility in Britain*, Routledge and Kegan Paul, 1954.

Glass, R. 'Introduction' in Centre for Urban Studies (editors) *London: Aspects of Change*, 1964.

Goldthorpe, J.H. 'Social stratification in industrial societies'.

Greater London Council *Employment in Greater London and the Rest of the South-East Region*, 1975, paper submitted to the Development of the Strategic Plan for the South East.

Halsey, A.H. *Educational Priority Volume 1: EPA Problems and Policies*, HMSO, 1972.

Harris, M. 'Some aspects of polarisation', in Donnison, D. and Eversley, D. (editors) *London: Urban Patterns, Problems and Priorities*, Heinemann, 1973.

Heraud, J.B. 'The new towns and London's housing needs', *Urban Studies*, December, 1966.

Hill, M.J. *et al Men Out of Work*, Cambridge University Press, 1973.

Howard, E. *Garden Cities for Today and Tomorrow*, Faber and Faber, 1946.

Inner Area Study Birmingham *New Housing Policies for the Inner City* (IAS/B/11), Department of the Environment, 1976.

Inner Area Study Birmingham *Progress Report: July 1973* (IAS/B/2), Department of the Environment, 1974.

Inner Area Study Birmingham *Project Report* (IAS/B/1), Department of the Environment, 1974.

Inner Area Study Birmingham *Small Heath Birmingham: A Social Survey* (IAS/B/5), Department of the Environment, 1975.

Inner Area Study Lambeth *Changes in Socio-Economic Structure* (IAS/LA/2), Department of the Environment, 1975.

Inner Area Study Lambeth *Housing and Population Projections* (IAS/LA/8), Department of the Environment, 1975.

Inner Area Study Lambeth *Housing Management and Design* (IAS/LA/18), Department of the Environment, 1977.

Inner Area Study Lambeth *Implications of Social Ownership* (IAS/LA/12), Department of the Environment, 1976.

Inner Area Study Lambeth *Interim Report on Local Services* (IAS/LA/3), Department of the Environment, 1975.

Inner Area Study Lambeth *Labour Market Study* (IAS/LA/4), Department of the Environment, 1975.

Inner Area Study Lambeth *Local Employers' Study* (IAS/LA/16), Department of the Environment, 1977.

Inner Area Study Lambeth *Local Services: Consumers Sample* (IAS/LA/9), Department of the Environment, 1975.

Inner Area Study Lambeth *London's Inner Area: Problems and Possibilities* (IAS/LA/11), Department of the Environment, 1976.

Inner Area Study Lambeth *Multi-Service Project: Report of the Working Party* (IAS/LA/14), Department of the Environment, 1976.

Inner Area Study Lambeth *People, Housing and District* (IAS/LA/5), Department of the Environment, 1975.

Inner Area Study Lambeth *Policies and Structure* (IAS/LA/7), Department of the Environment, 1975.

Inner Area Study Lambeth *Poverty and Multiple Deprivation* (IAS/LA/10), Department of the Environment, 1975.

Inner Area Study Lambeth *Project Report* (IAS/LA/1), Department of the Environment, 1974.

Inner Area Study Lambeth *Schools Project* (IAS/LA/13), Department of the Environment, 1976.

Inner Area Study Lambeth *Second Report on Multiple Deprivation* (IAS/LA/15), Department of the Environment, 1977.

Inner Area Study Liverpool *Area Resource Analysis: District D Tables, 1973–74* (IAS/LI/9), Department of the Environment, 1976.

Inner Area Study Liverpool *Area Resource Analysis: Methodology* (IAS/LI/5), Department of the Environment, 1975.

Inner Area Study Liverpool *Project Report* (IAS/LI/1), Department of the Environment, 1974.

Inner Area Study Liverpool *Proposals for Area Management* (IAS/LI/3), Department of the Environment, 1974.

Inner Area Study Liverpool *Study Review/Proposals for Action and Research* (IAS/LI/2), Department of the Environment, 1974.

Joseph, Sir K. 'The cycle of deprivation', in Butterworth, E. and Holman, R. *Social Welfare in Modern Britain*, Fontana, 1975.

Kinghan, M. 'Squatting in London', *New Society*, 2 May 1974.

Lewis, T. *The Haringey Rent Allowances Project: Second Report*, Department of the Environment, 1975.

Local Government Finance: Report of the Committee of Enquiry, HMSO Cmnd. 6453, 1976.

London Borough of Enfield *Report on the Changing Nature of Residential Areas*, (duplicated), Department of Architecture and Planning, London Borough of Enfield, 1969.

London Borough of Lambeth *Community Plan 1976 Volume 3: Housing Programme Area*, 1976.

Meacher, Mollie *Rate Rebates: a Study of the Effectiveness of Means Tests*, Child Poverty Action Group, 1972.

Metcalf, D. and Richardson, R. 'Unemployment in London' in Worswick, B.G.N. *Measurement of Involuntary Unemployment*, Allen and Unwin, 1976.

Miller, S.M. 'Comparative social mobility', *Current Sociology*, Vol IX, No. 1, 1960.

Mukherjee, S. *There's Work to be Done*, Manpower Services Commission, HMSO, 1974.

National Community Development Project: Inter-Project Report, Community Development Project Information and Intelligence Unit, 1974.

Newman, O. *Defensible Space*, Architectural Press, 1973.

Office of Population Censuses and Survey *The General Household Survey: Introductory Report*, HMSO, 1973.

Office of Population Censuses and Survey *The General Household Survey 1973*, HMSO, 1976.

Palmer, J. 'Using the results of action research in policy making', in *Report of the Colloquium on the Use of Action Research in Developing Urban Planning Policy*, Department of the Environment. 1975.

Pay Board Advisory Report on *London Weighting*, HMSO, Cmnd. 5660, 1974.

Pollak, M. *Today's Three-Year-Olds in London*, Heinemann, 1972.

Report of the Committee on Housing in Greater London, HMSO Cmnd. 2605, 1975.

Rex, J. and Moore, R. *Race, Community and Conflict*, Oxford University Press, 1967.

Rossi, P.H. *Why Families Move*, Glencoe Free Press, 1955.

Rowntree, B.S. *Poverty and Progress*, Longmans, Green, 1941.

Rowntree, B.S. *Poverty: a Study of Town Life*, MacMillan, 1901.

Royal Commission on Local Government in England *Community Attitudes Survey*, Research Report No. 9, HMSO, 1969.

Runnymede Trust *Race and Council Housing in London*, 1975.

Shankland Cox and Associates *Expansion of Ipswich*, HMSO, 1968.

Smith, D.J. *The Extent of Racial Discrimination*, PEP, 1974.

Smith, D.J. *The Facts of Racial Disadvantage*, PEP, 1974.

Smith, D.J. and Whalley, A. *Racial Minorities and Public Housing*, PEP, 1975.

SNAP (Shelter Neighbourhood Action Project) *Another Chance for Cities?*, 1972.

South East Joint Planning Team *Strategic Plan for the South East, Studies Volume 2: Social and Environmental Aspects*, HMSO, 1971.

South East Joint Planning Team *Strategy for the South East: 1976 Review*, Department of the Environment, 1976.

South East Joint Planning Team *Strategy for the South East: 1976 Review. Report of the Resources Group*, Department of the Environment, 1976.

Syson, L. and Young, M. 'The Camden Survey', *Poverty Report 1975*, Temple Smith, 1975.

Thatcher, A.R. 'The New Earnings Survey and the distribution of earnings', in Atkinson A.B. (editor) *The Personal Distribution of Incomes*, Allen and Unwin, 1976.

Thomson, C.W. *The Industrial Selection Scheme: A Study of Conflicting Objectives in Urban and Regional Planning*, CES, 1973.

Townsend, P. and Abel-Smith, B. *The Poor and the Poorest*, Bell, 1965.

Training Services Agency *Vocational Preparation for Young People*, HMSO, 1975.

Walker, P. 'Race and the inner city: an open letter to the Prime Minister', *New Statesmen*, 18 June 1976.

Wedge, P. and Prosser, H. *Born to Fail?*, Arrow Books, 1973.

Whyte, W.H. *The Organisation Man*, Cape, 1957.

Willmott, P. and Young, M. *Family and Class in a London Suburb*, Routledge and Kegan Paul, 1960.

Willmott, Phyllis 'Gains and losses in health and welfare', in Willmott, P. (editor) *Sharing Inflation? Poverty Report 1976*, Temple Smith, 1976.

Willmott, Phyllis and Challis, L. *The Groveway Project* (IAS/LA/17), Department of the Environment, 1977.

Wilson, H. and Womersley, L. *Expansion of Northampton*, Appendix, HMSO, 1969.

Wilson, S. and Sharman, A. 'Vandalism', *Municipal Engineering*, 7 May 1976.

Young, M. 'A new voice for the neighbourhood', *What?*, Winter, 1970.

Young, M. *Innovation and Research in Education*, Routledge and Kegan Paul, 1965.

Young, M. (editor) *Poverty Report 1974*, Temple Smith, 1974.

Young, M. and Willmott, P. *Family and Kinship in East London*, Routledge and Kegan Paul, 1957.

Young, M. and Willmott, P. *The Symmetrical Family: A Study of Work and Leisure in the London Region*, Routledge and Kegan Paul, 1973.

Index

Action projects, 184, 185, 188–193, 198
    community involvement in, 189
    initiation of, 189
    multi-service, 174, 175
    multi-space, 161
Age Structure (of population), 28–29
Amenities, 57
    shared, 71
Area Health Authorities, 10 footnote, 168
Area Management Teams, 195

Bi-polarisation, 33, 35, 206; *see also* social
    class
Birmingham, 4, 7, 61, 70, 185, 207; *see also*
    Small Heath
Birthplace, 29–32
Black people, 60, 70–73, 78, 89, 117, 124, 151;
    see also birthplace, colour, West Indians
Boundaries Committee; *see* Location and
    Boundaries
Boundaries,
    confusion of, 169–171
    co-ordination of, 171–173
    rationalisation of, 174–175
Brixton, 9, 12, 13, 14, 16, 18, 22, 29, 41, 78, 167,
    169, 215
    advice centre, 169
    employment exchange area, 78, 81
Brixton–Victoria Railway, 9
Building standards, 48
Burney Road, 17

Camden (London Borough of), 62, 64, 144,
    155
Census Material, 8
Child Benefit Scheme, 74
Child Density, 46–49, 141–143
Child Minding,
    salaried, 198
    unregulated, 80
Child's Play Provision, 40
Chronic Sickness, 57
Church Commissioners, 130
Citizens' Advice Bureau (CAB), 168, 178
Colour, 29–32
    influence of, 70–73
    and housing, 37, 42
Community, breakdown of, 37–40, 49–51
    development projects (Home Office), 68, 115
    Land Act, 96
    services, 74
    groups, local, 197
Conservation area, 20
Co-Ownership schemes, 147
Cost of living, 56
Crime, 43, 45, 50, 78
    mugging, 41, 43
    vandalism, 2, 18, 20, 26, 41, 43, 45, 47, 50,
        113, 156, 187
    of violence, 41, 43
Council housing lists, 107–114

Day care action project, 31, 80
    see also action projects; action projects,
    multi service

Day care,
    provision of, 80
Decants, 108, 151
Defensible space, 156, 163, 210
Deprivation,
    concentration of, 62–64
    experience of, 65–68
    forms of, 61
    housing, 57
    incomes, 63
    influences on, 64–65
    multiple, 59, 60–62, 63, 64–65
    thresholds of, 61
    explanations for, 68–70
Development, commercial, 22
Dirt and litter, 44, 45, 47
Disabilities, 57, 61, 63
Discontent, themes of, 42–45
Docklands, 3 and footnote, 77, 96, 128, 148,
    184, 185, 215
Durand Gardens, 13
Density, 141–143

Education,
    omission of, 186
Elections, local, 154
Employment, 77–95, 203, 206, 208
    exchange, 78–81
    Department of, 99, 167, 170, 208–211
    Services Agency (ESA), 99
    see also Jobs
Environment, Department of the, Introduc-
    tory note ix, 4, 167, 178, 183, 184, 195, 196,
    207, 208–211, 213
    improved, 34, 151
    physical, 42–45, 122
    social, 42–45, 122
    suburban, 121, 122
Equity sharing, 147, 185
Estate caretaker,
    resident, 155, 156
    mobile, 156
Estates, council, 151–154
Estates,
    Clapham Goods Yard, 22
    Coronation Buildings, 112
    Larkhall Park, 16, 22
    St. Katherine's, 155
    South Island Place, 160
    Springfield, 195
    Stockwell Park, 18, 20, 195
    Wellington Mills, 155
Expanding Towns, *see* New and Expanding
    Towns

Fairhazel Gardens (Camden),144
Families,
    anti-social, 154
    and their homes, 36–37
    multiple-deprived, 59
    problem, 58, 59, 67–68, 75, 112, 154
    single-parent, 57
Family, 55, 56
    structures, 30–31
'Four-day package', 151, 188

Garages,
  on estates, 160–161
General Household Survey, 28, 30, 38
General Improvement Areas (GIA), 20, 149
Gentrification, 3, 34, 37, 49, 112, 148
Government, Local and Central, 10
Grants,
  local authority improvement, 17, 34, 150
Greater London Council (GLC), 5, 96, 113,
  125, 128, 129, 133, 141, 143, 191
Greater London Development Plan (GLDP)
  and Inquiry, 22, 77, 127, 190
Green Belt, 126, 132–133
Growth areas, 133

Harleyford Road, 9
Halfway homes, 112
Health, Department of Health and Social
  Security (DHSS), 173, 174, 208–211
Health centres, 18; see also Services
  services, see Services
Highway schemes, 3
Home Office,
  see Community developments project
Homelessness, 78, 109–112
Household, structure, 28–29
  survey, 6, 8–9, 37, 40, 66, 103, 120, 125, 141, 186
Households, 36–37, 55
Housing Act 1974, 146
Housing,
  Action Areas (HAA) 18, 22, 26, 103, 142,
    149
  advice centres, 112, 167, 177
  allocation, 50, 129
  GLC allocation 129–131
  allocation, 'ready access scheme', 143
  amenities, 61
  Association, Lambeth Self-Help, 113; see
    also squatters
  Associations, 103
  costs, 128
  Co-operatives, 147
  deck access schemes, 159
  design of local authority h. 156–161
  'filtering', 135
  gains, 108, 135, 142, 149
  improvement, 44, 45; see also rehabilitation
  lettings office, 167
  Local Authority, private and public space,
    156–158
  market, 125
  multi-occupation, 102, 105
  national allocations pool, 135–137, 133, 144
  opportunities, 37
  pre-war council estates, 45
  private rented sector, 36, 125–126, 144–146
  protected low rent, 49
  purchase by local authorities, 132
  stress, 101
Housing types,
  artisan villas, 15
  five-storey walkups, 16
  high density low rise, 16, 18
  point and tower blocks, 16, 20
  semi-detached, 41
  slab blocks, 16
  tenement blocks, 15

terraced, 3, 36, 49, 102
terraces, 'two-up two-down', 15
terraces, Victorian, 14, 18, 25

Immigrants, 9, 10, 29–32, 45, 97
Immigration to London, 143–4
Income maintenance scheme, 73, 146
  maintenance and support, 73
  poverty, 55, 67, 73
Incomes, 83–85
Industrial Development Certificates (IDC), 93,
  96
Industrial Selection Scheme, see New and
  Expanding Towns Scheme
Industries, relocation of, 92
Industry, policies for, 95–97
  survey of, 186
Information shops, 40
Inner London Education Authority (ILEA), 5,
  166, 167, 174, 175, 186, 209
ILEA, divisional office, 168
Inner London forum, 191
Institute of Community Studies, 38, 62
Institutions, 193–197

Jobs,
  counselling, 99
  decline in number, 89–93
  instability of, 63
  market, 85–87
  mismatch, 88, 99, 203
  mobility, 99
  opportunities, 87–89
  survey, manufacturing sector, 91
  see also employment
Journeys to work, 85–86

Kennington, 14, 49
Knight's Hill (Lambeth), 142

Labour market, 8
  shortage, 93
  supply, 89
Lambeth (London Borough),
  Council, Introductory note ix, 18, 20, 22, 26,
    34, 78, 168, 169, 177, 185
    advice centres in, 169, 171, 177
    Directorate of Development Studies, 12
      Housing, 167
      Social Services, 10, 168
    Housing Action Areas, 103, 142; see also
      Housing
    Information Bureau, 168
    Officers and Councillors of, 123
    policy proposals for action by, 208–211
    Self-Help Association, see Housing Associa-
      tion, Squatters
    voluntary organisation in, 168
    waiting list, 107
    working party, on unemployment,
      96 footnote
    tenants' participation in management,
      155
Landlords, private, 45, 49, 144–145, 146
  resident and non-resident, 103, 105

Landor-Hargwyne, housing action area, 195
Landor Road, 18, 20, 22, 26
Lansdowne Gardens, 13
Layfield Panel (Report), 127, 192
Liverpool, 2, 4, 7, 70, 193, 207
Local Information Posts (LIP), 178, 179, 198
Location and Boundaries Committee, 174
London Boroughs Association, 131, 191, 194
London weighting, 56, 196

Maintenance, estates, 45, 155
Management,
  local, 155–156
  offices, 167
  tenants' participation in, 154–155
Manpower Services Commission, 98
Maud Commission, 39
Migration, 33, 35, 37, 123–124, 125, 128, 129, 136
Mobility, residential, 99
Motorway box, 22
Movers,
  desired districts, 120–122
  frustrated, Introductory note x
  intending, 117–120
  policies on movement and migration, 203, 209
  successful, 123–124
  transfers or mutual exchanges, 122
Multi service manuals and directories, 175

National Enterprise Board, 97
National Health Service, 168
Neighbourhood Councils, 9, 40, 166, 168
New and expanding towns, 35, 77, 125, 133–135
New and expanding Towns Scheme (NETS), 35, 122, 134

Oases, 13, 36, 37, 39, 41, 103
Occupational classifications, 32–35
Old people, 29, 57, 63, 75, 166, 168, 208
Old people's day centres, 18
Open spaces, 22, 44, 45, 51, 132, (156), 161; see also defensible space
Overcrowding, 61, 105
Owner-occupation, 1, 3, 36, 37, 42, 124, 148

Pedways, 18
Play facilities, 18, 44, 45
Planning policies for industry, 92, 96
Plans,
  local, 161
  structure, 161
Police, 169
Policy Proposals,
  boundary co-ordination, 205
  child densities, 204, 206
  deprivation, 206
  dispersal and renewal, 205, 206
  employment, 203, 206
  housing allocations, 204
  links between elements, 203–207
  management of environment, 204
  management of public housing, 206
  migration, 203, 206
  national income maintenance scheme, 206

population stability, 205, 206
rehabilitation, 204, 206
small scale rehabilitation, 205
training, 203, 206
welfare services, 205
Poor, breakdown of, 59–60
Population,
  age-structure, 28–29
  decline, 128
  dispersal, 127–137
  movement, 37–40, 45
Poverty, extent of, 55–59
  line, 55, 56, 60, 105
Prices and rents, 105–107
Programmes, American, 4
Property for sale, 106
Proposals, 206–211
  action, 211
  balanced dispersal, 209
  delivery of welfare, 211
  job market, 208
  planning and housing, 209
  poverty and deprivation, 208
  the immediate programme, 213–214
Public Sector services, 89, 91

Rate support grant, 192, 196
Recreational centres, 132
Redevelopment, 5, 16, 18, 22, 35, 38, 39, 40, 41, 49, 142, 148–151, 210
Refuse disposal, 44, 45
Rehabilitation, 5, 18, 41, 142, 148–151, 188, 204
Rehousing, 49, 128
Renewal proposals, 204, 211
Rent,
  Acts, 103, 144, 145, 146
  rebate schemes, 146, 165
  Tribunals, 103, 112, 167
Rent allowances, 165
Rented accommodation, 106
Rents,
  council, 106, 146
  'fair', 103, 145
  see also prices
Residents' Associations, 10
  Organisations, 9
Road-widening reservations, 22

Shelter Housing Action Centre, 122
Shopping precinct, 18
Sites, for improvement, 161–162
Sidney Road, 17
Slum clearance, 3, 4, 5, 16, 49, 101
Slums, 101
Small businesses, 187
Small Heath, Birmingham, 61, 62, 64, 74
Social class structure, 32–35, 36, 37
Social and community planning research, 62
Social services,
  careers officers (ILEA), 167
  community workers, 166
  Directorate of (Lambeth), 168
  education welfare workers, 166
  Health & Social Security, Dept. of (DHSS), 167, 173, 174, 208–211
  health visitors, 166
  home help organisers, 166

housing welfare, 168
    location of, 166–168
    probation office, 168
    social workers, 165
Socio-economic structure, 8, 32
South East Joint Planning Team, 127, 128
Squatters, 112–113, 147, 187
Standing Conference for the South East, 191
Strategic Plan for the South East, 133
Steering Committee, 6, 183, 184, 186
Stockwell,
    past, 13–16
    today, 16–20
    2000, 214–217
Stockwell Road, 18, 20
Stockwell Gardens, 20
Stockwell Park, 13
Stockwell Park Crescent, 17
Stockwell Underground Station, 18, 25
Supplementary Benefits Commission, 55

Task force teams, 195
Taxation, 192
Tenancies, controlled, 103
    exchange of, 125
Tenant-member committees, 154
Tenants, 3, 49
    associations, 9, 40
    conversion of leases, 146

council, 16, 36, 49, 122, 125
    furnished, 38
    private, 103, 144–146
    sitting, 49
    unfurnished, 30
Tenure, 36–37
    alternative forms of, 147–148
    security of, 103, 113, 145, 146
Terms of Reference, 5, 6
Town planning, 161–162
Training, 97–98
Training Opportunities Scheme, 98
Training and recruitment, 98–99

Unemployment, 58, 78–82, 88, 89
Urban renewal, 5, 155

Vocational training and schools guidance, 89,
    97, 99
Voluntary organisations, listed, 168

Waiting lists; see Council
Wandsworth Road, 9
Welfare, 167–179
West End, 28, 30, 42
West Indians, 18, 26, 29–32, 37, 41, 42, 70–73,
    81, 215

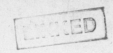
HER MAJESTY'S STATIONERY OFFICE

Government Bookshops

49 High Holborn, London WC1V 6HB
13a Castle Street, Edinburgh EH2 3AR
41 The Hayes, Cardiff CF1 1JW
Brazennose Street, Manchester M60 8AS
Southey House, Wine Street, Bristol BS1 2BQ
258 Broad Street, Birmingham B1 2HE
80 Chichester Street, Belfast BT1 4JY

Government Publications are also available through booksellers

Printed in England for Her Majesty's Stationery Office
by Ebenezer Baylis & Son Ltd., Worcester
Dd 587488   K 28 6/77